SSPR
Sage Series in Public Relations

COMMUNICATION
PLANNING
An Integrated Approach

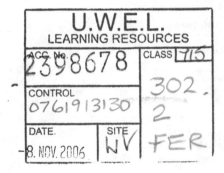

Sherry Devereaux Ferguson

SAGE Publications
International Educational and Professional Publisher
Thousand Oaks   London   New Delhi

For information:

SAGE Publications, Inc.
2455 Teller Road
Thousand Oaks, California 91320
E-mail: order@sagepub.com

SAGE Publications Ltd.
6 Bonhill Street
London EC2A 4PU
United Kingdom

SAGE Publications India Pvt. Ltd.
M-32 Market
Greater Kailash I
New Delhi 110 048 India

Printed in the United States of America

Library of Congress Cataloging-in-Publication Data

Ferguson, Sherry Devereaux.
    Communication planning: An integrated approach / by Sherry Devereaux Ferguson.
        p. cm. — (Sage series in public relations; v. 1)
    ISBN 0-7619-1313-0 (cloth: alk. paper)
    ISBN 0-7619-1314-9 (pbk.: alk. paper)
    1. Communication planning. I. Title. II. Series.
    P95.815.F47   1999
    302.2—ddc21   99-6168

This book is printed on acid-free paper.

05 06 07 08 09 10   10 9 8 7 6 5

Acquiring Editor: Margaret H. Seawell
Editorial Assistant: Renée Piernot
Production Editor: Astrid Virding
Editorial Assistant: Patricia Zeman
Designer/Typesetter: Janelle LeMaster
Cover Designer: Candice Harman

TO STEWART

Pilot, engineer, artist, professor, husband, father, friend . . .
Pour les bons temps

Contents

PART II: INTEGRATED PLANNING PROCESSES

PART III: COMMUNICATION THEORIES:
THE FOUNDATION FOR PLANNING

PART IV: STRATEGIC APPROACHES

Introduction

The goal of *Communication Planning: An Integrated Approach* is to expose students, practitioners, and consultants to the role of integrated communication planning in modern organizations. The book brings together several converging trends. First, the book recognizes the importance of integrating communication with business planning. Second, the book acknowledges the current trend toward a cross-functional approach to planning, which integrates public relations, marketing communications, and advertising strategies (integrated marketing communications [IMC]). Third, the book stresses the importance of establishing strategic planning cultures in organizations. Finally, the book acknowledges a trend toward integration of roles traditionally labeled as "organizational communication" and "public relations." A systems view demands that these two roles come together in the planning process.

The book is divided into four parts: strategic planning cultures, integrated planning processes, communication theories, and strategic approaches. Part I discusses the measures necessary to establish strategic planning cultures in organizations and the role of communication in these planning cultures. It also includes an analysis of the relationship between corporate, business, and communication planning. High levels of cooperation between communication and corporate planners ensure that communication plans reflect the priorities of the larger organization. Part II explores integrated planning processes and explains how to write the following kinds of communication plans:

- Multiyear (or annual) plans that suggest broad communication strategies for public relations, marketing communications, and advertising
- Multiyear (or annual) operational plans that explain how these strategies will be implemented
- Work plans that assign areas of responsibility, set milestones and performance indicators, suggest evaluation tools, and allocate budgets
- Support plans for information campaigns, advertising and marketing communications campaigns, issues management, and other action plans
- Plans for managing crisis communications

Part III examines the theoretical foundations for communication planning. Topics include the psychology of audiences, theories of media use and influence, source credibility, learning and persuasion theories relevant to message design, and considerations in choosing the channel of communication. These discussions integrate literature relevant to the design and execution of public relations, marketing communications, advertising, and employee communication activities and campaigns. Part IV examines strategic approaches to planning for issues management and the trend toward partnerships and sharing of resources, evidenced in relations within and between organizations.

This book offers value to the student of public relations, marketing communications, advertising, and organizational communication. The nature of the communicator's job has shifted dramatically in the past decade from a service-oriented to a management-oriented and strategic function. Communicators still perform services such as preparing speeches, advertising copy, press releases, and articles for corporate magazines and employee newsletters. An increasing number of communication managers, however, sit on executive committees and offer advice to chief executive officers and vice presidents. Others fill strategic roles that involve tracking issues in the media, consulting with stakeholders (inside and outside the organization), and evaluating their success against performance indicators. Those involved in planning processes often work together to ensure that their efforts are integrated—that they make maximum use of the organization's resources. In this book, I attempt to provide fresh, up-to-date perspectives on the changing role of the communicator in end-of-the-century organizations.

No other book on the market takes such a comprehensive approach to planning. A typical public relations text devotes one short chapter at best (a couple of pages at worst) to planning systems and processes, and most authors use the term *planning* to mean planning for a public relations, marketing communications, political, or health information campaign. This form of planning is only one type of planning exercise. Such discussions do not identify the range of plans that an organization can produce or talk about the relationship among the different layers of planning. This is the only book on the market that provides well-developed samples of strategic, operational, and work plans that can serve as models for communication planners.

Few authors stress the importance of information-based planning—that is, using opinion, attitudinal, and behavioral research as a foundation for communication strategies. None explain how to establish performance indicators that can tell the communication group when they have achieved success in their endeavors. In the same way, few books identify the strategic role played by communicators or talk about the necessity to integrate communication planning with business and corporate planning. Most authors fail to situate communication planning as a critical organizational communication function. This book is an attempt to correct these deficiencies.

A recent trend toward talking about the importance of integrating promotional, marketing communications, and advertising activities within the organization promises to close some of these gaps. Much of the current literature resides in the field of marketing, however, and the insights of communication researchers do not always appear in this literature. In this book, I try to integrate the perspectives of the three fields of study by examining communication planning as a generic organizational function. The more we apply systems theory to organizations, the more difficult it becomes to argue for territoriality, especially among communication-related functions. For this reason, I titled the book *Communication Planning: An Integrated Approach.*

In conclusion, *Communication Planning: An Integrated Approach* makes eight important contributions. First, the book acknowledges the current trend toward integrating the activities of public relations, marketing communications, and advertising in planning—that is, an IMC approach. Second, it establishes all these activities within the larger organizational context. That is, the book establishes a framework for communication planning, defining the relationships between the different kinds of plans and between communication and business planning. Third, the book argues that communication planning is a fundamental organizational function, which includes planning for internal and external audiences. If planning is a management function, it is also an organizational communication function. Fourth, the book defines the component parts of each type of communication plan that can be produced by the organization. It explains how to write an annual or multiyear plan that fits with the corporate or business plan, how to write an annual or multiyear plan that operationalizes the ideas in the strategic plan, how to write a yearly work plan and support plans for communication activities and campaigns, and how to write a contingency plan for crisis communications. Fifth, the book contributes to the development of a grammar for discussing planning products and processes. There is currently no common terminology for describing communication planning processes. Sixth, the book draws on many theories (audience psychology, theories of media use and influence, source credibility, and learning and persuasion) in discussing the design of communication strategies. Seventh, the book recognizes the importance of researching the opinion, attitudinal, and behavioral environment to develop information-based strategies. Finally, the book discusses the necessity to develop performance indicators to be applied in judging the effectiveness of communication strategies. Some performance indicators relate to outcomes and others to outputs, impacts, processes, and ethics. The communication plans include examples of performance indicators.

   I draw on a large experiential bank built on more than a decade of teaching communication planning to managers and executives who work in the fields of public affairs, marketing communications, and advertising. Market tested with government and business executives, this material has undergone extensive revisions over a period of years. The earlier incarnation of these ideas appeared in the book *Mastering the Public Opinion Challenge,* which received the 1994 National Communication Association PRIDE award for innovativeness of approach.

PART

I

Strategic Planning Cultures

1

The Making of
Strategic Planning Cultures

The new buzz words among managers are continuous planning and integrated planning. *Continuous planning* refers to ongoing planning efforts, at all levels of the organization, to ensure that the organization adjusts to changes in its internal and external environments (Redding & Catalanello, 1994). Distinctions in the management literature among long-term, middle-term, and short-term planning have all but disappeared as terms such as the *learning organization, strategic readiness, institutionalization of change,* and *proactivity* have come to dominate discussions of planning (Kaufman, 1992; Morgan, 1992). The days when organizations could follow a 10-year (or even a 5-year) strategic plan have disappeared. Frequent updates to relatively long-term strategic plans enable the organization to respond to threats from changes in the technological, economic, political, demographic, and other societal spheres. These societal shifts are occurring at an exponential rate as we enter the new millenium. From a demographic perspective, the face of the workforce is changing rapidly: It is growing older and is more culturally and racially diverse. Also, more often than in the past, it is female. The pace of technological change ensures the redundancy of knowledge, almost before it can be packaged and disseminated. The ability of publics to acquire information at the same time as their leaders has reduced—to unprecedented and dramatically low levels—response times available to politicians, chief executive officers, and bureaucrats. Despite the fact that "planning for change" may appear to be a contradiction in terms, much like "fighting for peace," many organizations believe that anticipating change is critical to their survival and prosperity.

Getting Ready for Strategic Planning

To prepare for these planning exercises, the organization must undertake three activities (Bryson, 1988). First, the organization must review its mandate. Second, the organization must develop or clarify its mission statement. Third, the organization must conduct a situation audit.

Reviewing the Mandate

A mandate specifies the organization's responsibilities and delegates authority to pursue these responsibilities. Usually contained in legislation, articles of incorporation, or charters, a mandate states the "musts" confronting an organization. The following illustrates a mandate statement: The Environmental Protection Agency is responsible for policies and actions to preserve and enhance the quality of the environment for the benefit of present and future generations of Americans.

Both governments and businesses have undertaken dramatic restructuring of their mandates in recent years, with many firms moving into new business lines. For example, many film companies also produce videos. Department stores sell insurance and eye care. Publishers market books, computer software, and videos. Some organizations have completely abandoned their former business lines and entered new markets. Federal governments have moved increasingly into the business of coordinating and communicating as state and local governments take over the design and delivery of programs. In other words, these organizations have rewritten their mandates—even if the changes do not always appear on paper.

Developing or Clarifying Mission Statement

The organization that wishes to engage in successful strategic planning must write or update its mission statement (Kaufman, 1992). A mission statement "defines the ultimate objective of the organization and the most important strategies to be applied in attempting to achieve the ultimate goal" (Ingstrup, 1990). Like the mandate, the mission statement responds to the most fundamental question: "What is the nature of our business?" The mission statement, however, also contains statements of purpose, strategy, values, behavioral standards, and sometimes guiding principles. Levi Strauss generated a document in the late 1980s titled "Crusaders of the Golden Needle" which demonstrated the first four components. The mission read as follows (Ireland, Hitt, & Williams, 1992):

> We seek profitable and responsible commercial success creating and selling jeans and casual clothing [purpose]. We seek this while offering quality products and service—and by being a leader in what we do [strategy]. What we do is important. How we do it is also important [values]. Here's how [behavioral standards]: By being honest. By being responsible citizens in communities where we operate and in society in general. By having a workplace that's safe and productive, where people work together in teams, where they talk to each other openly, where they're responsible for their actions, and where they can improve their skills. (p. 35)

Purpose statements in the mission suggest what the organization aims to produce or achieve. For example, Daimler-Benz aims to produce the best engineered car. The purpose of universities is to contribute to the knowledge of society and to transmit that knowledge to students. Police departments strive to protect society, and hospitals aim to alleviate the suffering of the injured, ill, and dying. The U.S. Department of Health and Human Services (1997) stated its mission in the following way: "To enhance the health and well-being of Americans [purpose] by providing for effective health and human services and by fostering strong sustained advances in the sciences underlying medicine, public health, and social services [strategy]."

Strategy statements suggest the means by which the organization will achieve its goals. For example, Wal-Mart's ability to offer high-quality discount goods (purpose) relates to its extremely cost-efficient warehousing system (strategy). Universities transfer knowledge (purpose) by hiring the best qualified instructors and researchers (strategy).

Mission statements also include statements of values. Core values in the mission statement for the U.S. Department of Justice include access to justice, honesty and integrity, pursuit of excellence, cooperation and partnership, importance of the individual, and openness in government. At the end of a lengthy process that involved 1,400 managers, Bell Atlantic managers reached consensus on five values: integrity, respect and trust, excellence, individual fulfillment, and profitable growth. The corporation then moved toward operationalizing these values in the form of concrete behaviors and work practices (Kanter, 1991). After establishing a committee to articulate corporate values for the Washington Mutual Financial Group, Chairman Lou Pepper appointed middle managers to roam the organization to find out where conflicts existed between "rhetoric and reality" (Tregoe & Tobia, 1990, p. 20). Where the two diverged, the managers reported back to Pepper, who made the necessary changes. Much of the cynicism concerning mission statements relates to the tendency of many organizations to tolerate inconsistencies between stated values and behavioral standards.

The fourth category in a mission statement is behavioral standards. Government departments and businesses often state their commitment to behave in ethical or socially responsible ways. Levi Strauss included an extended statement of behavioral standards in their mission statement. They observed that "what they do is important" but "how they do it" is also important. Finally, they detailed the specifics of how they intended to behave.

Other organizations include guiding principles in their mission statements. The mission statement for the Correctional Service of Canada (1990) demonstrates all these components. Their mission statement reads: "The Correctional Service of Canada, as part of the criminal justice system, contributes to the protection of society [purpose] by actively encouraging and assisting offenders to become law-abiding citizens [strategy], while exercising reasonable, safe, secure and humane control [behavioral standards]" (p. 4). The values of the Correctional Service of Canada are as follows (p. 4):

> *Core Value 1*: "We respect the dignity of individuals, the rights of all members of society, and the potential for human growth."
>
> *Core Value 2*: "We recognize that the offender has the potential to live as a law-abiding citizen."
>
> *Core Value 3*: "We believe that our strength and our major resource in achieving our objectives is our staff and that human relationships are the cornerstone of our endeavor."
>
> *Core Value 4*: "We believe that the sharing of ideas, knowledge, values and experience, nationally and internationally, is essential to the achievement of our Mission."
>
> *Core Value 5*: "We believe in managing the Service with openness and integrity and we are accountable to the Solicitor General."

Guiding principles are tied to core values (Correctional Service of Canada, 1990, pp. 8-16). Guiding principles for Core Value 1 were "We will accommodate, within the boundaries of the law, the cultural and religious needs of individuals and minority groups, provided the rights of others are not impinged"; "The disciplinary process, when used, will be fair, timely, and constructive"; and "Offenders, as members of society, retain their rights and privileges except those necessarily removed or restricted by the fact of their incarceration." Guiding principles for Core Value 2 were "We believe that offenders should be productively occupied"; "We recognize that the establishment and maintenance of positive community and family relationships will normally assist offenders in the reintegration as law-abiding citizens"; and "The involvement of community organizations, volunteers, and outside professionals in program development and delivery will be actively encouraged." Guiding principles for Core Value 3 were "We will be sensitive to the staff members' individual needs, interests, capacities, values, and aspirations in the workplace"; "We respect the need for employment equity achieved through a staff complement that represents a cross section of Canadian society"; and "We believe that our relationship with unions must be characterized by openness, mutual respect, and a desire to solve problems." A guiding principle for Core Value 4 was "We believe that we must actively encourage the gathering, creation, application, and dissemination of new knowledge if we are to remain a contributing member of the national and international correctional communities." Guiding principles for Core Value 5 were "We will endeavor to be a positive presence in the community and to be a social, cultural, and economic asset"; "We will ensure that appropriate segments of the public are consulted in the development of the Service's key policies"; and "We recognize the role of the media in a democratic society and we will work actively and constructively with them in order to demonstrate that we are open and accountable."

In short, a mission statement reflects the personality of the organization and distinguishes it from other organizations with similar business lines. Those who claim that mission statements are too broad to be meaningful should examine the implications in the mission statement for the Correctional Service of Canada. It should be obvious that countries such as Thailand have very different values and guiding principles for their correctional systems. Although the minimum period of imprisonment in Thailand for drug trafficking is 25 years, the average survival time is 12 years. Few graduate from Thailand's prison system, and China executes its drug traffickers. The same is true for many other countries throughout the world, in which a belief in rehabilitation of criminals does not figure into their justice systems. A mission statement written by these countries would appear quite different from American, British, or Canadian statements.

Conducting a Situation Audit

After clarifying the organization's mandate and writing its mission statement (purpose, strategy, values, behavioral standards, and guiding principles), the organization must conduct a situation audit. Situation audits examine

- The past performance of the organization (achievements, failures, trends in products and services, profits, and other indexes of performance)
- Forces in the organization's environment (economic, social, technological, and demographic)
- The identities, biases, and loyalties of stakeholders (clients and others who have a stake in the success or failure of the organization)
- Organizational resources

At this point, the organization has completed all necessary steps to prepare for the strategic planning exercise. The organization has reviewed its mandate, developed or clarified its mission statement, and conducted a situation audit. In some cases, the communication group will have contributed to the writing of the section on stakeholders in the situation audit. The organization is now ready for the strategic planning exercises.

Engaging in Strategic Planning

Strategic planning serves the function of determining where the organization wants to go, in the long term. From a policy perspective, a strategic plan constitutes a navigator's map for change and improvement—the "vision of a strongly desired future that the organization is committed to pursue" (Ingstrup, 1990). Strategic planning is the big picture, wide-screen, cinemascope vision.

Planning periods vary between organizations and over time. The time lines cannot always be specified. A recent U.S. government document (National Performance Review, 1997) found that most organizations viewed planning as an "evergreen process, one with no clear beginning and no clear end" (p. 4). They view the *process* of planning as more important than publication of the plan. They also see the ideal process as flexible and dynamic. Whereas strategic planning cycles used to involve 3 to 5 years, a growing number of organizations now update their plans every year (Brooker, 1991).

Similar to writing a mission statement, strategic and operational planning are cooperative, team-building exercises. Gaining commitment from the larger membership of an organization implies obtaining high levels of participation, involving all hierarchical levels (Burkhart & Reuss, 1993). In a 1990 speech, Ingstrup stated,

> Ownership in the plan is of paramount importance. The senior executives are responsible for the development of the plan, but a plan to which only a handful of people are committed has little chance of becoming more than a piece of window dressing to which people, at best, will pay little attention and which, at worst, will contribute to the image of the executives as unrealistic, uncommitted, or unable to do what they plan.

The U.S. government also affirmed the importance of upper management commitment to strategic planning: "Senior leaders own their strategic planning processes. Clear, consistent, and visible involvement of senior executives in the creation and deployment of the strategic plan was a hallmark of the best-in-class organizations" (National Performance Review, 1997, p. 4). Others agree that the best planning efforts are "visible, easily understood, and sufficiently important to motivate action" (Benveniste, 1989, p. 168).

Effective planning requires orchestration of efforts. In the 1980s, General Electric introduced a strategic management sector, one level above the business units, to ensure consistency between plans formulated at the business unit level and overall corporate objectives articulated in the strategic plan (Andriole, 1985). Following their study to identify "best-in-class" organizations, the U.S. government (National Performance Review, 1997) made the following comment:

> Effective strategic planning benefits from a consistent and cohesively structured process employed across all levels of the organization. Regardless of the type of partner studied, or the maturity of the planning process, the partners agreed on the importance of well-structured, well-understood planning process. Each of the study partners demonstrated an integrated approach to strategic planning that was linked from corporate down to business unit, and across all business lines. (p. 4)

The partners understood the process, the expectations of each level, and how the different parts fit together. This same logic extends to communication planning, which follows on the heels of corporate and business planning.

Conclusion

Many organizations abandoned their strategic planning functions during more than a decade of downsizing and restructuring. Many believed that it was pointless to plan in the throes of change. The dust has now settled, however, and organizations are talking about strategic planning with a new level of commitment. They are calling for continuous planning to facilitate ongoing adaptation to changes in volatile issue environments. After completing its National Performance Review (1997), the U.S. government required all government departments to post their strategic plans on the Internet. The weight attached to the planning function is greater now than at any time in the past. This chapter has laid the groundwork for the communication planning exercises that follow on the heels of corporate and business planning.

2

The Role of Integrated Communication Planning

During the past 5 years, an increasing number of academics have called for the involvement of communicators in strategic planning processes (Ferguson, 1993, 1994; Hon, 1998; Reddin, 1998). Living in an information age requires that businesses and governments communicate their intentions to constituencies. Moreover, the volatility of the issue environments of many organizations necessitates the presence of a strong communication component in corporate plans. A Conference Board report found that companies that value the "soft side" of strategic development involve communicators in the strategic planning process (Kinkead & Winokur, 1992). At companies such as Douglas Aircraft and John Hancock, communicators play an important role in planning. One public relations expert acknowledged the role that communication groups play in the strategic planning process at his company when he observed, "We help plan the parade, not just carry the shovels afterward" (Kinkead & Winokur, 1992, p. 23). Those who support this point of view see communication planning as part of the larger strategic planning process rather than as a separate and distinct planning exercise.

Different people and groups participate at different stages of planning that, much like Ukrainian dolls, nest one inside the other. The processes are integrated. The first and highest level of planning is strategic planning. Operational plans flow out of strategic planning, and work plans flow out of operational plans. Finally, support plans, which link back to the strategic and operational planning stages, emerge from work planning. It appears obvious that, as the first stage, strategic planning is critical to everything that follows. In this chapter, I discuss planning exigencies, communication planning systems, and the purposes and content of different types of communication plans.

Planning Exigencies

To carry out their planning tasks, communicators must understand the mission, mandate, and strategic objectives of the organization. Operating on the front lines of the organization, communicators act to convey the organization's messages to the public through direct or indirect means. As liaisons with the media, they produce press releases, feature articles, and other publications. In an indirect role, they research and write the speeches and press lines that organizational spokespersons deliver. Others design information, marketing communications, and advertising campaigns. How can they convey messages to which they have not been privy? When speech writers and media relations personnel do not obtain access to the organization's strategic documents, they must improvise and create their own messages. When these messages fail, critics say that communicators have only superficial knowledge of the organization and its policies and programs.

Worse, without knowledge of strategic objectives, the communication manager has no basis on which to reject any request that lands on his or her desk. In such a situation, the manager has no choice but to allocate human and financial resources to projects that often represent the whims of line managers (even if little justification exists, in strategic or communication terms, for the product). In a properly functioning organization, communication does not serve the whims of individuals. That is, communication campaigns and activities do not exist for their own sake. In ideal circumstances, they support the organization's efforts to achieve its strategic goals and to fulfill its mission and mandate. In other words, communication becomes a management function, and communication executives assume advisory roles (White & Dozier, 1992).

The volatility of the environment in which an organization operates and the character of its operations determine whether the planning period should be annual or multiyear. Corporations that compete in areas related to new technologies (e.g., computer and electronics firms) or require stable financial markets (e.g., the construction industry) experience rapid and often unpredictable changes. These changes make plans obsolete in a short period of time. The same is true for governments, which experience frequent changes in leadership. The external environment can change so rapidly that the organization may not be able to wait 3 years to adjust its communication priorities (Redding & Catalanello, 1994). Organizations with less dependency on the external environment do not need to update their plans as often.

Communication Planning Systems

Once the corporate planning group has produced its strategic plan, the communication group can undertake its planning exercise. Because communication always supports corporate activities, the communication planning exercise can never precede corporate planning. Communication groups should consider the following points in establishing strategic planning systems:

- The head of communication should be a member of the executive team that is responsible for strategic planning at the corporate level.
- The head of communication should be an active participant in the development of the mission plan and the setting of corporate goals.
- The head of communication should be the principal adviser on any communication-related matters.
- Ideally, strategic communication planning should follow closely corporate or business planning.
- The most senior members of the organization should share ownership in the strategic communication plan.
- An integrated approach to communication planning implies cooperation between members of public relations, advertising, and marketing communications.

Even when a planning unit assumes responsibility for generating the strategic plan, the commitment of upper management ensures broad-based support for the plan (Benveniste, 1989). When relegated to the division level, planning does not capture the "big picture" (Hiam, 1990, p. 25).

The same cooperative spirit should characterize operational planning efforts. Just as the head of communication ideally works with the corporate executive team or business managers to produce strategic communication plans, the middle-level communication manager typically cooperates with business planners to create the multiyear or annual operational and work plans. The writing of the numerous support plans, however, falls to lower-level communication officers in public relations or public affairs, marketing communications, and advertising. By contrast, planning for crisis management involves people at the highest levels of the organization. The heads of communication are active members of the crisis management team.

Different Types of Communication Plans:
Purposes and Content

The discussion that follows describes the purposes and characteristics of different kinds of communication plans: the strategic plan (annual or multi-year, at the corporate or business level), the operational plan (annual or multiyear, at the corporate or business level), the work plan (annual, at the corporate or business level), support plans (program level), and crisis communication plans (corporate level). Communication plans have value to the extent that they support corporate and business objectives. They do not exist in isolation; they are not creative efforts.

Strategic Plans

Annual or multiyear, the strategic communication plan supplements a corporate or a business/functional plan. Ideally, the plan includes a background statement; corporate or business/functional objectives; policy issues; external environment; internal environment; windows of opportunity; communication objectives; themes and messages; communication priorities; strategic considerations; consultation, partnership, and negotiation requirements; performance indicators; and anticipated financial resources. These points are discussed in-depth in Chapter 3.

Operational Plans

Like strategic planning, operational planning remains fairly general in scope. Operational plans specify how the organization will achieve its strategic objectives and establish the allocation of funds for different communication ventures. Planning processes become more concrete as planners rank order communication priorities, demonstrate the linkages to communication objectives in the strategic plan, identify key client groups, indicate

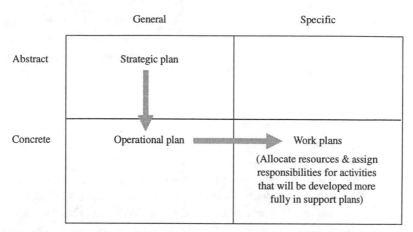

Figure 2.1. A Model for Integrated Planning (Robert Czerny contributed this figure, which appeared originally in Ferguson, 1994, p. 291; reprinted with permission)

complementary activities and services, and specify how the funds will be allocated among priorities.

Work Plans

An extension of operational planning (often performed in the same time period), work planning is more concrete and specific. Work plans identify the products and services to be delivered, designate responsible parties for delivering the products and services, identify performance indicators, set milestones, define evaluation methodologies, and allocate resources to specific products, services, and activities. Figure 2.1 illustrates the relationship among strategic, operational, work, and support planning. See Chapter 4 for a more detailed discussion of operational and work planning.

Support Plans

The term *support plan* refers to the most common kind of communication plan—a plan for managing a specific activity (e.g., a press briefing or a conference), initiative (e.g., a campaign to encourage people to purchase a new product), or issue (e.g., a transportation safety issue). A special kind of support plan is the "information campaign for social improvement" or social marketing plan, which provides people with the information they require to lead better, more healthy lives (Salmon, 1989). In organizations with well-developed strategic planning structures, communication planners may produce 30 or more support plans in any given year. Sometimes the planner creates 2 or 3 plans to accommodate different scenarios. This situation occurs frequently in governments, in which leaders often make last-minute decisions on policy initiatives.

A support plan can be extremely brief (1 page in length for a press conference or announcement of a new publication) or lengthy (e.g., 10 or more pages for a major environmental or marketing communications campaign). The average support plan is approximately 5 pages in length. Just as the length of a support plan depends on the subject matter, so do the categories included in such a plan. A well-developed support plan has strategic and operational components. Strategic elements in the plan can include the background statement that establishes context; crisis indicators (especially relevant to issues management plans); the opinion, attitudinal, or behavioral environment; communication objectives (linked back to the corporate or business plan); messages; target audiences; strategic considerations; and consultation requirements. Operational elements include tactical considerations and an assessment of financial requirements. Performance indicators and evaluation methodologies should also appear in a fully developed support plan. See Chapter 5 for a more detailed discussion of support plans.

Crisis Communication Plans

It has been said that the history of life contains "long periods of boredom and short periods of terror" (Gould as quoted in Meyer, Brooks, & Goes, 1990, p. 93). These moments of terror in the lives of organizations have been termed *crises*. The elements of surprise, immediacy, and reduced time for decision making characterize crises. This reduced time escalates the possibility that issues will become crises. For this reason, many organizations attempt to anticipate crisis situations. The crisis communication plan constitutes an integral part of the larger crisis management plan. The larger crisis management plan contains components such as acknowledgments, introduction, crisis profile, crisis management team, decision options, required support systems, and crisis management directory. The communication plan includes elements such as crisis indicators, communication team members, communication strategies, response and control mechanisms, evaluation of operations, and appendices with guidelines and formats for various communication activities such as issuing press releases and keeping logs of daily activities. See Chapter 6 for more information on this plan.

Conclusion

We are living in an age of accountability, and accountability implies responsibility. Accountability suggests, at the outside limits, the necessity for an individual or group to justify its continuing existence. Organizations have always held manufacturing, sales, and legal divisions accountable for their work. If a plant manufactures too many defective parts or a legal unit loses all its cases, the company will replace these groups. Until recently, however, both business and government held communicators to different standards. Organizations that invested in public relations or information campaigns did not expect communication managers to answer for the effectiveness of their efforts. The situation has changed in recent years—slowly but surely. Both private firms and public corporations demand new standards of accountability for all employees, including those who specialize in communication. These groups, like others in the organization, must document their successes if they wish to have job security. Strategic, operational, and work planning allow communicators to meet this critical objective. If the communicator sets no objectives or goals at the planning stage, the individual will have no way to know if he or she has met ultimate criteria. Meeting more limited objectives at the support plan level (advertising or marketing communications campaign) does not guarantee that the communicator has helped the organization to meet its ultimate strategic goals or to fulfill its mandate or mission. To ensure that strategic goals are met, the organization must establish a strategic and operational framework. If this framework does not exist, the communicator has no reference point for planning efforts.

Comprehensive planning is a critical new communication function—a strategic function that must be integrated into the planning cycles of the organization. Thus, this chapter considered planning exigencies, communication systems, and the purposes and content of different types of plans. Subsequent chapters will consider in-depth each of the major kinds of planning exercises.

PART

II

Integrated Planning Processes

3

Writing the Strategic Communication Plan (Multiyear or Annual)

Chapter 1 discussed what organizations must do to establish strategic planning cultures, and Chapter 2 examined integrated communication planning. This chapter explores the *who, how,* and *when* of writing a strategic plan in communication, principles for writing the plan, and steps in creating the plan.

Planning Processes: Who, How, and When

Who writes the annual or multiyear communication plan? Ideally, the head of communication oversees the process of generating this plan. As a member of the executive team, this individual comprehends the larger vision of the organization, including the corporate priorities. The communication executive consults with members of the public relations, marketing communications, and advertising groups in writing the plan and with other executive team members in gaining approval and commitment to the plan. Ultimately, the funding for communication comes from higher levels of the organization, which implies the need for the most senior levels to accept ownership of the plan. Moreover, the credibility of a communication plan depends, in no small measure, on the credibility of the chief communication executive. Communicators who can transcend the boundaries of their discipline and understand the needs of diverse groups within the organization are best suited to assume a place at strategy sessions. Typically, these individuals are widely read in areas affecting both the external and the internal environments of the organization (Kinkead & Winokur, 1992).

Once management has given its approval, the head of communication circulates the plan to all individuals who must implement it. Too often, organizations hide the results of their planning efforts (Benveniste, 1989; Redding & Catalanello, 1994). The futility of this approach becomes most evident in the case of communication plans. The messages articulated in these plans should appear in every communication product generated by the organization, including speeches, media interviews, press releases, brochures, and exhibitions. How can a communication practitioner know or convey messages from documents stamped "confidential" and "top secret" to which the person has had no access? Rather than being considered as an area suitable only for the "eyes and ears of chief executive officers (CEOs) and a few of their most trusted lieutenants . . . the effort to implement strategy must capture the heads, hearts, and hands of the entire organization" (Tregoe & Tobia, 1990, p. 20). Few employees feel motivated to work toward a vision about which they can only speculate. One middle manager of a New Jersey company aptly stated, "Don't ask me to kill for someone else's vision" (p. 20). At some point, all members of the organization (especially those who communicate the organization's vision) should keep a copy of the strategic plan in their top desk drawers. Canada Housing and Mortgage Corporation publishes and circulates its strategic plan to its employees and the general public.

By the same token, communicators require access to certain documents to write the strategic communication plan. The most useful documents are recent corporate or business plans (depending on the level of communication planning). If the communicator does not have access or the documents do not exist, the person will need to obtain the following supplementary materials: multiyear plans with budget allocations; mandate, mission, and vision statements (including statements of organizational values); annual reports; minutes of executive meetings; and other documents that could suggest current corporate or business objectives and priorities. The latter vary from organization to organization. For example, writing a plan for the U.S. government would involve examining the State of the Union Address, other speeches delivered by the president, and addresses by top advisers and Cabinet members (all of which suggest government priorities and future policy initiatives). Comparable corporation documents are annual speeches or statements to shareholders, major addresses by executives, and interviews with the press that suggest corporate direction and priorities. If a time gap occurs between corporate or business planning cycles and communication planning cycles, the communicator will require more than just the corporate or business plans.

Principles for Writing the Plan

The guiding principles for writing the annual or multiyear communication plan, intended to supplement the corporate plan, can be expressed in the following terms. Think broad. Think global. Write the plan from the perspective of the larger organization. When writing the plan for the corporate level, do not adopt a bias that is more appropriate to the level of the business unit. As noted in Chapter 1, strategic planning concerns itself with the big picture. Departments within government may vie for influence and status. Business units within a company may compete for prestige and funds. The annual planning processes at the corporate level, however, should not reflect these ethnocentric perspectives. The corporate planner should be a cosmopolite—capable of reaching beyond personal interests and prejudices to strive for the achievement of corporate objectives. The person should be flexible, familiar with the operations and procedures of the larger organization, and aware of its strengths and weaknesses. Most communication planners have this flexibility and awareness because they work on an ongoing basis with people throughout the organization. Part of their job involves consultation and facilitation of partnerships. Nonetheless, although a strategic plan for a business or functional unit reflects corporate priorities, this plan uses the objectives and perspective of the business or functional unit as a starting point.

In terms of length, the strategic communication plan should be relatively brief, concise, focused, and readable. Most plans mix essay style with bullet format. Statements of communication objectives and messages generally appear in a bullet format. By contrast, planners typically use a narrative style to discuss background and issues. Both narrative and bullet presentations have advantages and disadvantages. Bullet formats facilitate periodic updating of plans because the planner can add or drop sections without rewriting the entire plan. This more compact presentation style also requires fewer pages of text—a fact appreciated by top executives, who often read hundreds of pages of text in a week. Narrative presentations, however, have the advantage of being more coherent. They also allow an explication of points that may not be clear as bullets. Planners should remember, however, that the average reader of a communication plan will be an expert in the business of the company or government department. Therefore, detailed explanations may be unnecessary—even undesirable. A communication plan should not exceed 10 pages if the creators want others to read and use the plan on a daily basis.

Steps in Creating the Plan

As a stand-alone document, a strategic communication plan for the corporation or for the business unit can contain as many as 13 major sections: background statement; corporate or business/functional objectives (depending on the planning level); policy issues; external environment; internal environment; windows of opportunity; communication objectives; themes and messages; communication priorities; strategic considerations; requirements for consultation, partnership, and negotiation; performance indicators; and anticipated financial resources. If the communication plan fits inside the corporate or business/functional plan, the planner can begin with the background statement of policy issues instead of beginning with background or corporate objectives. The following discussion applies to writing or updating an annual or multiyear communication plan for the corporation as a whole or for a business or functional unit of the organization.

Background Statement

The background statement establishes a context for the rest of the plan. One or two paragraphs should be sufficient to position the organization or business unit, in broad terms, in the larger environment—noting recent events or developments that have focused attention on the corporation or business unit, general strategies pursued, and areas of emphasis. If the communication plan fits within the corporate or business plan (i.e., if the plan is not a stand-alone document), this context statement will be unnecessary.

Objectives (Corporate or Business/Functional)

Communication managers often find themselves in a situation in which business managers demand that they perform ad hoc service functions: "Prepare a brochure," "Design an advertising campaign," "Write a speech," or "Plan an exhibit." Sometimes these requests are germane to the priorities of the organization. At other times, the connections are strained or lacking. Even if the demands seem unjustified or inappropriate, however, communication managers may not be able to turn down the requests if they work in an organization without a planning structure. Organizations with strategic planning cultures, however, evaluate funding requests on the basis of a project's linkage to the corporate or business objectives. They ask, "Does this project or this activity help the organization to achieve its objectives?" In such a situation, those who make requests must justify their demands on the basis of fit with the organization's strategic objectives.

Like other groups in the organization, the communication group must justify its plans and its expenditures on the basis of ties to corporate or business priorities. Therefore, a statement of these objectives provides a logical starting point for the annual or multiyear communication plan. If no documents (corporate or business plans) explicitly or implicitly state corporate or business objectives, the communication planner must interview top executives to acquire this information. The communication planner must learn the objectives that exist in people's heads, even if they do not appear on paper. To write arbitrary objectives for the organization is to engage in "guess-ology." A communication plan built on erroneous objectives will have no credibility or utility. Many communication managers complain that others do not take their planning efforts seriously. The most probable explanation relates to this former point. Plans that emerge from the creative efforts of communicators (i.e., they bear no relationship to the larger picture) find their resting place in the nearest wastebasket. Where the efforts of corporate, business, and communication planners diverge, the organization follows the path of the corporate and business planners—and appropriately so. Communication's raison d'etre is to support these policies and programs.

The U.S. Department of Health and Human Services posts its corporate strategic plan on the Internet. The last update for the plan was September 30, 1997. Corporate objectives, the starting point for communication planning, are as follows:

- To reduce the major threats to the health and productivity of all Americans
- To improve the economic and social well-being of individuals, families, and communities in the United States
- To improve access to health services and ensure the integrity of the nation's health entitlement and safety net programs

- To improve the quality of health care and human services
- To improve public health systems
- To strengthen the nation's health sciences research enterprise and enhance its productivity

The strategic planning document for the U.S. Department of Justice (1997) illustrates how business or functional objectives tend to be more specific than corporate objectives. The strategic document for the U.S. Department of Justice contains objectives for each of its seven functional areas: investigation and prosecution of criminal offenses; assistance to state and local governments; legal representation, enforcement of federal laws, and defense of federal government interests; immigration; detention and incarceration; protection of the federal judiciary and improvement of the justice system; and management. In all probability, planning took place at the level of the functional unit, with different people involved in creating the objectives, strategies, and performance indicators for each functional area. In its October 1997 planning document, the U.S. Department of Justice identified the following objectives for the functional unit concerned with investigation and prosecution of criminal offenses (the equivalent of business objectives):

- To reduce violent crime, including organized crime and drug- and gang-related violence
- To reduce the availability and abuse of illegal drugs through traditional and innovative enforcement efforts
- To reduce espionage and terrorism (sponsored by foreign or domestic groups in the United States and abroad when directed at U.S. citizens or institutions)
- To reduce white-collar crime, including public corruption and fraud
- To coordinate and integrate Department of Justice law enforcement activities wherever possible, and cooperate fully with other federal, state, and local agencies that are critically linked to improved operation of the nation's justice system

Communication planners for the functional unit that investigates and prosecutes criminal offenses can refer to this document to generate a communication plan for their unit.

Management scholars disagree on the definition of *goals* versus *objectives*. Some authors and organizations characterize an objective as a "broad statement of purpose" and a goal as a "specific and quantified statement relating to operative and day-to-day activities" (Bergeron, 1989, p. 254). Using this definition, an example of an objective is "to improve service to the public." Related goals could be "to decrease the lag time between receipt of a complaint and mailing of a letter of acknowledgment to 1 week" or "to decrease the number of telephone calls forwarded to an automatic answering machine." Other authors and organizations employ the terms *goal* and *objective* in the opposite fashion.

Policy Issues

Some authors believe that planning should begin with analysis of the external environment (Brooker, 1990; Kaufman, 1992; Morgan, 1992). Others argue that such an "outside-in" approach to planning is reactive because it does not take corporate objectives into account (Robert, 1990; Seitel, 1984). In such a situation, it would seem to be easy for the organization to lose sight of its strategic issues and to take a scattergun approach to planning. An "inside-out" approach, however, selects the issues on the basis of fit with corporate and business objectives, mandate, mission, and values.

An increasing number of organizations have accepted the principle that every strategic plan must have a communication component that addresses management of the organization's critical and emerging issues. Thus, after identifying and articulating corporate objectives, the communication planner searches for evidence of policy decisions or strategies (already made or likely to be made in the planning term) that could have a significant impact on the communication planning activities of the organization. The following are examples of such policy decisions: The Olympic Committee votes to host a competition in a country with a record of human rights violations; a cosmetic firm approves the use of animals in product testing; an automobile manufacturer decides to relocate its operations to another country with lower labor costs; the government decides to lower the restrictions on testing of experimental drugs, transfer funding from breast cancer research to heart disease research, or approve more aggressive advertising against smoking; and an organization decides to place a new controversial low-fat oil on the market. Each of these decisions has the potential to stimulate acrimonious public debate and bad publicity for the organization. Advance knowledge of these decisions can assist the communication team in managing the debate that is almost certain to ensue. Therefore, this section of the communication plan states policy decisions or strategic choices that could have a significant impact on the organization in the coming months or years.

Where can the communication planner find these policy decisions and strategies? Corporate or business/functional plans typically identify decision options and their consequences. Sometimes they specify the approaches that will be taken to achieve strategic objectives. For example, the U.S. Department of Justice decided on the following strategies to achieve the objective of reducing the availability and abuse of illegal drugs: (a) Disrupt and dismantle major drug organizations along all points of the production, transportation, and distribution chain; (b) increase foreign government support for the successful investigation and prosecution of drug cartel members; and (c) gather, analyze, and disseminate intelligence regarding drug-trafficking organizations and the availability and abuse of illegal drugs to support investigative and prosecutorial efforts. It appears obvious that the communication planner for this functional unit should refer to these documents. If the documents do not exist, the planner must interview executives responsible for determining strategic direction for the organization.

Policy choices by government tend to generate issues for business and industry. Thus, communication planners for business and industry often seek to identify public policy decisions that could impact the corporation in the coming year(s). A clear statement of issues can assist the planner, at a later point, in framing communication objectives, messages, and activities.

After identifying and articulating policy decisions and strategies, the communication planner asks the question, "Which policy decisions and strategies will foster issues?" Governments deal with issues spawned by decades of uncontrolled spending, an aging population, increases in the number and frequency of violent crimes, unemployment, foreign affairs crises, failure to arrest the drug problem, and intermittent scandals. Corporations confront issues related to contentious environmental policies, flawed products, charges of tax evasion, allegations of insider trading, closing of plants, and so on. Strategic issues are policy questions that affect the organization's mandate, mission, and values (Bryson, 1988). These policy questions relate to what, why, and if. Operational issues address questions related to *how, when,* and *where.* The term *questions* is significant because issues arise from unresolved situations. Should an organization continue to pursue this option? Should the government levy further taxes? Should a pharmaceutical firm approve a new diet pill? Should a nonprofit organization reconsider its decision to use a particular spokesperson? Framing issues in the form of questions can help the planner to understand the debate that will erupt over the issue. Consider the example of the U.S. government's decision to eliminate affirmative action programs. To write an issues statement pertaining to this matter, the planner would not list the issue as affirmative action. Rather, the planner would focus on the strategic or operational questions relevant to affirmative action. The following might be a strategic question for the federal government: "Should the American government dismantle its affirmative action programs?" The debate over this issue would take place both inside and outside government as different parties take positions on the issue. The following might be a more operational question for those inside the organization: "Should the government announce its decision on dismantling affirmative action before the next election?" The debate over the latter issue would probably be restricted to those within the governing caucus. Bureaucrats and politicians often argue among themselves over the best timing for announcements.

Consider a second example. A few years ago, the Republicans attacked President Bill Clinton and the Democrats for hosting fund-raising dinners inside the White House. The issue for the White House was not fund-raising because all political parties engage in fund-raising. No one would dispute the necessity or rationale for fund-raising activities. The strategic issue was much more specific: "Should the president be allowed to hold political fund-raising dinners at the White House?" "Should the public pay for dinners used to fund political events?" A more operational issue was the following: "Should the president have given the videotapes of the fund-raising dinners to Attorney General Janet Reno at an earlier date?" By framing the strategic and operational issues as questions, the planner can anticipate the public debate. This knowledge can assist the organization in preparing for the debate—whether through plans for executive briefings, preparation of "Q's & A's" (questions and answers) on the topic, press releases, or other communication vehicles.

The previous examples illustrate the first characteristic of issues: their unresolved nature. The examples also demonstrate a second characteristic: Issues imply the existence of a debate, represented by at least two sides or points of view. This debate may be in regard to "ends (what), philosophy (why), location (where), timing (when), and who might be helped or hurt by different ways of resolving the issues (who)" (Dutton, Stempf, & Wagner, 1990, p. 144). Examining the nature of the debate reveals a third characteristic of issues: conflict of values. Issues are value-laced. For example, a debate over subsidized housing or social programs evokes arguments that pit economics against humanitarian and egalitarian concerns. The efficiency ethic becomes the foundation for arguments in favor of downsizing. The abortion debate arouses the strongest of emotions, with pro-life advocates arguing on the grounds of right to life and pro-choice advocates arguing for the right to self determination. During the 1960s, those who championed patriotism as the ultimate American value came into bitter conflict with those who gave a greater weighting to peaceful coexistence and pacifistic conduct. Americans value competitiveness and individual accomplishment. Many politicians brag about their rise from anonymity and poverty to a higher place in American society, a reference to the Horatio Alger myth of the self-made individual. Not all subcultures within America, however, place the same value on "getting ahead." Some place a greater value on cooperation and harmony in personal and work relationships. The differences in orientation toward the concept of competitiveness translate into debates over criteria for access to higher education, individual versus group bonuses in organizations, the use of steroids in athletic competitions, courtroom ethics, and many other issues. When governments decide whether to pay for "search and rescue" missions or to care for those with AIDS, they make a value judgment. "Yes" says that human life has a higher place than economics in our society. Issues with low value potency will probably not appear in the strategic plan. Because few organizations have the resources to deal with large numbers of issues, they tend to place their emphasis on those issues with the greatest potential to threaten the organization. This part of the communication plan should provide an overview statement that prioritizes organizational issues, taking value potency and other factors into account. (See Chapter 12 for a more detailed analysis of strategic considerations related to issues.)

Some issues do not emerge until the policy implementation stage. For example, Americans may accept the need for a policy such as stricter enforcement of drug laws at international borders. The same people may object strenuously, however, to longer waits at the airport or strip searches— ways in which the policy is implemented. Americans may believe in policies that protect against sexual harassment, but they may object to overzealous implementation of the policies. The passing of legislation or the implemen-tation of a policy does not necessarily mean that the accompanying issues will disappear. Issues persist until the organization's publics accept the legislation or policies as justified and legitimate. Until this acceptance occurs, the organization will need to adopt coping strategies.

Different groups "own" different aspects of an issue. Consider the Waco standoff. At one point in the confrontation with cult leader David Koresh, the office of the U.S. attorney general faced a strategic policy choice regarding whether to enter the dispute. The strategic policy issue was "Does the attorney general's office own part of the dispute?" Community churches and religious leaders had to decide their position on an issue that had potentially serious ramifications for people's right to worship as they wish. For these groups and individuals, the question was "Should the church approve state intervention in matters involving religion?" The issue for human rights groups was similar: "Should human rights organizations sanction government actions against private citizens?" The cult members had to decide the most critical issue: "Should we surrender?" With the unfavorable resolution of the issue (the burning of the compound and the loss of many lives, including children), the strategic issue for President Bill Clinton became "Should the office of the presidency distance itself from the decision made by the office of the attorney general?" The Clinton administration owned the political dimensions of the Waco issue. The U.S. attorney general and the state attorney general owned legal dimensions of the issue. Texas churches were concerned with the religious implications.

Within the same organization, different sectors or groups may own different aspects of an issue. For example, in the case of the Tylenol poisonings, the strategic policy decision for the CEO and his executive constellation was "Should the company remove all Tylenol products from the shelves?" For research and development, the policy issue revolved around the question "Should the company replace all capsule products with tablets or 'caplets'?" The legal team at Johnson & Johnson confronted the most difficult issue: "Should the company accept legal responsibility for the poisonings?" Overnight, a crisis generates many strategic issues to which an organization must respond. See Chapter 12 for further discussion of ownership questions.

Where does the communication planner go to locate the "hot issues"? In addition to identifying decision options, some corporate plans contain explicit issue statements. Even if the corporate or business plan does not explicitly state the issues, however, it will help the planner to identify current or emerging issues. Consultations with others in the organization should ensure that the planner is aware of all critical issues.

The statement of issues should appear in the same order as the decisions and corporate or business/functional objectives to which they relate. If the first objective of a municipal government is "to promote environmental awareness" (Objective A), a related policy decision could be "to charge for pickup of garbage bags containing nonrecyclable materials" (Policy Decision A). An issue arising from this policy decision could be "whether or not the city should charge for services that used to be free" (Issue A). A second objective of the municipality might be "to increase community participation in city life" (Objective B). A related policy decision could be "to build a pavilion for concerts and meetings" (Policy Decision B). A related issue could be "Should the city build a pavilion instead of a new ballpark?" Other issues (relating to Policy Decision B and Objective B) could concern the cost or the location of the pavilion. All these issues belong in the "B" category because they have linkages to Policy Decision B and Corporate Objective B. Arranging the issues in the same order as policy decisions and corporate objectives maintains a logical order of development in the plan. Some issues relate to more than one corporate objective.

In review, the policies articulated in corporate and business plans have the potential to generate debate, which can involve the general public, interest groups, or stakeholders within the organization. The corporation or government charges communication groups with the responsibility of managing this debate. To plan effectively, communicators must be able to articulate the policy issues that they will confront. They must also be able to distinguish between issues "owned" by their organization or business unit and issues for which they have no responsibility. The mandate and mission of the organization determine questions of ownership (see Chapter 1). Therefore, the first step in planning for issues management is to extrapolate, from the corporate and business (or functional) plans, the policy decisions and their spin-off issues.

External Environment

The role of the strategic planner is to provide management with an accurate analysis of stakeholder views and activities that could affect the operations of the organization. The term *external environment,* in this context, refers to the climate of opinion and knowledge outside the boundaries of the organization—that is, the levels of awareness, views, and related activities of external stakeholders (customers, shareholders, suppliers, the general public, special interest groups or activists, and others). This section of the plan outlines positive and negative factors in the external environment. What do Americans think about the policy decisions and strategies? How much do they know about the issues? Can behavioral patterns, relevant to the issues in question, be discerned? Do opinions vary in different regions of the country or among different clients or customers? If interest groups have been active on these or other topics, the external environment should also reflect their views and efforts at advocacy. Representative democracy demands that governments take the views of constituencies into account. Similarly, business and nonprofit organizations that ignore public opinion do so at great risk. Communication strategies (public relations, marketing communications, and advertising) must be grounded in a clear understanding of the levels of awareness, knowledge, beliefs, attitudes, values, and behavioral patterns of the audience.

External publics also have opinions on how the organization is performing. These views influence their willingness to accept organizational messages (Moffitt, 1994; Williams & Moffitt, 1997). This section of the plan documents these views with statements such as the following: "External clients are not happy with the amount of information that they are receiving from the organization" or "The pharmaceutical industry has expressed satisfaction with the increased opportunities for personal contact with agency representatives." Sometimes stakeholders do not know how to get information or services. They do not understand the distinctions between services supplied by municipal, state, and federal governments. They may become confused about who is responsible for supplying information, products, or services. This sort of confusion often accompanies restructuring. A statement could observe "Older Americans are unsure as to which government agency to contact for information on pensions."

Consistent monitoring of public opinion and customer attitudes provides the basis for the statements that appear in this part of the plan. Speculation is not in order. In other words, every statement that appears in the external environment section of the plan should be grounded in opinion, attitudinal, and behavioral research. The planner should be able to produce hard data to back up every statement. Common sources of information include the Internet (e.g., news groups and web sites), telephone inquiries, surveys, articles appearing in the print and electronic media, focus group reports, association and employee newsletters, correspondence, reports of House and Senate debates, interest group profiles, public consultation reports, correspondence, trade shows, and think tank reports (Table 3.1). Increased use of computer databases and on-line resources facilitate the monitoring of issues and the projection of trends (Johnson, 1997; Ramsey, 1993; Thomsen, 1995).

To write an environment statement, the planner refers to policy decisions and issues. As in the earlier sections, the order of presentation should conform to the initial ordering of corporate or business/functional objectives: Objective A, B, C, D, and E. Andriole (1985) speaks of the importance of causal considerations:

Strategic planning is grounded directly in judgments about environmental influences on corporate decisions and the operation of chains and networks of

TABLE 3.1   Information Sources

Business/industry	Special interest groups	Elected representatives
Internet (news groups, web pages)	Correspondence	Records of House & Senate debates
Interpersonal contacts (clients, consultants, competitors, suppliers, etc.)	Interviews with spokespersons	Interviews
Wall Street trading reports	Newsletters originating with interest groups	Speeches
Business & financial journals	News & feature articles	Comments in state legislatures
Trade journals and shows	Letters to the editor	Voting records of senators & congressional representatives
Technical journals & conferences	Group profiles generated by commercial firms	Court decisions
Academic journals & conferences	Position papers	Administrative decisions
Annual financial reports	Advertising	Media
Newspapers	Surveys	Household newsletter
TV & radio documentaries & news reports	Presentations to House & Senate committees	Internet (web pages)
Corporate magazines	Access to information requests	**Organized labor**
Employee newsletters	News releases	Interviews
Press releases & press conferences	Consultations	Print & electronic media
Hotlines	Records of lobbyist efforts	Trade magazines
Patent applications	Speeches	Newsletters
Sales reports	Reports of conferences & meetings	Internet (web pages, news groups)
Speeches	Ethnic media	Speeches
Brochures	Talk shows (TV & radio)	Correspondence
Advertisements	Internet (news groups, web pages)	Court cases
Correspondence		
International data bases		

General public	Government	Elite opinion leaders
Surveys & polls	State of the Union address	Interviews
Letters to the editor	Cabinet records	Journal articles
Correspondence	Annual reports	Reports by think tanks
Census reports	Speeches	Surveys
Focus groups	News releases & press conferences	Briefs to government committees
Evaluation & audit reports	Background papers	Correspondence
Customer & client service reports	Briefing notes	Letters to the editor
Public consultation reports	Interviews	Print and electronic media
Public inquiry records	Publications	Profiles generated by commercial firms
Records of complaints	Employee survey reports	Speeches
Speakers' bureau reports	Executive agenda	Association meetings
Court cases	Strategic plans	Talk shows
Print & electronic media	Requests for access to information	Internet (web pages, news groups)
Internet (news groups, web pages)	Internet (web pages)	

SOURCE: Reprinted with permission from Ferguson (1994, pp. 34-35).

causal factors. A strategic plan is really a set of objectives anchored in the matrix of a large and complex causal model. (p. 141)

Because some factors in the external environment are double-edged, having both positive and negative dimensions, some planners do not differentiate between positiveandnegativefactorsintheopinion,attitudinal,andbehavioralenvironment.

Statements that appear in long-term plans tend to be conclusive and broad. Because communication plans at the corporate level respond to the concerns of many business units, the planner cannot reference the results of every survey or media analysis. Therefore, it is unlikely that the statements will reveal specifics on the sources. Appropriate statements include the following: "Polls suggest that the large majority of Americans support government efforts to control deficit spending" and "Correspondence suggests that many shareholders support the acquisition of Company X." Alternatively, the statements could omit any form of reference to sources: "Americans support government efforts to control deficit spending" or "Many shareholders support the acquisition of Company X."

Statements in the external environment should reflect reality—the environment as it is and not as the organization would like it to be (Ferguson, 1994). The job of a planner can be very political. The desire to look good can drive management to ask for the nice parts of the picture. An inadequate statement of problem areas or one that "glosses over" potential obstacles, however, can result in the organization's being forced to respond reactively at some later date. Strategically inclined organizations not only tolerate but also encourage the discussion of bad news. They build this performance indicator into employee evaluation and reward systems. They give bonuses to whistle-blowers and employees and managers who expose "hidden dangers, malfunctions, or product defects" (Mitroff & Pearson, 1993, p. 123). Henry Kaiser once observed, "I always view problems as opportunities in work clothes" (as quoted in Fink, 1986). The planner's job is to turn negatives into positives (Morgan, 1992). At the same time, the planner should not neglect the positive elements. Directing excess energy toward the negative can be counterproductive, especially if the source of the negative comment is more shrill than representative.

The external environment links directly to corporate objectives. The corporate planner undertakes environmental analysis to predict how economic, technological, social, cultural, and political or legal forces can affect the organization. The communication planner undertakes environmental analy-

sis to predict how public opinion can influence the organization's capacity
to achieve its objectives.

Internal Environment

This part of the plan outlines positive and negative factors in the internal
environment. Much of the information incorporated into this section of the
plan pertains to employee perceptions, drawn from the results of communication audits. For example, surveys or interviews may determine that employees need more information on impending changes related to restructuring, relocation of offices, or other organizational changes; a new electronic
bulletin board may have increased the opportunity for branch managers to
contribute to corporate direction; and the establishment of "coffee shops" on
the internal computer network may have had a positive impact on employee
morale. How employees feel about their organization has a potentially huge
effect on their performance. Thus, this section of the plan includes references
to practices with a positive or, alternatively, a negative effect on employees.

Windows of Opportunity

Sometimes the organization wishes to relay information unrelated to
issues. For example, governments and politicians transmit information relevant to the health, education, and employment needs of their constituencies.
Many research organizations have ongoing educational programs to inform
the public about their research results. They may have few issues, apart from
concerns about testing procedures or use of animals in research. The following example illustrates this point. Approximately 10 years ago, the communication group at the National Research Council in Canada analyzed its press
clippings each month. They did not try to count the number of positive and
negative news items, as did most government departments. When asked why
they had chosen such an unusual performance indicator, one spokesperson
said that almost all their media coverage was positive. Their aim was to
generate more of the same. As a consultant to the National Research Council,
I had to modify the communication planning format to accommodate the
needs of a different kind of organization. Voluntary sector organizations fit
much the same pattern. Service organizations typically have few "hot issues,"
unless they face a crisis such as the one confronted by the Red Cross in
Canada. (The Red Cross failed to survive the bad publicity created by an

unwise administrative decision to continue infusions of untested blood, even after Red Cross administrators learned of the high risk of transmitting the HIV virus to patients.) With or without crises, service organizations have ongoing communication needs that serve their mandate, however. In many instances, organizations want to publicize "good news"—contributions to charity, support for community activities, the results of product research or other activities, or the expertise and accomplishments of their employees. To ensure the allocation of resources to publicity, the organization articulates the informational needs in the annual or multiyear plans.

Communication Objectives

Often, the objectives of communication are simply "to communicate" (Broom & Dozier, 1990), and completing the task becomes the goal (Pavlik, 1987). The endless recycling of communication activities from previous years means that the subsequent year's communication budget becomes "an incremental adjustment of last year's budget . . . institutionalized and routine" (Dozier & Ehling, 1992, p. 161). Objectives should not reflect last year's priorities. Nor should they be arbitrary. Communication objectives flow directly from the corporate or business objectives, policy issues, external environment, and internal environment of publics. As with the other sections of the plan, it is useful to organize the discussion so that the communication objectives appear in the same order as the corporate objectives to which they relate. Therefore, a communication objective that flows from "Corporate Objective A" would appear before a communication objective that stems from "Corporate Objective B" or "Corporate Objective C." The same is true for communication objectives that relate to business plans.

Communication objectives reflect attempts to

- Change or reinforce the audience's level of knowledge (cognitive influence)
- Change or reinforce how the audience feels about the subject (attitudinal influence)
- Change or reinforce audience behaviors (behavioral influence)

In other words, the communicator seeks to inform, persuade, or move to action. Communication objectives must be clearly relevant to the function of a communicator. Statements such as "to reduce inequities in access to . . ." or "to establish a new mechanism for . . ." are corporate or business/functional

tional objectives and not communication objectives. Examples of communication objectives that could flow from the corporate objectives of the U.S. Department of Health and Human Services are "to encourage Americans to lead an active healthy lifestyle" and "to inform Americans on major research funding priorities."

Several cautions apply in writing communication objectives. First, communication objectives to accompany a corporate plan should be broad in scale and scope. Second, they should reflect all communication activities required by the organization (the needs of public relations, advertising, and marketing communications groups). Third, they should reflect the interests, but not the biases, of individual business/functional units within the organization. Therefore, a statement such as "to convince marketing communications to work more closely with the public relations group" or "to convince research and development to work more closely with advertising" is inappropriate. The corporate communication planner wears the hat of all business units. Consequently, the statement must be neutral. If problems exist between groups in terms of communication flow, the communication planner can point to the need in the following way: "to encourage more communication flow between marketing communications and public relations" or, in another scenario, "to encourage more communication flow between sales and marketing communications." Moreover, the planner does not write the plan from the perspective of what is good for the communication group but rather from the perspective of what is good for the corporate entity. A communication plan written at the level of the business or functional unit, assumes the perspective of that unit.

Fourth, some communication objectives address the needs of audiences within the organization (employees or management), whereas others address the needs of audiences outside the organization (customers and clients). An example of a communication objective designed to address the employees of a large banking firm is "to inform employees of the changes that will occur subsequent to restructuring." An example of a communication objective written for the external audience of a bank is "to persuade older Americans to invest in registered savings plans." Fifth, the planner should limit communication objectives to realistic numbers. Plans with too many objectives are unrealistic, and no organization should have too broad an agenda. In most cases, budgetary restraints influence the range and number of communication objectives.

Sixth, an organization can address an issue on a rhetorical level or a pragmatic level (through policy, legislation, etc.). Communication objectives relate only to the rhetorical because a communicator does not undertake policy initiatives as part of his or her job. For this reason, the communication group may choose to be silent on some issues. The decision to include an issue in a strategic plan does not imply the need to communicate the organization's stance to external audiences. Sometimes, the issue may be so volatile that the public relations group advises the organization to adopt a low-key approach. Sometimes, the less communicated on an issue the better (particularly with no-win issues such as abortion and capital punishment or the use of animals in cancer research). On other occasions, the organization may not own the issue, even if the public thinks it does own it (see Chapter 12). If the organization does not own the issue, it may not be appropriate to communicate a position on the issue. For example, the public may blame a federal parole board for releasing an offender who later commits murder. In fact, the responsible party may be the Justice Department that frames the laws or the attorney general's office that implements them. The federal parole board, however, may not want to assign blame in a public way to other government departments or agencies. In this case, the representatives may choose to remain silent on the issue and accept the blame.

Finally, sometimes the organization chooses to communicate its internal strengths to external audiences (e.g., acknowledged scientific expertise or an international reputation for quality). Other times, the planner may include a communication objective designed to clarify the mandate or mission of the organization. When framing communication objectives related to image, the planner should take care not to write objectives such as the following: "to depict the company as concerned about environmental issues." This wording implies that the organization is not really concerned but would like to be perceived as conscientious. Others counsel that if the organization does everything it needs to do, a good image will be the end result—with or without an explicit communication objective related to image.

Themes and Messages

A theme is a general, overriding, often recurring idea that can encompass a variety of related messages. An organization develops themes to reflect areas to which they are directing their attention at any given moment. Examples of government themes are "reducing the deficit," "increasing employment opportunities," "protecting the environment," and "fighting drugs and crime." An example of a commercial theme is "customized or affordable services." Unlike themes, a message is a specific statement of limited scope, usually containing only one main idea. The organization sends messages to audiences inside and outside its boundaries. Any individual message will be a variation on a particular theme. An organization has more messages than themes. This section of the strategic or business communication plan should express, in the simplest terms, the themes and messages to be carried in all its communication products. Corporate messages ultimately appear in press releases, speeches by CEOs and other officials, conference presentations, brochures, slide shows for community groups, and media interviews. These messages relate to communication objectives. They also respond to the needs and opportunities identified in the external and internal environments.

The formal statement of messages in a strategic communication plan can also serve as a reference point for those who write messages for support plans. The messages in the strategic communication plan, however, will be broader than those that appear in support plans for marketing communications or advertising campaigns, information campaigns, and other communication activities. For example, an appropriate message for the corporate level might be "Government is pushing industry to adopt more environmentally friendly practices." At the level of a support plan, the same message could become "The government passed Bill 209 to force chemical plants to conform to more rigorous emission standards." Messages should appear in the same order as the communication objectives to which they relate. Messages in business plans will be more specific than messages in corporate plans but less specific than messages in support plans.

Communication Priorities

Usually, communication executives assume responsibility for planning at the corporate level. Middle-level communicators assume responsibility for writing business/functional and support plans. This hierarchy of job duties influences the level of specificity in plans. That is, whereas senior communication managers typically determine the broad direction of communication, they do not design the individual activities. For this reason, the communication priorities section of the plan, written by senior-level managers and their assistants, will be reasonably broad. The planning team may suggest that an emphasis should be placed, in the coming year, on more open communication with employees, community outreach and partnerships, improved communication with shareholders, developing web sites on the Internet, and a campaign to inform the public of the results of recent research activities. These senior-level planners, however, do not specify how these priorities will translate into specific communication activities. Middle managers and planners working at lower levels, charged with bringing life to the priorities, develop the more concrete approaches that surface in later planning stages (operational, work, and support plans).

Decisions on communication priorities can be justified to the extent that they relate to earlier sections of the plan. Communication priorities must respond to the needs of both external and internal audiences. Priorities related to the internal environment will influence every aspect of the organization's functioning. These statements should appear in the same order as the communication objectives to which they relate. Therefore, a priority designed to respond to Communication Objective A would appear in the plan before a priority designed to respond to Communication Objective B. Maintaining this presentation order keeps the planner focused on the linkages between different parts of the plan. The communication priorities section of the strategic plan becomes the starting point for subsequent operational planning exercises.

Strategic Considerations

The term *strategic considerations* refers to recommended approaches to communication activities. This section of the plan can be speculative. The planner "adds value" to the hard data acquired through research and analysis. For example, the planner can comment on

- Cautions in proceeding with communication activities
- The level of desired visibility for the activities
- Target audiences to be reached
- How the organization would like to be positioned in the public view
- Opportunities for "piggybacking" some activities on others
- Implications in the general level of support expected from constituencies

Consultation, Partnerships, and Negotiation Requirements

The current emphasis on partnerships means that most planning exercises require consultation. The strategic communication plan, written to complement the corporate or business/functional plan, necessitates consultations with internal and external stakeholders. Thus, this section of the plan states anticipated requirements for consultation, coordination, or the active cooperation of other individuals or groups. The planner asks "Who are the relevant actors? . . . Into what networks do they tap?" (Benveniste, 1989, p. 162). The plan can be so specific as to designate individuals or executives who should be consulted or so general as to indicate corporate entities or business/functional units. Government communicators often consider other government departments as internal stakeholders and the general public, interest groups, and others as external stakeholders. Within the organization, consultations can involve more than one functional or business unit or more than one communication group (advertising, promotion, and marketing communications). In addition to specifying consultation needs, the plan can suggest partners for communication activities. Coalitions help to ensure that plans are realized. Negotiation can also be important. Many public disputes require consensual approaches to problem solving. See Chapter 13 for a detailed discussion of consultation and negotiation.

Performance Indicators

A process begun in 1993, the National Performance Review examined planning processes and performance in government agencies and "best-in-class" organizations. At the end of the study, they concluded that all levels of the organization must evaluate their performance and tie incentives and compensation to this performance. Although performance measures varied from one level of the organization to another, each level of the organization linked its performance measures to achievement of overall organizational objectives (National Performance Review, p. 5). Redding and Catalanello (1994) said that learning organizations typically strive to achieve a "continuing series of ambitious, short-term benchmarks" (p. 71). They sprint after relatively short-term targets, even though they have a long-distance goal. At their best, annual and multiyear planning documents establish a series of performance indicators to be assessed at regular intervals throughout the planning period. Several recent conferences (1998 and 1999)—sponsored by the International Quality and Productivity Center, the International Communications for Management, and the Institute for International Research—addressed the need for performance indicators in communication.

Applied in the context of annual or multiyear planning for communication, performance indicators suggest the need to measure outcomes (the extent to which the organization met its overall communication objectives for a given fiscal year). If the communication objective was "to encourage increased public knowledge, interest, and involvement in the environmental movement," performance indicators for outcomes could be

- The level of knowledge demonstrated by the public
- The number of new members who gave financial support to the organization
- The number of people who volunteered for activities

Ideally, the communication group should have the results of exercises that measured the extent to which the organization achieved its many individual communication activities (information, marketing communications, and advertising campaigns); issues management; relationship building; and other communication activities designed to inform, persuade, or move audiences to action. The cumulative results of these evaluations should enable the communication or planning group to evaluate the achievement of broad objectives. If no hard data exist, the conclusions will be much more subjective and thus more unreliable and probably self-serving.

Anticipated Financial Resources

The strategic plan provides the basis for resource allocations. It has been said that "planning drives the budget" (National Performance Review, 1997, p. 3). This section of the plan identifies the budget, developed in concert with the financial planning processes of the organization. In some organizations, communication groups obtain their money from a central budget. In others, the communication group receives funding directly from clients in business or functional units. In either case, the communication executive uses the strategic plan to justify budget requests. The appendix provides a sample strategic communication plan.

Conclusion

The organization's strategic plan is a "motherhood" document that lays out strategic direction in broad, visionary terms. This level of planning does not contain the specific language that is used in later stages of planning. Although some firms may believe that information on their strategic direction should be safeguarded, most would be more concerned about sharing the specific, concrete information that appears in support plans. For communication planners, closely guarded corporate and business plans pose a particular problem. How can communicators engage in coherent and proactive planning if they do not know where the organization is heading or what it is doing? Piecemeal, reactive communications do not work. Progressive organizations have instituted integrated planning systems in organizations.

Appendix

The following plan was written by Sherry Devereaux Ferguson and Ginette Lauriault. The plan is based on a fictitious government agency. The letters A, B, C, and D are used to demonstrate how all parts of the plan link to corporate objectives. The letter I refers to statements on the internal environment, which can influence the achievement of all the objectives of the organization. In the same way, the letter G refers to statements on the external environment that can relate to all organizational objectives, such as "research and analysis of public opinion."

Strategic Communication Plan for the
U.S. Drug Administration (USDA)

Background Statement

This part of the plan establishes the background for the communication plan. For example, the planner may point to restructuring efforts, broad initiatives undertaken, and demographic trends influencing what is happening.

The USDA has just undergone a major review. Management is anxious to begin to address some of the major issues that face the organization, as external stakeholders have become increasingly active in the past year.

Corporate or Business/Functional Objectives

Corporate objectives or business/functional objectives provide a reference point for strategic planning in communication. For the purpose of this case study, the USDA would have the following mission statement and functional objectives.

The mission of the USDA is to contribute to the health and safety of Americans. The USDA achieves this goal by ensuring that Americans have safe, effective, high-quality drugs and sufficient information to use the drugs properly. The following functional objectives flow from this mission:

A • Assess the safety and efficacy of drugs and manage the risks.

B • Provide Americans with the information they require to make rational use of drugs and become equal partners in protecting their health and safety.

C • Develop sharing, cooperative relationships with industry, academics, and professional organizations.

D • Establish the United States as a cooperative and productive player on the international drug regulatory scenes.

Policy Issues

Current and emerging policy debates for the USDA concern whether or not:

A • Americans are being provided with safe and efficacious drugs.

A • Americans are being provided with new products in a timely fashion.

A • The United States has a safe and effective surveillance program.

A • The government should deregulate low-risk products.

B • The government is providing sufficient information to the public on how to use drugs safely and effectively.

C • The USDA is providing clients and partners with useful information.

D • The United States should harmonize its system with that of other industrialized countries.

D • The United States should link its surveillance program more closely to other countries.

External Environment

The external environment documents the opinions and actions of stakeholders outside the boundaries of the organization. The opinions may relate to policy issues or the performance of the organization.

Positive Factors

A • A recent review found that experts regard the American drug regulatory system as one of the most thorough and comprehensive in the world in terms of offering protection.

A   • The public perceives that, in general, the government is fulfilling its responsibility to protect people against risks.

B   • A 1998 survey indicates that Americans who know about the USDA see it as a useful and credible source of information.

B   There is a growing acceptance of government's position that there may be better ways to achieve societal goals than relying strictly on governments.

C   • Industry recognizes the value, in financial terms, of work undertaken by the USDA.

D   • Visiting delegations from other countries often request presentations on a wide variety of topics.

Negative Factors

A   • Governments have to take the economy into account in their planning and allocation of budgets, but people are unwilling to accept even low-hazard risks.

A   • The public perceives that the government does more in the way of regulating and testing than it actually does; this situation leads the public to assign blame when the government fails to perform in these areas.

A   • Consumer and patient associations, large segments of the academic and professional communities, and some industry groups criticize the government for delays in releasing new products.

B   • Even while there is a growing recognition that government may not always be the most efficient or effective agent for achieving societal goals, Americans continue to ask the government for better services, better protection, and more involvement in determining the nature and delivery mode of those services.

B   • The Bruner report found that consumers cannot always understand the reports released for public consumption.

C   • Some professional groups complain that reports are released too late to be of any real value or are directed to the wrong people; others say that they receive multiple copies of the same data.

D   • Stakeholders who are more knowledgeable about scientific process want the government to make better use of studies carried out by other countries.

Internal Environment

This section describes the opinions and actions of internal stakeholders. What are their information needs? How do they feel about the communication practices of the organization? What are the positive and negative factors in the internal environment? The internal environment has a strong influence on the organization's ability to achieve corporate and business objectives.

Positive Factors

I
- Employees find the biannual information sessions, sponsored by upper management, to be very useful; they would like to meet more often with upper management.

I
- Employees appreciate the opportunity to receive training in interpersonal and intercultural communication.

Negative Factors

I
- Employees complain about insufficient information and feedback, favoritism that results in only a select few being "in the know," and an active grapevine that results from lack of openness and timeliness in communication.

I
- A recent review agreed that the USDA requires a more effective internal communication system to inform employees of changes in policies and practices.

I
- The review identified a need for more face-to-face meetings, involving all staff, to present an opportunity for questions about change processes underway in the USDA.

I
- Employees have voiced the need for greater recognition by peers and management when they complete regular tasks or special assignments in an exemplary way.

Windows of Opportunity

The organization may want to communicate good news, actions, or research undertaken to benefit internal and external stakeholders.

External Clients

A
- The USDA has already begun to identify opportunities to publicize its role and activities with academia, professionals, and the general public.

B   • The USDA often acts in partnership with other government departments, industry, and professionals.

C   • The USDA is compiling an inventory of the contents of all publications for the purpose of determining areas of overlap.

D   • The United States participates in a number of international conferences on drug testing and surveillance.

Internal Clients

I   • The USDA has initiated "Thank-You" and "Employee Recognition" campaigns.

I   • An electronic suggestion box has been established to collect the views of employees.

I   • A committee has been appointed to head up a "Let's Talk Campaign" to promote two-way communications.

I   • The new electronic mail system makes it easier for employees to communicate with each other.

I   • Other ongoing initiatives include focus groups and surveys to determine staff needs.

I   • Periodic updating of a comprehensive electronic directory of all employees facilitates regular contact between employees.

I   • A pilot project, under way in Corporate Services, is expected to lead to a proposal for a department-wide feedback system.

Communication Objectives

The following communication objectives link directly to the external and internal environments and actions being undertaken by the organizations to respond to these environments.

External Audiences

A   • To create a better understanding of how the USDA performs its safety and regulatory functions

A   • To promote better awareness of the sound scientific foundations that underpin regulatory decision making

A   • To communicate America's leadership role in developing and adopting effective evaluation and surveillance practices

A	• To educate audiences on the relationship between the advance of science, the globalization of markets, and changes in how low-level risks are regulated and managed
B	• To promote safety awareness among Americans
B	• To encourage Americans to share responsibility with government on matters that affect their health and safety
C, D	• To encourage partnerships with public and private sector organizations (state, national, and international) engaged in research, assessment, and control
D	• To communicate the nature and extent of America's cooperation with other countries—in terms of both giving and receiving information

Internal Audiences

I	• To encourage timely and open two-way communications with stakeholders
I	• To help create an environment in which the USDA employees feel recognized and appreciated
I	• To promote a better awareness of the benefits of the change process and the role played by individual employees

Messages

This section of the communication plan expresses, in the simplest terms, the messages that the administration hopes to convey to its target publics. Variations on these broad messages should be carried in all of the USDA's products during the coming year—internal memoranda, press releases, ministerial and executive speeches, brochures, and other publications.

Messages to External Audiences

A	• Managed risk is today's reality; no product is 100% safe.
A	• America is a recognized leader in protection.
A	• The USDA makes an ongoing effort to improve its evaluation and surveillance systems.
B	• Protection is the shared responsibility of individuals and governments.
B	• Information is the key to sound decisions.

C, D   • Learning organizations share information.

C, D   • Partnership is the key to success.

D   • The USDA wants to work with its international colleagues.

<u>Messages to Internal Audiences</u>

I   • The USDA values open, personal, and timely communications.

I   • Employees are our most important resource.

I   • Opportunities will be available to ask questions about change
           processes.

Communication Priorities

Communication priorities refer to areas of emphasis implied in the preceding section of the plan: an emphasis on employee communications, research and analysis, or increasing the visibility of the organization; an information campaign; a conference; or other broad undertaking.

A   • Information campaign to increase the visibility of the USDA

B   • Advertising campaign on safe, effective use of drugs

C   • Communication of changes under way at the USDA to client
           groups who believe the system is too slow to be effective: for
           example, consumer and patient associations, academics and
           professionals, and members of the pharmaceutical industry

D   • Greater communication with other countries—in terms of both
           giving and receiving information—is necessary to achieve a
           leadership position in product assessment

I   • A major employee communication initiative to improve
           employee morale as it relates to communication practices in the
           organization

G   • Research and analysis of the external environment to determine
           levels of awareness, attitudes, and behaviors

Strategic Considerations

Unlike the statements on internal and external environments, which are based on hard data obtained from monitoring efforts, this section of the plan is speculative, with value-added judgments, cautions in proceeding, and recommendations for action.

A	• Any public communication strategy, designed to communicate systemic changes, should assure the public that the planned changes will not compromise the safety of the review process.
B	• A number of other government initiatives are currently emphasizing the need for grassroots ownership of problems and solutions; thus, the public should be more receptive to the USDA's attempt to get people to share responsibility and take individual action.
B	• There needs to be a greater effort to communicate with the general public on their level so that the public can apply the information in their everyday lives.
C	• The USDA enjoys general industry support; to maintain this good will, however, it needs to maintain timely communications.
C, D	• Opportunities for "piggybacking" other activities should be explored: for example, conferences sponsored by other private sector firms, nonprofit groups, professional associations, and state or municipal agencies; gatherings of seniors' groups; and annual meetings of manufacturers.
C, D	• Efforts should be made to build on existing partnerships; the USDA particularly needs to capitalize on existing interest in industry and professionals.
I	• Any system to inform employees about changes in policies, practices, and systems should include all USDA managers and staff and involve multiple channels of communication.
I	• Any communication strategy should be based on a coordinated USDA-wide commitment.
I	• To effect changes in the corporate culture, the USDA should encourage activities that allow informal—as well as formal—sharing of information among USDA employees: for example, social occasions.
I	• Communications should be an agenda item for all USDA staff meetings.
I	• Emphasis must be placed on releasing information to all employees at the same time to eliminate the necessity for grapevine communications; all communications within the USDA should be dated.

I   • Employees will become less cynical about change activities once they perceive the USDA is serious about implementing their recommendations; thus, an emphasis should be placed on communicating all implementation efforts.

Requirements for Consultations, Partnerships, and Negotiation

This section of the plan outlines requirements for consultation with stakeholders, suggests partnerships that could be established, and points to situations that could benefit from negotiations.

G   • The following groups should be consulted in planning communication activities in the coming year: the Pharmaceutical Association, the International Drug Standards Commission, and the employees association.

G   • Potential partners for activities include the National Organization of Seniors and the Lifestyle Division of the Department of Health.

G   • The USDA should consider undertaking negotiations with groups that are urging the government to lower its safety requirements for new products. These groups include the Cancer Research Society and the AIDS Research Foundation.

Performance Indicators*

Performance indicators establish a standard by which communication efforts can be measured. The USDA will measure its success by whether it achieves:

A   • Public understanding of the mandate and activities of the USDA

A   • General awareness of the scientific bases on which decisions are made

A   • Increased willingness to rely on the government's judgment on matters pertaining to low-hazard risks

B   • Public awareness of what constitutes safe behavior in using drugs

B, C, D • Communication products and services that are useful, professional, and respected by clients, partners, and the general public

C, D   • Increased numbers of partnerships with many different groups

I   • Employees who feel involved and appreciated

I   • Greater understanding of the change processes by employees

*This section of the plan can go a step further to translate the more qualitative indicators into statistical indicators of performance.

4

Writing the Multiyear or Annual Operational and Work Plans

Operational planning establishes the means by which the organization will pursue its strategic objectives. Whereas strategic planning represents the "what" in planning, operational planning represents the "how." The strategic plan identifies a destination—where the organization wants to be at the end of its journey. The operational plan suggests the mode of transportation, the route to reach this destination, and the stops along the way. In other words, strategic planning decides organizational goals, and operational planning defines how to achieve those goals. How will the organization put its strategic plan into action? Allocate financial and human resources? The operational plan also provides direction for the formulation of work plans.

Operational Communication Planning

Whereas the strategic plan is forward-looking, the operational plan is backward-looking. That is, the operational plan looks backward to the strategic plan for direction. The plan

- Uses communication priorities from the strategic plan as a starting point
- Reviews and orders these priorities

- Points to the linkage between communication priorities and strategic communication objectives
- Identifies key client groups (external and internal) to whom messages should be targeted
- Identifies complementary activities and services, not necessarily performed by the communication group, that can contribute to the achievement of communication objectives
- Identifies the allocation of resources to support communication activities and services

Communication Priorities

The communication priorities, identified in the strategic plan, become the starting point for the multiyear or annual operational plan. The term *communication priorities* refers to areas of emphasis in communication activities. Communication priorities can include advertising or social marketing campaigns, publications, special events, conferences, consultations, audiovisual activities, exhibits, media relations activities, research and analysis, and activities to improve employee communication. Notice that almost all these categories imply multiple activities. The annual operational plan does not break down the clusters into individual activities. The breakdown occurs only at the work planning stage.

To write this section of the plan, the communication planner refers to the "communication priorities" articulated in the strategic communication plan. All subsequent sections of the operational communication plan follow from these initiatives.

Rank Ordering Communication Priorities

The operational plan explains the emphasis to be placed on each communication initiative. That is, the planner establishes a rank order for the communication priorities. At the same time, the plan refers to any changes from priorities designated in the earlier strategic planning phase. An organization may face a crisis situation, cutbacks in people or resources, or reorientation of product or service lines between the time that it formulates or updates its strategic plan and the time that it writes a follow-up operational plan. This possibility for changes in priorities is more likely in the case of multiyear strategic and operational planning. The organization may have transferred funds from one of the priorities in the strategic plan to an unplanned crisis management activity. Some government departments argue that strategic planning is made more difficult by the lack of predictability in their external environments. For example, a wildlife agency may experience many crises during an El Niño year, and the Air Force may discard a campaign (planned at the strategic level) to urge new recruits into the service so that it has money for communication activities stimulated by an unantici-pated conflict with Iraq. This same need to shift priorities can occur with reorientation of the organization (e.g., downsizing). In other words, unex-pected expenditures or shifts in organizational direction can mean that operational planners have to drop some priorities (ones that originated at the strategic planning stage). Some organizations discontinue strategic planning in periods of massive reorganization and restructuring.

If the organization places a rank order on priorities at the time of writing the operational plan, the decisions on priorities will be approved in a rational, unpressured environment. If operational planners find that they must drop some strategic initiatives, they should indicate the reason for the changes in the operational plan. Budgetary considerations drive operational plans. Bringing a strategic objective to life requires financial investment. Increases or decreases in the coffers of the organization can thus influence the ability of the communication group to realize its objectives. The operational plan recognizes these organizational realities.

Top executives often play an important role in establishing issue priorities. A 1992 survey of *Fortune* 500 companies found that 6 of 15 companies confirmed executive involvement in prioritizing the company's issues (Fer-guson, 1994). In government, these individuals are positioned at the highest levels of the bureaucracy and political structures. Their involvement will have taken place at the strategic planning stage. The operational planner, who generally occupies a position in the middle ranks of management, refers to the strategic planning documents to accord priorities to communication initiatives that involve issues management activities.

Linkages to Strategic Plan

This section of the plan articulates the communication objectives that were formulated at the strategic planning stage. As previously noted, different individuals engage in strategic and operational planning. That is, senior executives engage in strategic planning, whereas middle managers carry out operational planning. The senior executives decide the strategic direction and priorities of the organization. The middle managers implement these ideas. The need to restate the communication objectives ensures that the operational planner will refer to the earlier planning efforts.

Key Client Groups

The term *key client groups* refers to internal and external stakeholders who comprise the main audiences for communication products and services. Clients can include employees, managers, customers, or community and society (Kaufman, 1992). They may be interest groups, specific units or divisions of the company, shareholders, upper level executives, the general public, or others. The term *client groups* can apply equally to the public, private, or voluntary sectors.

Complementary Activities and Services

Organizations have ongoing activities and services on which they can draw when they plan special events, advertising or marketing communications campaigns, or issues management activities. A community health organization, planning an antismoking campaign, may find that state health clinics publish brochures on the same topic. The use of some of the materials produced by the state health clinics can reduce the cost of the community campaign. If the U.S. Department of Health and Human Services is planning an information campaign on AIDS, it can identify community groups to help to distribute its educational materials. Policy groups within bureaucracy monitor newspapers, television, and radio stations on an ongoing basis. Communicators charged with developing an issues management plan can use these reports for additional information. Different departments monitor controversial issues from slightly different perspectives. For example, the Department of Justice, the attorney general's office, and the Bureau of Consumer Affairs are probably all involved in the management of issues regarding sweepstakes scams. Although not all their research will apply to every department or agency, some aspects of the research will be germane to each organization. In other words, planners should search for activities and services, inside and outside the organization, to complement their efforts. Economic restraints, attempts to avoid redundancy, and budgetary limitations justify the need to specify existing complementary resources in other organizations or sectors of the same organization.

Financial Resources

Communicators must identify the resources required to carry out each major communication initiative or set of activities. The planner divides the total budget, first identified in the strategic plan, into smaller units. The allocation of funds reflects the priority status of each initiative or cluster of activities. A sample operational plan is shown in Table 4.1.

Communication Work Planning

Work plans grow out of operational planning. Work planning, which takes place on an annual basis, is the most specific, concrete level of planning. Work plans detail actions to be taken by the organization in achieving the operational plan. Work plans accomplish the following:

- Translate communication priorities into products and services to be delivered
- Assign responsibilities—who will deliver which products
- Set milestones—the dates by which communicators will accomplish each task
- Specify performance indicators to be used as a basis for evaluation efforts
- Identify evaluation methodologies for measuring the achievement of goals

Priority Initiatives and Activities

Like the annual or multiyear operational plan, the work plan begins with a statement of strategic communication priorities. The intent is to ensure coherency in planning from the strategic to the operational to the work planning levels.

Products and Services to Be Delivered

A major communication initiative (e.g., a campaign to inform the public of a new electric-powered bicycle) could generate many potential communication products and services. Examples include pamphlets publicizing the new bicycle, press releases to announce when the bicycle will be on the market, feature articles for leisure magazines, speeches for executive officers, and focus groups to determine the best marketing appeals to use in publicizing the new product.

TABLE 4.1   Operational Communication Plan for the U.S. Drug Administration

Communication Priorities	Priority Level	Links to Strategic Communication Objectives	Key Client Groups	Complementary Activities/Services	Budget Work Years	$
Advertising campaign on safe use of drugs	I	To promote safety awareness	General public, seniors & veterans organizations, youth groups, industry partners, physicians	Council for Older Americans and federal & state agencies publish materials on drug safety	X	$
Employee communication initiative	I	To help create an environment in which employees feel valued and recognized	All employees, middle & senior management	Human Resources sponsors "Employee Days" and workshops to sensitize managers to employee needs	X	$
Research and analysis of client awareness & views	II	All objectives	Relevant policy groups in the Department of Health & Safety; senior management	Research and analysis carried out by H & S policy groups & the Addictive Drugs Research Agency; surveys conducted by Human Resources	X	$
Information campaign to increase visibility of USDA	II	To create a better understanding of the role and activities of the USDA	General public, partners at state, national, & federal levels, seniors organizations	Speakers Bureau, media interviews, special events, exhibitions at trade shows	X	$
International conference on managing risks	III	To share findings on the best ways to manage risks and to determine mutually acceptable levels of risk	Partners and clients in industry, professional groups, and academia; other government agencies; international drug regulatory agencies	Academic research findings (published and unpublished)	X	$

Changes in communication priorities from strategic communication plan:

Reasons for the above changes:

NOTE: The format for this plan was developed by Stewart Ferguson. The plan is fictitious.

Responsible Party for Delivering Products and Services

The work plan constitutes "an agreement between the supervisor and the responsible employee, which can be appraised" (Privy Council Office, 1989). Within any firm or bureaucracy, certain designated individuals assume responsibility for delivering or overseeing the delivery of specific products and services. This section of the plan designates those individuals.

Milestones

Milestones specify the deadlines for accomplishing different stages of a project. Typical deadlines for communication undertakings are the dates by which (a) bids should be requested, received, and evaluated (if the organization contracts out the work to an outside firm); (b) the design of a project should be completed; (c) any necessary research should be completed or data collected; (d) the product or service should be delivered; (e) product approvals should be obtained; (f) publication should occur, where applicable; and (g) distribution of the product should occur, where applicable. Although communicators may make changes during the process, they establish an initial schedule for reaching the different steps of the project or campaign. The planner often works backward. That is, the person begins with the last step (when distribution is required) and works backward. Sometimes, the deadlines are very tight.

Performance Indicators

Vince Lombardi, American football coach, once wryly observed, "If you don't keep score, you're only practicing" (as quoted in National Performance Review, 1997, p. 25). Evaluation results provide a rationale for later adjustments or shifts in strategies. A recent survey of public relations practitioners in 13 different countries confirmed a growing awareness of the need for evaluation of communication efforts in organizations (Synnott & McKie, 1997). Performance indicators tell the organization when it has achieved its objectives (Walker, 1994). A communication objective may aim to create awareness, such as "to inform the public of a new opportunity to conduct banking over the telephone." In this situation, performance indicators are the number of people who use the service in the first months of its operation and the number of inquiries received about the service. Another objective could be "to inform potential applicants of the requirements and procedures for obtaining citizenship." Performance indicators are the number of individuals who call the citizenship office for clarification of the requirements, the number of complete and appropriate answers to questions on the application form, the number of trips that applicants make to the citizenship office before they possess all the documents that are required, and level of awareness of the requirements when applicants speak with citizenship office personnel. Other objectives aim to change or reinforce attitudes. If a bus company conducts a campaign to improve public attitudes toward its services, performance indicators are the number of complaints to bus drivers and the head office, the frequency with which the public expresses satisfaction with the service, and numbers of users. in other situations, objectives aim to change or reinforce behaviors. If a telephone company seeks "to encourage people to take care of the equipment in its public telephone booths," performance indicators are the cost of replacing equipment in public booths in the months following the communication campaign, the number of complaints about broken equipment, and the number of hours spent repairing the equipment (Ferguson, 1998b).

Tools and Methodologies

This section of the chapter does not aim to be comprehensive in its coverage of tools and methodologies for measuring communication. The discussion below, however, identifies the most common approaches to evaluating communication products and services (for a detailed discussion, see Ferguson, 1998a).

Outcomes

Audits measure outcomes. For example, the public relations audit seeks to "describe, measure, and assess an organization's public relations activities and to provide guidelines for future public relations programming" (Simon, 1986, p. 150). Through interviews and content analysis of external communications, the research team identifies the most important publics. Then the researchers ask how these audiences view the organization (their opinions, attitudes, and perceptions). The team also judges the audience's knowledge of the organization (whether members recognize the company logo and products, understand the mission statement, and know the name of the president). A public relations audit compares the views and knowledge of different groups, inside and outside the organization. Audits often employ ranking scales. On the basis of what they learn, organizations can improve communications with their publics. Hon (1997, 1998) argued for the necessity to evaluate outcomes in public relations programs. Other kinds of communication audits (e.g., the International Communication Audit) examine the opinions, attitudes, and behaviors of employees.

Outputs

Organizations use quantitative and qualitative methodologies to evaluate their communication outputs. The most common quantitative methodology involves *counting*. The evaluator counts the number of press releases generated, speeches written, exhibits prepared, public service announcements produced, or audiovisual presentations created. The person measures column inches of space, frequency of appearance of concepts, or minutes of broadcast time. This methodology does not attempt to determine the number of readers, listeners, viewers, or participants who received the communication. *Usage counts,* however, determine if (and how much of) the message reached the public. How many press releases and public service announcements appeared in the media? What parts of the message reached the public? How many organizations booked speakers from the Speakers' Bureau? How many times did seniors' groups request a video on healthy living? How many viewers watched the television program? How many listeners tuned into the radio program? How many people attended the meeting? How many people requested or inquired about an advertised product or service? Whereas the first methodology is *organization* centered (how many speeches were written), the second methodology is *audience* centered (how many people heard the speech). Circulation data and information on audience size are available for many print and broadcast media outlets. For example, the Audit Bureau of Circulation reports data for member newspapers and magazines. A. C. Nielson and Company and the Arbitron Company publish estimates of television viewership for more than 200 markets. Arbitron also conducts research for local and network radio (Cutlip Center, & Broom, 1994). These kinds of systems use meters to record the times at which audiences activate their television sets and the channels that they select. In the same way, Internet sites record the number of visitors.

Ketchum Communications, which tracks messages in the top 120 American markets, developed a publicity tracking model. This model generates a computerized audience analysis of groups reached by messages (Dozier & Repper, 1992). The Newlin company uses a similar publicity tracking system that equates product publicity with advertising value (Dozier & Ehling,

1992). Other firms that track placement of messages in print and electronic media include "Bacon's PR and Media Information Systems (Chicago), Burrelles's Press Clipping Service (Livingston, NJ), the Delahaye Group (Hampton Falls, NH), Luce Press Clippings, Inc. (New York), and PR Data Systems, Inc. (Wilton, CT)" (Cutlip et al., 1994, p. 421). One service places an invisible code on client videos that activates a monitor signal decoder whenever video excerpts appear on television. The decoder detects and records air time, date, station, and content aired. Computer programs can quantify the appearance of messages in print media and on the Internet. Such programs can identify, for example, where ideas originate (the source and location), mutations in the message as it moves from one medium to another, and the source of mutations. Clients can suggest key names, topics, or words to be tracked: "organization's name, staff names, products or services, and even similar or competing organizations" (Cutlip et al., 1994, p. 421).

Other readership and viewing tests go a step further than usage counts. Not only do they identify who received the message but also they attempt to measure the extent to which the audience recalls the content. Do people remember the communication product? Do they associate the product with the sponsor? Did they read or view the whole message? The technique devised by Daniel Starch separates readers into three groups: viewers who recall having seen the advertisement, those who remember the name of the advertiser, and those who recall enough to support their claim to have read at least half the copy (Cutlip et al., 1994). The methods used to answer these questions can include diaries, telephone interviews, surveys, and focus groups.

Researchers also seek to determine the quality of communication products generated in organizations. A quantitative measure to assess the quality of communication outputs is the readability test. Formulas constructed by Flesch (1948), Gunning (1968), and Fry (1977) enable the evaluator to determine the comprehensibility and readability of print materials. The person assigns the materials a readability score (Flesch uses "very easy," "easy," "fairly easy," "plain English," "fairly difficult," "difficult," and "very difficult") and grade level (Flesch's levels range from fifth grade to college graduate). The evaluator determines these scores by computing the average number of letters and syllables in words and the average number of words in sentences.

Other methodologies applied to the evaluation of outputs are more quali-tative in nature. Communicators can place inserts in magazines or other products that users remove and use for evaluation purposes. Users reply to specific questions and make general comments about their reaction to the product. Another evaluation technique is the theater test. Political figures often use this device to learn audience reactions to their political speeches and platforms. This test takes place in a controlled environment, often a theater-type setting, in which people press different buttons on a handheld device to indicate the parts of a message they liked or disliked. Electronic monitors chart the results in the form of graphs. The same test can be applied to the evaluation of commercial products or public service announcements.

Focus group testing brings together clients or customers to discuss their feelings and attitudes toward communication products or services. Focus groups respond to questions such as the following: What do you like or dislike about the service that you received from the communication group? The company's new product? What caught your attention in the last brochure that you read? What do you remember from the advertisement that aired on television? How do you feel about the format of the last report that the communication group presented to the executive committee? Which company logo do you prefer? Which cover do you prefer? Were you satisfied with the last media analysis that you received? Why or why not? and What could be improved? A variation on this technique is use of the panel of experts, who assess the quality of some communication product or service. Alternatively, a panel composed of members of the public can react to the questions mentioned earlier. This type of review often takes place during political campaigns, when audience members comment on the strategies and platforms of the candidates. On other occasions, expert review, which refers to subjective assessments of product quality by a single individual with expertise in the area, can be employed. For example, an experienced editor might be asked to evaluate the quality of a pamphlet.

Process and Efficiency

Many methodologies can be used to evaluate process and efficiency of operations, including surveys, interviews, observation, and other means.

Impact

The use of pretests and posttests enable researchers to measure impact or changes in levels of awareness, knowledge, acceptance, attitudes, relationships, or behaviors. Common tools for acquiring this information are surveys, focus groups, expert panels, and interviews. Evaluators can ask selected individuals to record their attitudes and behaviors over a period of time in a diary. Longitudinal studies are useful in tracking long-term changes in attitudes and behaviors.

Advertisers also use dummy tests to predict the impact of a message on the audience. They place the material to be evaluated by a test group of users in a medium similar to that in which it will eventually appear. Other tests measure recall of details from test and control advertisements or other communication products. Social scientists and advertisers use galvanic skin tests and pupillometers to learn more about how people respond to other individuals, photographs, or ideas. These tests measure degree of liking for an individual or concept.

Ethics

Social audits seek to determine how well the organization is fulfilling its social responsibilities: "The audit provides feedback on company-sponsored social action programs such as minority hiring, environmental cleanup, and employee safety. This is the newest form of public relations research and the most challenging" (Wimmer & Dominick, 1997, p. 335). The organization can also assess ethical performance by auditing publications for use of gender-free language, avoidance of stereotypes, and responsible language.

Resources

This part of the work plan identifies resources required to deliver each product or service. The communicator breaks down these resources into work years (the cost of time used by company employees to perform a certain cost) and the cost of supplies and materials, outside expertise, and equipment not owned by the organization. A sample communication work plan is shown in Table 4.2.

Conclusion

In an ideal model, operational and work planning flow from the strategic planning process, and each stage of planning results in corollary documents. These documents explain how the organization will implement and evaluate the extent to which it has achieved its communication priorities.

TABLE 4.2 Work Plan for the U.S. Drug Administration

Communication Priorities	Product/Service to be Delivered	Person to Deliver Product/Service	Milestones	Performance Indicators: Impact, Outputs, or Process	Evaluation Component	Budget Work Years	Budget $
Advertising campaign on safe use of drugs	Video	Person 1	Bids in by 2/3/99 Contracted by 2/22/99 Submitted by 4/15/99 Approved by 4/30/99 Circulated by 5/30/99 Evaluated by 7/14/99	Increased public awareness of safe practices (impact)	Focus groups & telephone interviews	X	$
	Pamphlets	Person 2	Prepared by 1/15/99 Approved by 2/5/99 Distributed by 3/8/99 Evaluated by 6/5/99	Knowledge demonstrated in quiz included as mail-back insert (impact) Readability of materials (output)	Content analysis of responses Flesch formula	X	$
	Bumper stickers	Person 2	Ideas requested by 2/28/99 Ideas submitted by 3/6/99 Committee decision by 3/15/99 Contract for design signed by 4/3/99 Stickers produced by 5/1/99 Stickers distributed by 6/2/99	Numbers of cars with stickers (output) Numbers of people who submitted ideas for bumper stickers (process)	Counts Counts	X	$

NOTE: The format for this plan was contributed by Stewart Ferguson. The table demonstrates how one communication priority has been broken down into three different communication products. The planner subdivides each priority into individual products and services. This plan is fictitious.

5

Writing the Communication Support Plan

Planning for Special Events, Campaigns, and Issues

Organizations with well-developed strategic planning cultures produce many support plans each year. These plans anticipate upcoming events and activities (e.g., the announcement of a new product, service, policy, program, or capital expenditure; employee communication survey; tabling of legislation; executive involvement in a conference or proceedings; or the release of a new publication), campaigns (clusters of related activities that characterize social marketing, public relations, and advertising campaigns), or issues (e.g., a controversy over a new medication, the location of a new highway, or the decision to restructure the health care system). Crisis-prone organizations produce more issue management plans than less crisis-prone organizations. A typical government department may produce 30 or more support plans for issues management purposes in the course of a year. When decisions are pending, some organizations produce multiple plans to accommodate different scenarios. Once the decision is made, the organization puts the appropriate plan into action and discards the others. This chapter considers the purposes and characteristics of support plans and the optional components of a support plan.

Purposes and Characteristics of Support Plans

The term *support plan* derives from the fact that these plans support the achievement of broader communication objectives, delineated in the strategic communication plan. A similar term exists in the management literature to refer to the many plans that support business objectives. The scope of a support plan can be broad or narrow. For example, an organization can write a support plan for an information campaign on the environment called Environment 2000. Subsequently, the organization can write a separate plan for any one of the activities that emerge from the Environment 2000 campaign. No matter whether the support plan addresses a single activity or a group of related activities, it is more limited in scope than annual or multiyear plans, which address many issues and many different topics. A support plan typically deals with a single issue, campaign (cluster of related activities), or special event. A special kind of support plan is the social action or "information campaign for social improvement" (Salmon, 1989). The social action campaign provides people with the information they require to lead better, more healthy lives.

According to Rogers and Storey (1987), campaigns are (a) purposive, (b) aimed at a large audience, (c) restricted to a predefined time frame, and (d) characterized by an organized set of communication activities. The hierarchy of effects model (Backer, Rogers, & Sopory, 1992) states that campaigns aim to accomplish one or more of the following goals: exposure, awareness, information, persuasion, intent to change behavior, actual change in behavior, or maintenance of behavior change. Some campaigns (e.g., antismoking and antidrug campaigns) aim to effect long-term social change. For additional information on social marketing and political campaigns, see Pollay (1989) and O'Keefe (1989).

A support plan will rarely be more than five to seven pages in length. For activities of a limited nature (e.g., an announcement of a new research initiative), a plan may be very short (one or two pages). A pressing concern or major event, however, may warrant a longer communication plan. The writing style for the plan should be plain language. The planner should avoid bureaucratic jargon, lengthy sentences and paragraphs, and unnecessary detail. Typically, the users of the plan are experts in the area of concern.

The organization should update its plans on a regular basis. The frequency of updates depends on many factors: the importance of the event or activity, the dependency on events outside the control of the organization (e.g., a volatile political, social, or economic environment), and the responsiveness to internal influences (executive priorities, budgetary restraints, or other variables).

Components of a Support Plan

A communication plan, framed to guide the management of a single issue or activity, has strategic and operational components. Strategic elements include the background statement that establishes context; decision points, trigger events, and crisis indicators; the knowledge and opinion environment; communication objectives; messages; target audiences; strategic considerations; and requirements for consultation, negotiation, and partnership. Operational elements include tactical considerations and financial requirements. Performance indicators and evaluation methodologies also appear in a well-developed plan. In the following sections, a breakdown of what could appear in a support plan, produced in anticipation of a communication event, activity, or issue, is presented. Not all categories will appear in every plan.

Background Statement

This first section identifies the nature of the activity or issue to be addressed by the plan (e.g., the announcement of a new service or product, an upcoming conference, the withdrawal of a controversial product, a rate increase, an executive resignation, or the allocation of new funds to a project). This part of the plan also positions the event or issue relative to the past. The planner describes, in one or two paragraphs, the origins of the issue or rationale for the product or activity. He or she describes the forces that have driven its development or the backdrop to the event or activity (including the most recent developments).

For example, a communication plan to announce new funding priorities for health research can include the following in its background statement:

- History of the organization's funding priorities
- Recent studies that have demonstrated the seriousness of risks faced by women in regard to heart disease
- Recent studies that have revealed the need for counseling services for men who are recovering from heart attacks and strokes

- A brief reference to escalating public discussion of this issue (developed in more depth in the environment statement)

- Current priority of the issue on the organization's research or policy agenda, relative to other organizational issues

- Likely media reactions to the announcement or event (developed in more depth in the environment and strategic considerations sections of the plan)

The planner could say "Based on the company's experience 2 years ago and the current sluggishness of the local economy, the proposed utility rate increases may unleash a tidal wave of protest from interest groups; the media is likely to give extensive coverage to this outcry." The analyst can anticipate the lineup of media for and against the proposal: "It is anticipated that 60% of news coverage willbefavorabletowardtheorganization'sannouncement,30%willbeunfavorable, and 10% will be balanced." The planner can propose best-case and worst-case headlines: "Parole Laws Give First-Time Offenders Second Chance" or "Parole Laws Turn Hardened Criminals Free." A second example is "Allergy Medication Safe If Used Properly" or "Company Irresponsible for Not Withdrawing Allergy Medicine." Such headlines serve to focus the organization on how the public debate could evolve.

Decision Points, Trigger Events, and Crisis Indicators

In the case of an issues management plan, communicators should note pending policy decisions or events that could positively or negatively influence the development of the issue. Also, they should identify warning signals in the external or internal environment that could suggest the movement of an issue to crisis status or suggest the impending failure of a campaign or the decline of customer confidence in a product. These signals could be increased numbers of phone calls from irate constituents or customers, increased activity among interest groups, many negative articles in the press, or other indicators. Indicators of an ineffectual information campaign could be growing numbers of people who have abandoned safe sex practices, continuing confusion regarding what levels of government provide health services, or increased levels of smoking among youth. This section of the plan should help the organization to be proactive in its approach to issues management or to diagnose early problems in the conduct of information campaigns or performance of a product.

Knowledge or Opinion Environment

Statements regarding the opinion or attitudinal environment (external and internal) should appear in the plan. For example, if a company executive or a government official intends to announce a new policy or legislative agenda, the organization will want to have a clear indication of the public opinion environment. The communication plan should identify trends in public opinion and client behaviors and should suggest likely reactions to the announcement or planned activity. The plan should suggest current sensitivities on the topic and expectations of different groups. Information or advertising campaigns also include a statement on levels of awareness and attitudes. The campaign planner needs to know how the target audiences view the subject of the campaign—how much they know about the topic and their opinions of it. For example, a communication planner for an antismoking campaign might write the following: "Public attitudes toward smoking have changed dramatically in the past 10 years; a majority now support restrictions on smoking in public places." A marketing communications director might state "Customer attitudes toward domestic products have changed markedly in recent years, as more turn to the Internet for options."

Sources of information on opinion and attitudes include news groups, web pages, and chat rooms on the Internet; print and electronic media (mainstream newspapers, radio, TV, ethnic press, magazines, and journals); correspondence (expert and general public); think tank reports; interest group profiles; association proceedings and newsletters; speakers' bureau reports; records of congressional and Senate debates; court cases; studies of social indicators; interviews with elite opinion leaders; surveys; union proceedings; focus group reports; and international databases. Table 3.1 provided a detailed list.

It is important to note that opinions and attitudes may (or may not) correspond to reality. Client publics may have an accurate or a completely distorted view of the organization's position on any given issue. Whether accurate or inaccurate, the organization should be aware of these perceptions. Decision makers require advance notice if the general public or special-interest groups strongly oppose forthcoming legislation or entertain decidedly hostile views of a product or service offering. By the same token, if opinion favors particular options, decision makers may see opportunities for acceptable resolution of an issue. In regard to customers, a business may see the possibility to adopt an alternative approach to a product or service offering.

Analysts should represent the opinion environment as it exists and not as top executives would like it to be. If upper management does not receive bad news in a strategic or support plan, they may not receive it at all because subordinates limit the type and quantity of information that passes up the chain of command. Downs (1967) demonstrated that top managers receive only 1/64 of an original message that passes up a hierarchy of four levels. The tendency of employees to protect themselves by passing only positive information to the next level has been well documented in the organizational communication literature. The press secretary for the minister's office in one Canadian government department ordered that a media analysis be shredded because he feared that the report would make him appear incompetent at managing public opinion. To alleviate this problem, a few years ago another government department paid a consulting firm to convey bad news to the top levels of the organization because top bureaucrats believed that they were receiving an incomplete—and potentially distorted—view of the public opinion environment. Higher levels of the organization can encourage or discourage open and honest disclosure. If the organization rewards the bearer of good news and punishes the messenger who brings bad news, the analyst will report only the good news. Organizations must encourage a climate wherein bad news can travel, as easily as good news, up the organizational hierarchy (Kaufman, 1992). Task forces working on *La Releve,* a Canadian government initiative designed to reenergize the public service, identified the "challenge" function as an important responsibility of government communicators. By challenge, they mean the willingness to take a stand and challenge the common wisdom. Such an approach typifies learning organizations.

This section of the plan should be completely factual, based on hard data: the results of surveys, media analysis, focus group tests, tracking issues on the Internet, and other means. Sample statements that could appear in a support plan for the announcement of shifts in research funding priorities are as follows:

- Several national women's groups have staged demonstrations in Washington, D.C., demanding additional funding for heart disease research.

- AIDS activists, concerned that increased funding to other areas could result in losses to AIDS research, have increased their lobby efforts during the past 6 months.

- Correspondence from interest groups, supportive of the move to place heart disease higher on the research agenda, has increased in the same time period.
- Analysis of newspaper coverage during the past year demonstrates growing levels of media interest in the funding debate.
- Reference to the House and Senate debates suggests that politicians from states with large numbers of people with AIDS (e.g., New York and California) or high rates of cancer (e.g., Louisiana and Michigan) fear a backlash from these constituencies if funding priorities shift dramatically.

The following are sample statements that could appear in a support plan on gun-control legislation written by the Justice Department:

- Gun-control lobby groups have grown increasingly active during the past year, indicating that a renewed push for legislation could be in the offing.
- Urban newspapers have tended to give more favorable publicity to the pro-gun control groups, whereas rural newspapers have tended to favor the stance of the Rifle Association.
- The volume of correspondence has increased dramatically since the recent shopping-mall killings, as many writers call for more rigorous laws and better enforcement.
- A growing number of fiction shows on television have dealt with the topic of accidental killings and the role of guns in family violence. These shows may increase public awareness of the dangers inherent in keeping guns in the home.
- Recent values studies indicate that Americans may be more apt today, than in the past, to support the balancing of individual rights with social responsibility. If this trend continues, it is possible that this theme may carry over to the debate over gun control.

Sample statements that could appear in a plan for an environmental agency are as follows:

- Greenpeace continues to set the media agenda for environmental groups concerned about the seal hunt.
- The environmental movement appears to be gaining momentum in the southeastern United States, where a number of oil spills have occurred in Gulf Coast waters.

- Americans living in the Southwest are concerned that industrialization could pose a long-term threat to the attractiveness of the region to tourists. Regional surveys and focus group testing have documented these concerns.

- Studies of interest group activities suggest a trend toward the proliferation of many small, single-issue environmental groups rather than increasing enrollment in national organizations.

Support plans also include statements of employee opinions, attitudes, and behaviors relevant to the topics. The extent to which employees support or oppose a company policy can influence the likelihood of its successful implementation. In the same way, employee morale can have a dramatic impact on the success of everything that an organization undertakes. The level of employee expertise makes it easier or more difficult to achieve organizational goals and objectives. Thus, plans should indicate the level of internal support for policies, new product lines, and other activities; levels of employee expertise; employee morale; and other relevant factors. Some departments within governments have a large internal clientele (e.g., the Library of Congress, used by many senators and congressmen and congresswomen, and the public service commission). In some cases, the internal component is more important than the external component. The following examples illustrate the type of statements that could appear in a support plan:

- Support for the new accountability policy is greater among senior than middle managers.

- High levels of employee participation in a recycling campaign suggest that employees will actively support the company's new environmental policy.

- Analysis of suggestion box contributions reveals that employees favor work sharing.

- A high level of esprit de corps exists among those who worked on the matrix management team for project X. Their enthusiasm will probably translate into support for this project.

Some issues interest only internal constituencies. For example, if a company decides to switch from a seniority-based system to a merit-based reward system, those most strongly affected will be employees and their families. The following statements could appear in a plan designed to address the proposed change in reward systems:

- Support for changing from a seniority-based reward system to a merit-based system is strongest among the employees who work in sales.

- Strong opposition by union members is evidenced in recent association newsletters.

- The strongest criticism for the proposed changes continues to come from older workers.

- Members who work in human resource capacities argue that it is not possible

n and attitudinal environment
r others. If an activity or event
the plan can be brief in its

h a clear understanding of the
values, and behaviors of
provides the basis for this
d prioritizes target audi-
cal, regional, or national;
ic, or political in orienta-
. The following example
related to a new equity

Note that some target audiences are internal, whereas others are external to the organization. This section of the plan should not repeat points covered in the preceding section of the plan (opinion environment).

Communication Objectives

The communication objectives that appear in the support plan are more specific incarnations of those that appeared in the annual or multiyear plan. Consider the following example. A communication objective, taken from a multiyear strategic communication plan, could be "To make the public aware that Murdock Chemicals is a good corporate citizen." A more specific form of this objective, appearing in a support plan to announce a new company policy on plant emissions, could be "To inform the public that Murdock Chemicals contributes to cancer research." A second outgrowth of the parent message could be "To inform the public that Murdock Chemicals sponsors high school athletic teams." Communication objectives seek to (a) create awareness, (b) intensify or reinforce existing attitudes or behavior, (c) convert from one set of attitudes or behaviors to another, or (d) build relationships. Note that each communication objective suggests only one outcome. The ordering of the objectives reflects their priority.

The following are additional examples of communication objectives:

- To allay fears that Murdock Chemicals may be downsizing their operations in Cleveland
- To provide information on research initiatives in the area of biodegradable detergents
- To stimulate community support for a new baseball league sponsored by Murdock Chemicals
- To urge local businesses to contribute to the building of a community recreation hall for which Murdock Chemicals is providing the first wave of funding

Other communication objectives will be directed at internal audiences:

- To explain the new promotion policies to all employees
- To promote networking between the design and planning sectors
- To encourage at-risk employees to participate in the "Drugs in the Workplace" program

- To encourage employees to attend more social functions sponsored by the company

- To generate support among middle managers for the new employment-equity policies

If the organization has not engaged in annual or multiyear planning for communication activities (the reference point for the support plan), the communication planner must conduct interviews with managers and corporate executives to determine corporate and business objectives. Alternatively, the communication planner can use, in the fashion described in Chapter 3, relevant corporate and business documents (e.g., executive speeches, policy documents, and strategic plans) to determine policy directions and to frame appropriate communication objectives. These objectives then offer a reference point for support planning.

Messages

This section of the plan identifies the principal messages to be conveyed to stakeholders. Corporate messages in a communication plan for Environment Week could be as follows: "Murdock Chemicals is doing its part to ensure that Americans can breathe clean air," "Murdock Chemicals is making major changes to plants to ensure that emissions conform to national safety standards," and "Murdock Chemicals is doing its part to ensure that the ozone layer is not depleted." Messages in the support plan relate back to the more general messages that appeared in the annual or multiyear plan: In this case, the parent corporate message is "Murdock Chemicals is concerned about the environment." The following are additional examples of corporate messages:

- Gerald's Furniture is a traditional company with a modern outlook.

- Bayside Optical gives affordable eye care.

- Molly's Designer Wear will not open shop in countries that exploit factory workers.

- The government has balanced its budget.

- First National Bank offers personalized banking services.

Examples of messages directed at internal audiences are as follows:

- Job sharing allows employees the opportunity to work flexible hours.

- Drinking in the workplace is not an acceptable practice.

- The enhanced software creates new opportunities for networking with regional representatives.

- A new on-site day care facility will allow working parents to be closer to their young children.

Corporate messages should appear in every communication product: speeches, press releases, brochures and booklets, and so on. For this reason, all communicators should be aware of the organization's messages as articulated in the annual or multiyear communication plans. If communicators receive a copy of the annual or multiyear plans, they can generate compatible messages for support plans. The messages will link back to the needs articulated in the opinion environment and the communication objectives.

The more specific and concrete the message, the easier it is to track the extent to which the media carried the message. Organizations sometimes quantify the number of newspapers, radio stations, television stations, or other media that conveyed their messages. Consider the following messages: "The U.S. government will not trade with China until the United Nations has removed that country's name from its list of countries that abuse human rights," "Refugee claimants will not be allowed to work while awaiting status," and "The IRS will clean its own house." These messages are clear, understandable, and sufficiently explicit as to be "trackable." Artfully constructed messages are "uneditable . . . concise, and synoptic" (Jamieson & Campbell, 1988, p. 96). The best messages employ the language of newspapers, not bureaucratic jargon.

Strategic Considerations

This section of the support plan suggests strategic approaches to communication activities and campaigns. The planner offers personal insights, speculates about what could happen in the future, and "adds value" to the facts and statistics that constituted the opinion and attitudinal environment. The right strategic choices depend on a knowledge of the theories discussed later in this book (e.g., persuasion, learning, and media theories). Planning an information campaign requires examining (a) the types of collaboration that will be required among individuals and organizations, (b) the context or environment in which the campaign will occur, (c) principles for what has been found to work in the past, and (d) desired effects of the campaign (Backer et al., 1992). The communicator considers the following:

- Desired level of visibility for the activity (high or low profile)
- Types of appeals to be used in messages (emotional, fear, logical, and credibility)
- Issues management approaches
- Consultation requirements
- Level of involvement by senior executives

Organizations adopt a high-profile approach to some communication activities and a low-profile approach to others. For example, issues such as abortion and surrogate motherhood are no-win issues, incapable of generating consensus. Gun-control questions likewise provoke heated debate. The population is so divided on such questions that no politician or government likes to deal with them. In such cases, the organization may choose no publicity over negative publicity. If a company is building a new child care facility for working mothers, however, it may want a high-profile billing for this announcement.

In deciding on issues management strategies, the analyst will need to ask whether the organization owns the issue. He or she will need to assess the power capability of the organization (in terms of resources and credibility) to manage the issue. He or she will need to ask whether the opposition stakeholders have sufficient power capability to present a challenge. The analyst will need to understand the extent to which the issue has pathways into the central value systems of audiences, activates networks of other issues, has reached maturity, and possesses other characteristics that could influence the choice of strategies. He or she will need to consider the existing level of media interest in the issue. Where does it rank on the media agenda? Some of the factors that influence media interest, as discussed in other chapters, are degree of controversy attached to the issue (controversial issues are more media worthy), extent to which the issue can be sensationalized (media thrives on the unusual and bizarre), celebrity support for the issue, and the attractiveness of the issue to political parties and interest groups. The following are statements that could appear under "strategic considerations":

- The anticipated popularity of the new state tax incentives for small business justifies giving a high profile to this policy announcement.

- Because there may be some confusion regarding how the new provisions will interact with existing tax legislation, a campaign to inform small business is in order.

- Because the current state government has a proven track record in supporting small business, it seems appropriate to emphasize this record in communications to the public.

- Those who have been pushing for increased spending in the public sector may need to be reassured that these new incentives for private business will not adversely affect the state's potential to maintain its commitments in other areas such as education.

- Discussions over tax incentives for small business may stimulate multinationals to ask "What are you doing for me?"

- Small business may query the criteria that have been set to qualify for the incentives.

Other examples relate to internal communication policies:

- Raising the issue of merit pay increases for employees will probably generate renewed discussion of promotion criteria; senior managers should be prepared to respond to these questions.

- Although women at middle-management level will probably support the new employment equity policy, they may feel that it does not go far enough.

- Personnel responsible for processing new employees are in a good position to influence initial attitudes of employees toward sick-leave policies.

- All employees affected by job reclassification will be targeted in the initial flurry of communications; those not affected will receive a second wave of information.

In developing a message, a communicator can use logical, emotional, and credibility appeals. Logical support materials include evidence and reasoning (the use of statistics, quotations, or facts to back up a position). Emotional appeals tap into the needs and wants of the audience. Credibility appeals ask an audience to accept a message on the basis of the organization's reputation or prestige. Most messages involve all three types of appeals. The reliance on logical appeals, to the exclusion of the other appeals, would make the communicator sound like Dr. Spock on *Star Trek*. Asking an audience to accept a message solely on the grounds of credibility, however, may be expecting too much, unless the organization has the status of Amnesty International. In recent years, many have questioned even those messages originating with the president of the United States. At the same time, strong fear appeals rarely work. The strategic considerations section of a support plan can suggest approaches to the use of fear, emotional, logical, or other appeals. For example, a plan may state "The use of fear appeals is unlikely to work with young audiences involved in illicit drug use." Alternatively, the plan could note "Rational appeals will be extremely important with this well-educated, relatively affluent audience."

The plan can also specify the way in which the organization will involve other departments, opinion leaders, groups, or individuals in its planning exercise. There is a growing recognition of the importance of consulting with clients, customers, and other stakeholders (see Chapters 12 and 13). Organizations, public and private, have found it increasingly difficult to ignore the views of stakeholders—inside and outside their boundaries. They have learned that discussions with advocacy groups and their opinion leaders can help to avoid many painful confrontations. As activist groups mature and professionalize their operations, businesses and governments engage more frequently in negotiation of differences (Pattakos, 1992). An increasing number of organizations have realized that the most satisfying successes come from the extensive involvement of members in all parts—and at all levels—of the organization. The support plan identifies groups and individuals to be consulted in writing and implementing the plan. The planner also notes requirements for senior management or executive involvement. The following kinds of statements can be included under the heading of strategic considerations:

- Branch offices in Chicago, Lansing, and Boston have cooperated in planning the marathon for "Progress against Poverty." The Austin and San Diego offices should be consulted.

- Consultations with voluntary groups should include the Salvation Army, the Good Neighbors Association, and Good Will.

- Concerned government entities include the Education Department, Welfare, and Finance.

- Officials in United Automobile Workers should be consulted on plans for downsizing.

- Senior managers should be brought on board early to help in communicating the necessity for the revised equity policies.

- Executives will need to be available to act as liaisons with community groups.

Tactical Considerations

Tactical choices include the appropriate medium to carry a message, the best time to release news, requirements for supporting materials, requirements for briefing the press, and responsible individuals to carry out the various components of the plan. In writing this section of the plan, the communicator needs to identify channels and delivery systems for messages. Obviously, some tactical choices also have a strategic dimension. Therefore, where the communication planner chooses to place the statements is somewhat arbitrary.

As discussed in Chapter 11, television can be an effective vehicle to reach national audiences, radio to reach young audiences, and newspapers to reach more politically aware and educated audiences. Anniversary celebrations provide a good occasion to announce a new policy, product, or research initiative. Groundbreaking ceremonies, conferences, and exhibitions offer opportunities to "piggyback" on others' activities, saving the organization human and financial resources. A cross-country executive tour can become a useful vehicle for speaking out on economic or sociopolitical issues. A Farmers of America Association meeting could be a good occasion to announce a new agricultural subsidies program. It is important to take particular care in selecting the vehicle for the announcement: "Often this means bypassing standard and routine communications vehicles . . . in favor of more creative methods such as audiovisual presentations, news conferences held in environments that typify the subject matter, teleconferencing, and regional tours" (Privy Council Office [PCO], n.d.).

The planner should also note appropriate media for reaching internal clients. Management should not rely solely on written communication to reach employees. Oral communications (or a combination of oral and written communications) continue to be important means to reach employees (Tompkins, 1984). Chief executives prefer informal, spoken communication (even rumor) to formal, written messages (Mintzberg, 1973). The choice of an appropriate medium depends on both content and audience. Financial and technical data are conveyed more effectively in writing, often supplemented by oral explanation. Written messages can be risky, however (Garnett, 1992):

> Written messages often have a life of their own—ending up in the hands of unintended audiences and showing up years after they were written. Written

messages are also more likely to be interpreted as official and thus harder to recant or alter later. (p. 58)

Moreover, members of the public and journalists can request written documents from public institutions.

The following examples suggest appropriate media for reaching audiences:

- Reaching street youth with messages on the dangers of AIDS necessitates using alternative media and techniques such as distributing leaflets on streets inhabited by youth.

- Because the announcement will have statewide impact, television is the best first-contact medium for reaching these audiences.

- The employee newsletter is a "friendlier" vehicle for informing rank-and-file employees of sick-leave policies than is the corporate magazine.

- Armistice Day will be a good occasion to announce the restructuring of the military and to emphasize its new peacekeeping functions.

Appropriate timing is also important in releasing news. Organizations often seek to release news at a time when the largest number of people can receive the news. Many interest groups plan their events for times when the media can cover the events (prime time for live broadcast coverage). Political parties plan their conventions so that chosen leaders make their acceptance speeches at peak viewing times. Information released in the opening week of the fall television season reaches optimum numbers of viewers. The support plan specifies the timing for any announcement or news release (date and hour) and the location at which the announcement will be made. The plan also notes special requirements, such as a "lock up" of journalists before a budget announcement.

Providing prepackaged materials increases the chances that the media will air the organization's viewpoint. Many reporters working on tight deadlines make only minor changes to materials received in press kits. Similarly, layout editors often fill last-minute news holes with materials prepared by public relations personnel. The following are typical requirements:

- Information kits for media personnel (describe contents and distribution requirements)

- Background material for briefing party members, legislators, interest groups, and other stakeholders
- Briefing notes, press lines, and question-and-answer (Q's & A's) packages for the chief executive officer or other lead officials
- Materials that legislators may want to give to their constituents (e.g., inserts for newsletters and pamphlets) or materials that organizations may want to give to their customers or clients

The plan should also specify areas of responsibility—for example, individuals or groups responsible for coordinating activities, announcements, or campaign components. Finally, requirements for follow-up activities should be noted: "speaking tours, advertising, brochures and booklets, direct mail campaigns, follow-up media interviews, or radio 'hotline' programs" (PCO, n.d.). The planner makes the following kinds of statements:

- An article that outlines the major points of the law will be submitted to *Physician's Quarterly* to explain the implications of the new family violence legislation.
- Videotapes, distributed to seniors' organizations, will alert viewers to signs of elder abuse.
- The Christmas newsletter will introduce employees to the revised bonus system.
- Feature articles on the new warrantee will be posted at all dealerships, and a brief description of the revised policies will be included in mailings to customers.

Performance Indicators

Performance indicators (at the level of the support plan) allow the organization to measure process, outputs, impacts, and ethics. (Strategic planning at the corporate or business level establishes desired program outcomes. The organization, however, does not measure outcomes at the level of the support plan.) Examples of a performance indicator for process are "the extent to which the organization involved all the partners in the planning and designing of information campaigns" and "the engagement of senior executives in the early stages of planning." Performance indicators for outputs include "the readability of a brochure" and "the number of telephone calls answered." Examples of performance indicators for impact are "changes in the buying habits of people who have heart disease" and "increases in the sales of government bonds." Performance indicators for ethics include "the use of gender-free language in all publications" and "the representation of ethnic minorities in print and electronic advertising campaigns."

A performance indicator is "a clear, unambiguous statement of desired or required results" that specifies "precise rigorous criteria to measure actual results . . . who or what will demonstrate the intended results . . . and under what conditions" (Kaufman, 1992, p. 130). Performance indicators can include a qualitative and quantitative dimension. That is, the planner can translate a qualitative statement of desired results (greater employee participation) into a statistical indicator (5% increase in employee participation) *if* the higher level of specificity seems appropriate. This level of specificity requires the establishment of benchmarks at some early point. The statement does not include a reference to means or resources.

Evaluation Methodology

The planner specifies evaluation instruments and procedures to be applied in evaluating the organization's performance in communication. Many different techniques and tools can be used to evaluate communication products, activities, and services:

- Surveys (general public, clients, and customers)
- Focus groups
- Media tracking and analysis
- Analysis of correspondence
- Inquiry tracking
- Pull-out inserts in publications
- Readability assessments
- Expert reviews
- Theater tests
- Readership and viewership tests
- Content analysis
- Pretests and posttests
- Dummy tests
- Audits (social, public relations, and communication)

The researcher should not be afraid to use unorthodox means to document the organization's successes and failures. For example, a visit to the local pub or the nearest senior citizens' home can yield valuable information. Informal conversations with travelers on a cross-country train can provide an immense wealth of information, particularly if one travels coach in one direction and first class on the return. In the last election in Great Britain, the taverns sold ale from kegs marked with the candidates' names. The results obtained in this less than orthodox vote mirrored the final count at the electoral booths. Evaluation can be so expensive as not to be affordable if organizations fail to use imagination and creativity in determining their methodologies.

Budget

This final section of the plan identifies the resources (human and financial) required to implement the plan. There should be an indication of the stages at which funding will be required. If the budget for communication activities does not appear in the work plan, the support plan should indicate the fit with the operational plan. For example, "Cost for the announcement should be less than $2000.00, well within the amount budgeted in the operational plan."

Conclusion

The most common communication plan is the support plan. Examples include information campaign plans, advertising and marketing communications campaigns, employee communication plans, public relations plans for special events or activities, and issues management plans. This chapter suggested a set of generic categories that can be applied to most kinds of support planning. The communication planner, however, rarely employs all these categories in a single plan. For this reason, the length of support plans is highly variable. See the Appendix for an example of a support plan.

Appendix

The following plan was prepared by Steve Collins, University of Ottawa. The plan is fictitious.

Support Plan for a Campaign to Legalize Marijuana for Medical Use for the Foundation for AIDS Research (FAR)

Background Statement

The debate over the legalization of marijuana is both complex and emotional. Stories rarely appear on the front pages of newspapers or in the television news lineup. Nonetheless, the issue possesses longevity, partly because of the polarization of public opinion on the topic. Those for and against the legalization of marijuana hold strong feelings. Advocates believe that the right to use marijuana involves personal choice and civil liberties, and they do not believe the government should be legislating on such matters. Recently, those suffering from AIDS have given increased visibility to the issue because they demand the right to use the drug to ease their pain. The case of Joel Kinsley of California has fueled recent press coverage of the issue.

Corporate or Business/Functional Objectives

- To improve the quality of life for those suffering from AIDS
- To support the availability of products that can ease the suffering of those with AIDS
- To serve as a credible information source for facts on AIDS

Opinion Environment

Positive Factors

- Analysis of print media coverage of this issue reveals a slow, but steady, increase in support of legalizing marijuana.
- Nationally, legalization has received support from some influential members of the House and Senate, as well as Ilsen Svenberg, lawyer for the American Foundation for Drug Policy.
- Correspondence and personal interviews confirm a high level of support from those suffering with terminal illnesses.
- Other supportive correspondence comes from those who have acquired a criminal record for possession of marijuana.

- A growing number of members of the health care profession have been speaking out in favor of marijuana as a palliative drug.
- People in favor of legalizing marijuana argue that people with terminal illnesses should be allowed to take low-level risks to improve the quality of their lives.
- Civil rights activists believe that prohibition of marijuana violates civil rights.
- FAR experienced significant increases in organizational membership this past year.

Negative Factors

- The majority of negative press has come in the person of Ian McAffey, the drug policy chief to the Clinton administration.
- There is a general public perception that people who smoke "pot" are "pot-heads" or criminals.
- The drug rehabilitation and treatment professions oppose the legalization of marijuana.
- Many doctors are afraid to speak out on the issue because they believe that people would think badly of them.
- Pharmaceutical companies, which have a vested interest in more conventional treatments, lobby strongly against the legalization of marijuana.
- Arguments against the legalization of marijuana sometimes appear on television shows that are sponsored by breweries.
- Some argue that legalization in the United States could cause a strained relationship with Canada.
- Those opposed to the legalization of marijuana argue that legalization will lead to increased numbers of users, who will subsequently progress to using hard drugs.

Communication Objectives

- To inform the public that the FAR supports the movement to legalize marijuana
- To relay the importance of this issue from the perspective of the terminally ill
- To inform the public of the legal dimensions of the issue
- To correct and clarify misconceptions regarding the dangers of using marijuana
- To encourage cooperation between different advocacy groups

Messages

- The Foundation for AIDS Research supports the legalization of marijuana for medical purposes.
- Marijuana reduces pain and nausea and stimulates the appetite of those suffering from AIDS and other serious illnesses.
- Smoking marijuana does not mean that one will become a heroin or cocaine user.
- Denying the chronically ill access to marijuana violates their civil rights.

Target Audiences

- General public
- The terminally ill
- Doctors and other health care workers
- Governments
- Law enforcement
- Civil rights activists

Strategic Considerations

- The Foundation can sponsor a series of feature articles for community newspapers to stimulate awareness of the issue.
- Regional speakers' bureaus can offer presentations on the topic to community and professional groups.
- Producers of network soap operas can be approached about running a story line consistent with the Foundation's perspective.
- The Foundation should consider planning some joint functions with citizens' rights groups and the American Cancer Research Group.
- Those suffering from AIDS should be made aware of efforts on their behalf.
- The large numbers of AIDS victims and the recent publicity on the Joel Kinsley case should translate into significant support for FAR initiatives on the West Coast.
- FAR can ask well-known and well-respected physicians to contribute articles that explain the improved quality of life that marijuana can give to terminally ill patients.
- All communications will need to stress that FAR is not asking for marijuana to be legalized for general public consumption.

Tactical Considerations

- National AIDS Awareness Week will provide an excellent opportunity to obtain television and radio interviews.
- A large number of the newspaper stories should appear during National AIDS Awareness Week to build momentum for the cause.
- Information on the issue of legalization can be posted on FAR's web site.
- A press conference during AIDS Awareness Week would draw attention to the cause. Celebrity spokespersons could lend credibility to the event.
- Information packages on the medical uses of marijuana should be distributed at the press event.
- Members of the House and Senate should also receive copies of the information.
- FAR should establish a 1-800 line for people who seek information on the subject or who wish to become involved, on a local level, in advocacy efforts.

Performance Indicators*

- Increased awareness of the facts on medical uses of marijuana
- Understanding of FAR's position on the legalization of marijuana
- Greater awareness of the legal implications of the issue in terms of civil rights
- Increased support from the medical community and the general public
- Larger numbers of cooperative efforts by advocacy groups

Evaluation Methodologies

- Monitoring of 1-800 line
- Intercept survey at shopping malls
- Analysis of media and print coverage of the issue before and after AIDS Awareness Week

Budget

$$$$ to be allocated in the following way:

*The performance indicators can be expressed in statistical terms (e.g., percentage increases expected in levels of awareness, understanding, support, or cooperation).

6

Writing the Contingency Plan for Crises

Written in Chinese, the word *crisis* has two characters. One character represents danger, and the second signifies opportunity. (President John F. Kennedy referred to this definition of crisis in a speech delivered on April 12, 1959, to an audience in Indianapolis, IN.) The ultimate danger or cost of a mismanaged crisis is the demise of the corporate entity or the fall of individual actors in the crisis. In 1999, Bill Clinton came closer than he would have liked to that precipice. Pan American Airlines no longer exists consequent to revelations of a cover-up that followed the downing of a passenger jet over Lockerbie, Scotland. Contained within every crisis situation is a Pandora's box of risks and dangers. For example, when an innocuous-looking man opened fire on observers at the Empire State Building, New York City officials faced accusations that their security system failed. Also, female engineering students at a technical university in Montreal, Canada, died when a crazed gunman entered their classroom, ordered them to lie down on the floor, and shot them, execution style. Campus police were accused of acting too slowly and, more important, too late. Although the dangers to organizations that experience crisis situations are obvious, the opportunities are less obvious. Nonetheless, to those prepared to learn, crises can offer valuable lessons. The benefits of a properly managed crisis can be an improved understanding of clients and constituencies, the infusion of new life into the organization, and newfound respect in the community. Crises give organizations a chance to demonstrate their concern for the community and leadership: "Just as a fire department gets credit for its heroism—and a boost for its next year's budget—by minimizing the damage, so a company can get some benefit in good will by handling itself conspicuously well in a crisis" (Stephenson, 1984, p. 17). Successful negotiation of periods of conflict and war can give new life to tired governments. Margaret Thatcher experienced higher levels of popularity in the days following the Falklands conflict, and George Bush gained new support after the Gulf War. Some accused Clinton of seeking to emulate their successes when he deployed missiles against Iraq on the day that Monica Lewinsky testified before Ken Starr.

What an organization does and says in a crisis situation can permanently influence the organization's image and its policy and business agendas. To ensure that the organization remains in control, maintains public confidence, and avoids escalation of the crisis, those in positions of authority often commission the development of contingency plans. Such plans provide crisis managers with a sense of purpose and direction at a time when they could easily succumb to panic and fear. Every crisis management plan has a communication component. The final product of these efforts is a crisis management manual, which the organization updates on an annual or biannual basis. Copies of this plan should be kept at an off-site location.

Writing the Crisis Management Plan

All crisis management team members sign an affidavit to acknowledge that they have received and read a copy of the crisis management plan. The signatures also confirm that the members are prepared to put the plan into action should the need arise. This affidavit appears at the beginning of the crisis management document.

Introduction

The crisis management plan begins with a message from the chief executive officer (CEO), chairperson, or government executive. Statements of mission, mandate, and organizational objectives offer a reference point for planning. Almost by definition, a crisis occurs when an organization faces the possibility that it will not be able to achieve its objectives. A gap occurs between expectations and realities. Crises affect the company's reputation, its ability to transact business, and ultimately its bottom line. This introductory material also includes principles for operating in times of crisis, with the lynchpins being openness, integrity, consistency, flexibility, and accuracy.

Crisis Profile

Type of Crisis

In one survey, *Fortune* 500 CEOs unanimously agreed that the following areas tend to be common sources of crises: industrial accidents, environmental problems, union problems and strikes, product recalls, investor relations, hostile takeovers, proxy fights, rumors and media leaks, government regulatory problems, acts of terrorism, and charges related to fraud and embezzlement (Fink, 1986). Mitroff and Pearson (1993) reproduced a "laundry list" of approximately 130 different kinds of crises. Governments often face crises of a political nature, including revelation of impropriety or scandal of a personal nature, conflict of interest in business dealings, or highly controversial policy decisions. Governments also confront emergency situations that originate with nature (e.g., ice storms, floods, and earthquakes).

No organization can anticipate every kind of crisis. For this reason, organizations create typologies. A typology of crises for an airline could include airplane crash, hostage taking, hijacking, worker layoffs, discovery of structural fault in aircraft design, and merger. Crisis types for a chemical company might include toxic emissions, fire, product failure, worker layoffs, and strike. Crisis typologies for a local department of health could include outbreak of a virulent form of influenza, threat of typhoid fever from flooding, E. coli food poisonings, and other health threats.

Obviously, the closer the fit between the crisis characteristics and the category, the more likely the plan will be appropriate. For example, a crisis management plan for an oil spill will be quite different from a plan for a fire involving one of the offshore oil drilling rigs. Similarly, a plan to deal with revelations of E. coli outbreak or manifestations of mad cow disease will be different from a plan to deal with employee layoffs. A crisis management plan for a fire will include floor plans with exits clearly marked, lists of the nearest hospitals and fire stations, the location of fire extinguishers, and copies of policies related to building materials. A plan for managing an airplane crash will include aircraft manufacturing information, access codes for retrieving passenger manifests, maintenance schedules, and current in-

formation on the aircraft's performance record. Other kinds of information appear in almost every crisis management plan, regardless of type. For example, responsibilities for notifying families of the victims and names of individuals who can act as liaisons with families will be common to most plans.

Probability of Occurrence and Potential for Impact

An organization can rank a potential crisis on the basis of probability of occurrence and potential impact. Plotting probability and impact scores on a grid allows the organization to visualize the importance of the crisis issue relative to other potential crisis situations. For example, crises with a high probability of occurrence and a potentially serious impact occupy the red zone. Those with a high probability of occurrence but low impact appear in the gray zone. Crises with a low probability of occurrence but high impact fall into the amber zone. Finally, crises with a low probability of occurrence and low impact appear in the green zone (Fink, 1986). Plotting all the organization's issues on the same grid enables the organization to determine where it should assign priorities in planning. The value of the crisis barometer depends on the quality and appropriateness of questions that have been asked. Asking the wrong questions or omitting important questions can result in errors of judgment regarding probability of occurrence and impact. If the organization places a crisis in the wrong danger zone, crisis managers may assign insufficient resources to the issue or monitor its development in an inappropriate way.

The crisis barometer was created by Fink (1986) to predict probability and impact. This barometer measures probability on the basis of (a) the organization's safety record, (b) past crises, and (c) the experiences of similar organizations. The organization rates the probability of a crisis on a scale that ranges from 0% to 100%. The barometer measures impact on a scale of 0 to 10. Five impact-related questions concern (a) intensity of the crisis, (b) the likelihood that the organization will come under the scrutiny of the media or a government regulatory agency, (c) the extent to which the crisis could interfere with the ongoing operations of the organization, (d) the extent to which the crisis could damage the organization's bottom line, and (e) the extent to which the media and public will perceive the organization as a victim or a culprit. In the case of governments, judgments on impact should consider the issue's ability to influence the achievement of organizational objectives because the government's bottom line is service to the public.

Other questions that could prove helpful in determining the impact of an issue are the following: What is the potential for media engagement? How many stakeholders are interested in the issues at stake in the crisis? What is the intensity of their interest? What is the value of objects or goals threatened by the crisis? Are lives at stake? Health? Economic viability? What is the potential for adverse reaction by employees? By investors? By unions? Has the organization suffered long-term or short-term damage to its reputation? and What is the field of influence of the issue, both in terms of geography and in terms of interaction with other issues? An earthquake or hurricane can generate minicrises associated with transportation, clean water, bacterial infections, diseases such as typhoid fever, and communications. The resignation of a chief executive can bring the viability of the firm into question. Employees may begin to speculate about why the CEO resigned. Is the company being acquired? Has the president been charged with wrongdoing? These kinds of speculations and rumors can provoke other resignations and sales of stock. A leadership crisis, unchecked, can become an economic crisis. When several people died from cyanide-laced Tylenol capsules, Johnson & Johnson had several crises to manage, including the immediate threat of poisoned capsules, the larger issue of diminished credibility that could affect the sale of other products, loss of public confidence, and widespread fear. They also had to contend with the issue of reengineering, on very short notice, their packaging plant.

Like migraines, crises tend to occur in clusters (Fink, 1986). The effects of these secondary crises can persist longer than the original catalytic event. For example, a police shooting or riot squads can provoke further outbursts of violence from groups that perceive themselves to be at risk. Bad feelings can permeate the community for a long period of time. In other instances, the organization may need to proceed with caution in enforcing certain policies or invoking certain procedures. For example, the public may accuse the government of overreacting if it calls out the National Guard or military to deal with a domestic crisis. Some interest groups or opposition forces will use opportunities created by crisis situations to undermine the organization, particularly in cases in which misconduct or mismanagement is alleged. Governments frequently undergo this type of testing. The organization may want to create influence diagrams that chart the development of a crisis, once in progress. In other words, if this event occurs, what event will follow? Will a chain of events be activated by some catalytic occurrence? The death of Diana, Princess of Wales, provoked a series of events that almost toppled the British monarchy. Some say that the historical moment determines the significance of people and events. Perhaps the scene was set, waiting for the single event that would trigger a social and political revolution. The violent death of a twentieth-century princess in a Paris tunnel may have been that catalyst.

Crisis Indicators

The organization should try to identify "trigger events"—events or activities that could focus public concern on a potentially highly contentious issue (Brody & Stone, 1989). Crises often have historical precedents—a series of prior crises in the same or related areas. In general terms, technical, human, and organizational factors trigger crises (Mitroff & Pearson, 1993). Donald Stephenson (1984), director of corporate communications at Dow Chemicals Canada, suggested that more detailed content groupings help the crisis manager to identify potentially vulnerable or high-risk areas. The organization can designate crisis indicators for each of the following areas:

- Products or services—their safety, their effects on the environment, the company's use of scarce materials in manufacturing the products, and choice of firms for contract awards

- Processes—vulnerabilities in areas such as manufacturing, transportation, or finance

- Locales—potential problems related to where operations, suppliers, and buyers are located (e.g., Columbia [drug cartels], Italy and Japan [earthquakes], Brazil [debilitating levels of inflation], Florida [hurricanes], the Middle East [political instability], the prairies [drought], and California [forest fires]), workplace safety, and how the company handles hazardous products

- Officers and executives—corporate practices, private or company associations, activities, and sponsorships

- Personnel—hiring and firing practices, equity policies, benefits, job security, tasks assigned employees, or union-related activities

Organizations must be prepared to respond to all potential threats. Being prepared means having accurate, current information on all vulnerable products, policies, services, locales, and operations. The generation of crisis indicators can help the organization to recognize emerging problem areas.

Crisis Management Team

Managing a crisis implies the need to agree on jurisdictions. All parties with a stake in the crisis must decide on areas of responsibility. Management of the crisis will proceed more smoothly if these decisions take place before the onset of a crisis. A crisis management plan specifies the membership of the crisis management team and the roles and responsibilities of each person. The chain of command is clear. Who is in charge? Who answers to the person in charge? Someone has the authority to delegate responsibility. The CEO typically heads the crisis management team, and an executive officer with communication training acts as lead spokesperson. An individual with a clear understanding of the "nuts-and-bolts" functioning of the organization coordinates operations. Someone other than the CEO assumes responsibility for coordinating operations, and others take control of specific operational areas, such as command, security, safety, engineering, personnel, data processing, and communications. These operations link up at the central spot, occupied by the coordinator. All support functions report to this individual (ideally, a senior-level manager with at least some technical knowledge). The coordinator chairs crisis management meetings, and the CEO listens, observes, questions, and reacts to the group's decisions. Ideally, the coordinator is not chosen from a business unit with special interests because such an affiliation can bias the person's handling of the crisis situation. The organization selects alternates for the position of coordinator of operations.

The team should not exceed 10 members. Common areas represented on crisis management teams are finance, human resources, law, science, medicine, occupational health, risk management, safety and security, international affairs, and communications. The specific makeup of the team will vary according to the nature of the crisis and the perceived needs. Generally, team members should possess the creativity to invent solutions, the perspective to understand the inner workings of the organization, the power and authority to command resources, and the knowledge of how and when to communicate to the public (Meyboom, 1989). Outside experts from areas such as investor relations or financial relations can be valuable additions to a team.

Decision Options

The organization cannot control every potential crisis source. Nonetheless, crisis managers can prescribe, in advance, options for action in such circumstances. Contingency planning for crises involves anticipating the decision options and deciding on the criteria by which the organization will make its selection (Andriole, 1985).

Required Support Systems

The crisis management plan designates a preferred site for an operations center and alternative sites. These centers should be as close as possible to the crisis site but not located in a restricted zone (Bouchard, 1992). The following description applies to a typical operations room (Meyboom, 1989):

> This is a special room, generally with limited access and equipped with special telephones, maps, computer terminals, and audiovisual equipment. Blackboards, flip charts, and modest kitchen facilities are other essential elements. The room should be close to typing and transmission facilities. (p. 28)

Backup generators should be installed in the event of power failure. In the event of a crisis, team members need food, drinks, bedding, flashlights, battery-powered lamps, and first-aid kits. The organization must arrange for the transportation of required supplies and equipment to the central operations site and to other locations.

Requirements for communication equipment include telex, telephones, line-load control for telephones, word processing equipment, typewriter (in the event of power failure), facsimile machines and lines (incoming and outgoing), modem, conference call networks, photocopying machine, police scanner, walkie-talkies, cellular phones, and extension cords. Several different telephone lines should be available for communications between the chief spokesperson, those who are at the scene of the crisis, other experts, and the media. The organization should establish separate communication channels for employees, distributors, wholesalers, retailers, and suppliers. Media personnel at the crisis management center also require access to telephones. Some 1-800 numbers may be necessary. Battery-powered radios and televisions enable the crisis management team to monitor press coverage of the crisis. A videotape recorder enables playback and analysis of the coverage. A camera, film, and video equipment are useful to record crisis events and the crisis environment.

Useful documents include executive profiles, photographs, location of branch offices, fact sheets on organization (e.g., numbers of employees, products or services, operations, management, and clientele), annual reports, quality control procedures, safety records and procedures, crisis management manual (including crisis communication plan), telephone and media directories, site maps, street and highway maps, building plans showing emergency exits, schedules, and press kits (Fearn-Banks, 1996). Other necessary supplies include pencils, pens, paper, company stationery, news release paper, camera, and film.

Requirements for support staff include administrative help, telephone staff, typists, computer specialists, equipment maintenance operators, and messengers capable of carrying information in the event that telephone service is disrupted. These personnel requirements may be necessary 7 days a week, 24 hours a day, until the emergency ends. Team members may require transportation to crisis management headquarters or to a site location. The organization will need to locate the nearest restaurants and stores for purchasing food and other supplies that run low and the closest motels and hotels. The crisis management plan should specify all of these material, equipment, and support staff needs.

Systems must be in place to deal with recovering lost information and restoring data processing functions in an organization: "Industry-wide statistics show that essential company functions can continue for only 4 to 5 days after a disaster to its data processing applications" (Ginn, 1989, p. 3). Sources of the problem include industrial espionage, hacking, terrorism, and growth in fraud. The warnings about the probable failures of computer systems in the Year 2000 can be classified under this category. Prearranged service and vendor agreements, which include agreements to provide alternate facilities and equipment, can help the organization to cope in such circumstances. Backup copies of all information, in appropriate formats, should be kept at an off-site facility that is physically isolated from the main facility. These kinds of measures ensure continuity in business operations, even in a period of crisis. Although budgetary requirements cannot be firmly fixed in advance of a crisis, approximate costs for carrying out certain kinds of activities can be estimated.

Crisis Management Directory CAJETE .

The plan should contain complete information on where and how to reach all team members and their alternates at all times. The company should print a directory of crisis management team members and alternates that includes references to where they can be reached, including work, home, cottage, and other places. This directory should include telephone and fax numbers, cellular phone numbers, and e-mail addresses. Names, addresses, and telephone numbers of neighbors, friends, and family can prove useful in times of crisis. The directory should list the names and contact numbers for groups such as police, fire stations, emergency response teams, hospitals, paramedics, local health departments, utility companies, consumer associations, unions, regulatory agencies, relevant city and state officials, other government or political figures with a stake in the crisis, key community organizations, media outlets, and journalists with expertise or interest in key areas.

Communication Component

Crisis communication plans can be supplementary to or part of the crisis management plan. Many believe that a crisis communication plan is key to survival of an organization—knowing what to say, when, and to whom. The following discussion proposes relevant content for such a communication plan.

Crisis Indicators

Like the larger mother plan, the crisis communication plan should include a set of indicators to suggest when crises are imminent (i.e., when organizational objectives are at risk) or when a crisis is due to move to another level of seriousness. These indicators will be specific to communication. For example, press coverage typically escalates as crises grow near. Rumors abound inside and outside the company or government department. The press may report cynical comments by competitors or hint of the impending failure of the organization. Journalists may inquire about some aspect of the organization's operations. Receptionists and telephone operators may witness an increase in unpleasant telephone calls to the firm. A government may witness its popularity plummeting in the polls or major pieces of legislation defeated in the House of Representatives or the Senate. The mention of specific topics, with connections to the central value systems of publics, may herald a new stage in the crisis. These warning signs typically occur during an extended period of time. Governments may fall and corporations collapse, but their demise rarely occurs overnight. It has been said that disaster occurs slowly and in stages. Communication monitoring systems (monitoring the Internet or media) can identify these early warning signs or indicators (Johnson, 1997).

Communication Team C A JETE

Manager

The head of communications or public relations usually (but not always) leads the crisis communication team. Responsibilities include briefing and advising top management, drafting or approving official statements, and coordinating the efforts of the crisis communication team. Alternates assume responsibility when the lead person is unavailable.

Spokesperson(s)

Many experts suggest that a single spokesperson should represent the organization in a crisis, and some believe that the spokesperson should always be the CEO or company chairperson. Interviews with 71 bank executives, representing 35 commercial institutions, confirmed this dominant point of view (Reilly, 1991). Others argue that the CEO has little credibility in a crisis because he or she, more than anyone else, has more to lose when crisis strikes. This camp of opinion further contends that experts are best able to answer specialized questions. The president of an oil company may understand the political implications of a spill in the Gulf of Mexico, but experts in ecology can answer questions on the long-term implications of the spill for the environment. Others believe that decisions on spokespersons should relate to the content of the planned communication. For example, when injuries result from the crash of a subway car, the head of the transportation carrier will be the best person to apologize to the victims and their families. This individual, however, may have no understanding of the mechanical failures responsible for the crash. Scientists can answer technical questions more convincingly than can executives, and financial analysts can predict the economic consequences of events. Sometimes, regional spokespersons are the best interpreters of what a crisis means to the local population. At other times, volunteers man hotlines and give orchestrated responses to questions and concerns.

The seriousness of the crisis also influences the choice of spokespersons. For example, General H. Norman Schwarzkopf (commander of Allied Forces in the Gulf), Dick Cheney (secretary of defense), and Colin Powell (Joint Chiefs of Staff chairman)—all high-ranking officials—shared the duties of spokespersons for the armed forces in the Gulf War. Some believe that more serious crises merit more senior spokespersons. If a top executive represents a firm on a matter of moderate importance, onlookers will attach more significance to the event than it merits. If a junior spokesperson represents the organization on a critical issue, however, the public will view the company as placing little importance on the outcome of the crisis. Some believe that the head of public relations should act as spokesperson only when the crisis is minor in nature because this individual will not have the stature of a CEO in the public view.

Whoever speaks for the organization must coordinate his or her messages with other spokespersons. Otherwise, inconsistencies will undermine the best efforts of the organization to contain the crisis. Also, the organization should appoint alternates in the event that designated spokespersons are not available. Advance agreement on replacement individuals will facilitate the process. Most corporations accept the necessity for spokespersons to receive training in media interviewing techniques, and most newly elected governments enroll their executives in media training seminars. The leaders learn through simulations and role plays. Many engage in semiannual reviews to ensure they maintain the facility acquired in initial training sessions.

Liaison With Victims' Families and Hospitals

In crisis situations, there are strong emotional dimensions for which organizations must plan (Pauchant & Mitroff, 1992). For example, a crisis communication plan should specify who will contact the families of victims, who will decide questions related to the release of victims' names, and how to accomplish these tasks. The liaison to victims' families should be someone with an empathetic manner and strong interpersonal skills. This liaison, however, may need to do more than just assure and comfort the families. The person may also need to assume the management of details such as arranging transportation, meals, and lodging. Most experts agree that, to the extent possible, the victims' families should be kept in a location separate from media headquarters. Crisis communication teams will need to provide local hospitals with copies of the communication plan for notifying victims' families, releasing names, and other similar information.

Public Relations Personnel

Many communicators become engaged in the daily management of crisis communications. They prepare press releases, document the daily activities of the crisis communication team, and liaise with the media. Other individuals approve media access to disaster sites, arrange for specialized services (e.g., the services of a photographer), or give refresher courses in interview techniques to organizational spokespersons. Some assume responsibility for contacting regulatory agencies. The head of public relations sometimes acts as spokesperson.

Communication Strategies

Information Flow Patterns

The crisis communication plan can include anticipated information flow patterns. This analysis identifies formal and informal information networks (inside and outside the organization) that could be activated by the crisis, including identification of key opinion leaders [not necessarily top management]). Studies in disaster management have determined that information moves in particular ways in crises. Some classical message diffusion studies (DeFleur & Dennis, 1985) determined that 93% of the people who eventually knew about a message acquired their information on the first day. Nonetheless, some groups receive information before others. In addition to identifying first-, second-, and third-wave populations for information, this section of the plan should identify groups that might not receive the information from normal channels of information (e.g., street people, housebound individuals, those who are hearing impaired, or others). Disaster plans must consider these special populations.

Key Messages

The organization frames key messages to be delivered to its publics, and spokespersons deliver these messages in clear lay language, avoiding jargon and "bureaucratese." The most successful media interviews are "message-driven, not question-driven" (McLoughlin, 1990), and the most important message that the organization can transmit in the early hours of a crisis is concern. Neither explanations nor assignment of blame is appropriate at this time. The organization demonstrates, through its actions and words, that it is searching for solutions to the problem. In a time of crisis, it is inappropriate to mount a defense of the organization based on past performance, superior products or services, or exceptional policies. The organization should communicate these messages in noncrisis periods. If an organization has a laudable performance record, others will speak on the organization's behalf. The public has a preexisting image of the organization, which should influence the choice of communication strategies (Coombs & Holliday, 1996).

Target Audiences for Messages

Chapter 12 describes a stakeholder identification tool appropriate to issues management. This same tool can identify the stakeholders in a crisis situation. All of the following can help the organization to manage the crisis: police, fire, and hospital officials; emergency preparedness personnel; key government leaders; civil servants; politicians; directors and members of the board of trustees; print and electronic journalists (especially those with interest and knowledge in the affected areas); and consumer, special interest, and advocacy groups. Many "bad news" situations create a need to involve government officials.

This part of the crisis communication plan should prioritize publics in terms of their need to receive information and their ability to contribute to crisis management efforts. The planner must decide on a contact order. Who should be called first? The media? Employees? Managers of specialized functions? Union representatives? Visiting groups and tour companies? The board of directors? Shareholders and investors? Customers or consumers? Government or regulatory agencies? Suppliers? The general public? Those who live near the crisis site? The nature of the crisis, the level of risk to different populations, and the information flow patterns described previously decide the answer to these questions. The organization must update contact lists on a regular basis. Plans for communicating with target publics should take into account the need to notify families of victims before notifying the general public of any injuries or deaths resulting from a crisis event.

Communication Materials

Question-and-answer kits anticipate the questions most likely to be asked in a crisis situation and suggest appropriate responses. Fact sheets inform the media about the organization's products, operations, services, and management. These fact sheets, prepared in advance, ensure that the media has relevant names, dates, and statistics. As the crisis progresses, press releases keep the media informed on how the organization views key issues.

Assessment of Media Expertise

The circulation of inaccurate information is common in the acute phase of crises, when confusion abounds. For example, the national media made many mistakes in reporting the 1991 Gainesville, Florida, murders of university students (Tuggle, 1991). The press reported the following myths: (a) The university administration had suspended classes, (b) the notorious Ted Bundy killings had occurred in Gainesville, and (c) a $1 million bond is common in cases involving battery. A similar situation occurred at Oka, Quebec, where Mohawk Indians set up a barricade to prevent the movement of individuals or vehicles onto the tribe's sacred burial grounds. The barricade was a protest against the municipality's plans to build a golf course on the land. The journalists who covered the events admitted that they were seriously handicapped by their lack of familiarity with the history of Oka, a dispute that dated from the 1700s. As a consequence, the journalists published many inaccurate facts (Post-Oka Symposium, 1990). Because spot news reporters often cover crisis situations, it may be necessary to educate reporters on the history of an event.

Principles for Dealing With the Media

Every crisis communication plan should include a set of principles for dealing with the media. It has been said that only fools enter a war of words with an enemy that "buys ink by the barrel, paper by the ton, and controls the airwaves" (Fearn-Banks, 1996, p. 65). Many believe that the media has the power to define a situation as a crisis. According to this view, an event becomes a crisis only when the media, government, or influential interest groups attach the label of crisis to the event (Privy Council Office [PCO], 1989). Sometimes, a conflict arises between the mandate of the media to provide information to the public and the need of the organization to control the flow of information in a crisis environment. Media coverage of a crisis follows predictable lines of development. Early stories focus on fatalities and destruction: "First come the colorful descriptions of personal heroism, grief, and suffering by individuals. . . . Next come discussions of property damage and cost. . . . Finally come the discussions of preparedness and competence of response by authorities" (Hume, 1989, p. 19).

Media tend to ask the following questions (PCO, n.d.): Who is at fault? When will the responsible party be punished? When did the organization learn about the problem? How did it respond to the discovery? What is the organization doing at this time? and How should the organization compensate or protect at-risk individuals or groups? The media want to know details on time and location, fatalities and injuries (numbers, names, addresses, and length of time with the company), property damage (estimates of extent and cost), the company (number of employees, products manufactured, safety record, and prior incidents), and potential harm to the environment. They also want to know the continuing level of risk to individuals, property, the organization, and the environment. In such a charged atmosphere, the organization must not treat confrontations with the media as a zero-sum game. Crisis situations demand open communication policies, and crisis communication plans include a strategy for dealing with the media. Rumors and cries of alarm fill any information vacuum, and the media go elsewhere if they do not get information from the concerned organization (Picard, 1991).

Although openness in communication should be the norm, the following cautions are in order:

- Never offer an opinion on the cause of a problem until a thorough investigation has taken place.
- Do not assign blame.
- Be succinct and keep interviews focused on key messages.
- Be alert to legal implications in statements.
- Avoid speculation at all costs.
- Double-check all facts before communicating the information to the media or the public (some organizations use a spiderweb procedure for verifying information).
- Avoid going "off the record" because journalists often ignore such labels.
- Avoid responding with "no comment" because many will interpret silence as guilt.
- Avoid defensive statements because observers will suspect guilt behind the defense.
- Demonstrate compassion but do not apologize.
- Do not talk about successes that predated the crisis.
- Do not be afraid to say "I don't know."
- Respond first to human safety concerns.
- Avoid jargon and bureaucratese.

Television visuals and photographs pose the highest risk to organizations faced with a crisis. Sometimes, spokespersons for the organization hold press conferences off the premises to prevent journalists from taking unauthorized photographs. At other times, they provide photographs and videotaped materials to journalists.

The role of spokespersons shifts with the progress of a crisis. In the acute phase of a crisis, the major role of the spokesperson is to express concern.

Improperly briefed spokespersons inform journalists that they will respond as soon as possible, but they do not attempt to answer questions to which they do not know the answers: "The implications of naming the wrong manufacturer, of placing blame on the wrong party, of announcing wrong names insofar as victims are concerned are too horrific to consider . . . from both personal and legal standpoints" (Baugniet, 1984, p. 7). There are also insurance implications in many organizational crises. The organization must obtain legal advice on the limits of disclosure. Attorneys are an indispensable part of the crisis management team, especially with issues involving land use and development, municipal and private labor negotiations, and political referenda (Cooper, 1992). For this reason, attorneys should participate in the organization's crisis simulation exercises. A problem sometimes arises, however, because most attorneys value silence over disclosure. The following is a typical response: "We will try this suit in the courtroom, not on the front page of the newspaper"(Howard & Mathews, 1985). Communicators, however, tend to value openness, and they believe that spokespersons can describe the nature of an incident without speculating on the cause or costs. They argue that the court of public opinion will render a verdict on the organization's case, even if people lack vital evidence. Also, history has demonstrated that efforts to conceal information, once exposed, can generate more publicity than the event they are intended to cloak. The impeachment proceedings against Bill Clinton offer a classic example from which organizations can learn. The public tends to receive bad news more graciously if it comes from the responsible person or organization (Howard & Mathews, 1985):

> You want to be the first to reveal bad news. . . . You are more likely to get your story accurately reported by the media. You are less likely to be on the defensive. You may get credit for honestly admitting a mistake—and caring enough about your customers and the public to speak up and let them know about it. You will establish yourself as the source of information. . . . Taking the initiative may avoid making a hero out of your attacker. . . . You are also more likely to have the story covered for one day and then forgotten. Your objective in handling bad news is to get it out of the way and prevent it from becoming a continuing news story. Forthrightly explaining the situation and emphasizing remedial action will usually accomplish this objective, since there will be little of the charges and countercharges between two sides that characterize ongoing news stories." (p. 146)

Johnson & Johnson answered 300 calls from reporters on the weekend following the revelation of the Tylenol poisonings. Chairman James Burke answered questions on television shows such as *Donohue* and *60 Minutes*. The company hosted a massive news conference to respond to reporters' questions. The company subsequently regained more than 80% of its previous market share, a virtual miracle according to many (Knight as cited in Howard & Mathews, 1985, p. 162).

If the organization decides to restrict access to information, the spokesperson must explain the rationale. One of the best ways to ensure fair coverage during a crisis is to develop good media relations prior to the time of the crisis. The quality of media relations depends on factors such as the extent to which management appreciates the importance of communicating with media on a regular basis, understands and respects media deadlines, and treats all reporters and media organizations in the same way. As the crisis progresses, the organization regains control by finding opportunities to disseminate preferred messages to stakeholders. The Seattle-First National Bank described how it co-opted employees to assist in disseminating messages to publics in a crisis situation (Howard & Mathews, 1985):

> Get management and staff . . . involved in telling your story. We did that in
> the branches—we even had branch managers writing articles for the op-ed
> pages of their local newspapers. And we used our executives in talking to the
> media. It humanized us as an institution in a tough spot. (p. 143)

In other instances, the organization may need to avoid overreacting to situations that are localized. The involvement of regional offices can imply a broader scope to a problem than actually exists.

Guidelines for Issuing News Releases

The following are common rules for writing a news release:

- Place the most important information in the lead paragraph, in descending order of importance.
- Answer who, what, when, and where.
- Do not speculate on why something happened.
- Avoid jargon and bureaucratese; explain any technical language.
- Do not minimize or exaggerate the situation.
- Do not release specifics on damage or injuries.

Response and Control Mechanisms

Alert System for Activating Crisis Management Network

As noted earlier, a crisis communication plan specifies indicators to warn the organization of an impending crisis. Prior to the time that a crisis strikes, the organization agrees on a sequence of actions to be taken during crisis periods. If an organization has a hotline, callers can activate the crisis management network by reporting threatening events. Many organizations use a chain procedure in which each contact calls the next individual in the telephone tree. The first person to learn about the crisis calls the CEO, the head of public relations, and the head of the affected business unit. These individuals activate the telephone tree according to predetermined procedures.

Daily Operations

The plan specifies communication activities to be undertaken once a crisis is in progress. For example, some individuals monitor media coverage of the crisis, some meet with key opinion leaders from the community, and others write daily strategic communication overviews based on environmental intelligence acquired through media monitoring, interviews with opinion leaders, and other information sources. The plan identifies the sources to be monitored in a crisis and the individuals responsible for completing these tasks.

Once activated, the crisis communication team assigns tentative times and locations for committee meetings and debriefings. They record all communications with the media and other groups in a daily logbook along with the times of the communication and the telephone numbers of reporters. Accurate record keeping preempts the possibility for circulating contradictory information or duplicating information. These records also protect the organization from critics who charge that the organization did (or did not) take certain actions during the crisis.

System for Deactivating Crisis Management Network

Many years after Japan surrendered to the Allied Forces, pockets of Japanese soldiers were still hiding on remote Pacific islands. The soldiers were unaware that World War II had ended. Crises are not unlike wars. The organization prepares, does battle with the forces that threaten its survival, and then dismantles its operations. Organizations establish alert systems to activate and to deactivate crisis management networks. For example, following the discovery of a hypodermic needle in a Pepsi can, the company conducted an extensive investigation. After exposing several hoaxes, Pepsi officials believed that they could say that the crisis had ended. Pepsi announced the end of the crisis in the form of a letter to customers and an advertisement published in newspapers throughout the country (Fearn-Banks, 1996).

This section of the crisis communication plan details the actions that must be taken to facilitate a return to normalcy: "People cannot psychologically cope with crisis for an indefinite period. . . . Failure to announce resolution can lead to confusion, which prolongs the chronic phases of crisis or complicates recovery" (Garnett, 1992, p. 215). Nonetheless, no one should interpret the term *normalcy* to mean that the organization will necessarily be the same after the crisis. The crisis may have changed, forever and irrevocably, the character and structure of the organization. The communication group should thank not only those who acted in the crisis but also those who offered to act.

Evaluation of Operations

Pretesting of Systems and Procedures

Trial runs and simulations allow crisis management members to practice how they will behave in a crisis. Simulations, based on games theory, enable team members to test assumptions, establish norms, and analyze the outcomes of various behavioral options. Hypothetical situations provide participants with an opportunity to make decisions and negotiate the release of sensitive information. Many of these simulations focus on interaction with the media under crisis conditions. Rehearsal dates appear in the crisis communication plan. Some individuals (e.g., media relations officers and executive officers) require specialized training.

Postcrisis Debriefing

Postcrisis debriefings allow the organization to judge how well its plan worked. Those most directly affected by the crisis (the media, emergency centers, employees, selected community members, and corporation or government executives) participate in this assessment of organizational performance. Logbooks, newspaper articles, videotapes, audiotapes, and transcripts of radio and television coverage provide data for the evaluation. Outside experts help to ensure objectivity.

Updates

Some recommend that no crisis communication plan should remain unchanged for more than 2 years. Situations change, personnel change, and the company must integrate the results of learning into the plan. The organization circulates the updated plan to all crisis management team members and collects all outdated copies. At the time that a crisis occurs, the crisis management team tailors the generic plan to the specifics of the crisis situation.

Conclusion

Crisis communication team members act as part of a larger crisis management team with delegated authority. They play a critical role because the public has a great desire for knowledge in such situations. The role of the crisis communication team in the larger picture, the components of the crisis communication plan, principles for functioning in a crisis communication capacity, and supplementary data and materials that should be available to the crisis communicator were discussed in this chapter.

Appendix

The crisis management plan should contain an appendix that includes timetable and daily log forms (technical and communication) as well as the following regulations and procedural guidelines:

- Regulations governing decision-making procedures in times of crisis (procedures to be followed, roles of resource persons, ethical guidelines, etc.)

- Regulations governing delegation of authority when previously designated individuals cannot be reached

- Regulations governing intelligence-gathering operations
- Regulations governing dissemination of information (how to interact with media and other stakeholders, responsibilities of spokespersons, procedures for dealing with families of victims, procedures for verifying information, procedures for clearing press releases, etc.)
- Regulations governing the keeping of a logbook that details the technical aspects of a crisis (what is happening, what damage has occurred, who has been injured or killed, etc.)
- Regulations governing the keeping of a communications logbook that would include the date and time of information releases, logs of calls in and out (e.g., media and other inquiries and responses to media, community leaders, shareholders, and others), what was published or aired in the media, and key issues
- Procedures for updating lists of those who hold crisis management manuals
- Procedures for activating and deactivating the crisis communication networks
- Guidelines for writing press releases
- Guidelines for interacting with the media
- List of maps, fact sheets, personnel sheets, and other data required for use in crisis operations

Communication Theories:
The Foundation for Planning

7

Understanding the Psychology of Audiences

Beliefs, Attitudes, Values, and Needs

Audience response to information or persuasion strategies depends on their beliefs, attitudes, and values. Studies of perception indicate that we are most likely to attend to—and recall—information that fits well with existing belief systems. In this chapter, theories related to beliefs, attitudes, and values are reviewed to assist the communication planner in developing effective strategies and designing appropriate messages. Audiences are the starting point for all planning efforts. The latter part of the chapter considers audience needs for achievement, power, and affiliation and the impact of personality on how audiences receive messages.

The Influence of Beliefs, Attitudes, and Values on How Audiences Receive Messages

Beliefs

Belief systems, which act as filters between individuals and their environments, screen out potentially threatening stimuli and admit rewarding and nonthreatening stimuli (Best, 1970). According to Rokeach (1968), each individual holds five types of beliefs: types A, B, C, D, and E. These beliefs are structured in layers, like an onion, with Type A in the center and the others in concentric rings around Type A.

Type A beliefs, within the most central core of the belief system, constitute basic truths about physical reality ("This is a tree"), social reality ("I live in New York"), and the nature of the self ("I am a woman"). Type A beliefs require 100% consensus for the person to be comfortable with the beliefs; they are seldom controversial. People acquire Type A beliefs early in life, and they continue to validate these beliefs as they age. A person learns the beliefs by direct encounter with the belief object, and unanimous social consensus reinforces faith in the beliefs. Because of object constancy, person constancy, and self-constancy, the individual maintains a certain stability. Beliefs that concern existence and identity and the physical world have many connections with the other parts of the belief system. If a belief that has consensus within the society (e.g., Type A beliefs) comes under assault, the resistance to change will be great. For example, when Galileo argued that the earth revolved around the sun (a belief contrary to the long-standing belief that the earth was at the center of the universe), the Church authorities threatened to excommunicate him unless he recanted. Galileo had brought into question a Type A belief about physical reality and the nature of the universe.

In the same way, Type B beliefs (which form the next layer of the belief structure) are highly resistant to persuasion efforts. Ego-centered Type B beliefs require zero consensus. A person learns these concepts by direct encounter, but external authority does not necessarily support the concepts. The concepts may be either positive ("I am intelligent") or negative ("I am unattractive"). Phobias, delusions, and hallucinations exemplify negative Type B beliefs ("People hate me"). Psychiatrists seek to effect changes in negative Type B beliefs. Unshared beliefs (Type B) have fewer connections with other parts of the belief system than do shared beliefs (Type A).

Changing Type C beliefs, or authority beliefs, is easier than effecting shifts in Type A and Type B beliefs. People develop authority beliefs to deal with facts of physical and social reality that have alternative explanations. These beliefs, not personally experienced, are often controversial. Reference persons and reference groups help individuals decide which Type C beliefs to accept. Authorities may be "positive" (the person likes the authority) or "negative" (the person dislikes the authority). The individual typically regards statements originating with positive authorities as credible and discredits the views of negative authorities. Hare Krishna, Fidel Castro, and Pope Paul are positive authorities to some individuals and negative authorities to others.

Type D beliefs emanate from authority figures: "Believing in the credibility of a particular authority implies an acceptance of other beliefs perceived to emanate from such authority" (Rokeach, 1968, p. 10). Type D beliefs have fewer connections with other parts of the belief system than do authority concepts. For example, if a voter rejects President Clinton's explanation of the Monica Lewinsky affair but accepts the president's right to stay in office, the person will probably experience limited changes in the belief system. The individual will probably still vote, pay taxes, and sing the national anthem at football games. If the person rejects Bill Clinton as an authority symbol, however, more far-reaching changes will result in the person's belief system. The person may no longer attach much value to the office of president. This devaluing may result in the person not voting in the next election, attaching less importance to the rituals that show loyalty to the country and government, and not trusting future presidents. Events such as Watergate and Vietnam resulted in a wave of cynicism and distrust of authority and set the stage for the questioning of Nixon's successors.

Types C and D are easier to change than Types A and B because not all persons share these beliefs (Rokeach, 1968):

> Beliefs about such issues as birth control and sin, communism and fascism, Russia and the South, and beliefs about such personages as Hitler and Krushchev, Lincoln and Christ do not seem to be among the most deeply held of man's beliefs. More resistant to change . . . are those taken-for-granted beliefs about identity that are incontrovertible either because they are shared by virtually everyone or because they are not at all dependent on social consensus. (p. 57)

Type E beliefs, situated on the periphery of the belief structure, involve arbitrary and essentially inconsequential matters of taste. The maintenance of these concepts does not require social consensus. Because Type E beliefs have the fewest connections with other parts of the belief system, they respond more readily to attempts at persuasion than do more centrally placed beliefs. Despite the fact that a person may hold peripheral beliefs just as intensely as more central ones, they will relinquish these beliefs more readily because the beliefs have fewer connections with the rest of the belief system. The advertiser often achieves a persuasive goal by associating Type E beliefs with more psychologically central beliefs, such as A, B, and C. The advertiser who connects a Type E belief with a negative Type B belief may be exploiting a person's primitive fears to achieve change in inconsequential beliefs. Mouthwash and deodorant commercials illustrate attempts to appeal by making such connections. Other persuasion attempts link Type E beliefs to Type C authority concepts to achieve change. Testimonials exemplify this variety of persuasion.

Attitudes

Attitudes have been defined as predispositions to respond, either positively or negatively, to an object situation (Jahoda & Warren, 1966). Classical consistency theories seek to explain how audiences respond to information that does not fit with existing perceptions and attitudes. Many different terms have been used. Heider (1946) applied the terms *balance* and *imbalance*. Osgood and Tannenbaum (1955) talked about *congruity* and *incongruity*. Festinger (1957) referred to states of *consonance* and *dissonance* in which people tend to avoid (or, alternatively, rationalize) these psychologically uncomfortable situations. All these situations involve internal conflict, in which the person confronts inconsistencies in what he or she knows and believes. Newcomb (1953) discussed a situation in which cognitive imbalance results when two people, who like and respect each other, disagree on an issue. In such circumstances, the desire to maintain the relationship can stimulate attitudinal shifts on the part of both people. The final position will be somewhere in-between the two original positions. Newcomb said that a person can restore psychological balance in one of several ways. First, the person can experience attitude change toward both the object of discussion and the person, with the greatest attitude change occurring toward the least valued. Second, the person can distort the position of the other person in his or her own mind. Finally, the person can disassociate his or her thoughts (even his or her physical self) from the uncomfortable situation.

Many later researchers embedded the idea of co-orientation in their public relations models. *Co-orientation* refers to the extent to which parties are willing to change to accommodate the position of persons or groups with opposing viewpoints. Newcomb (1953) defined co-orientation as "perceived consensus" in systems "straining toward symmetry" (p. 393). Grunig and Hunt (1984) discussed the mutual adjustment processes that occur at the organizational level. They said that the public should be "just as likely to persuade the organization's management to change their attitudes or behavior as the organization is likely to change the public's attitude or behavior"

(p. 23). Dozier and Ehling (1992) said that "communication managers are more successful moving two parties closer together than converting one party (publics) over wholly to the other party's (dominant coalition) perspective" (p. 178). More in-depth consideration of attitudes is provided in Chapter 10, which reviews persuasion theories.

Values

Studies in perceptual psychology indicate that the extent to which the audience accepts the message of a communicator will depend on whether the message unlocks the value system and appears congruent with the existing value priorities of the reader.

Attempts to Identify Audience Values

Interest in measuring values has grown steadily during the past half century since Allport, Vernon, and Lindzey (1950) published their first values research. The Rokeach Value Survey, first published in 1968, laid the groundwork for almost every values study that followed. Rokeach (1973) defined values as "enduring beliefs that specific modes of conduct (instrumental values) or end-states of existence (terminal values) are personally or socially preferable to opposite or converse modes of conduct or end-states of existence" (p. 5). Values may be inferred from what a person says or does. According to Rokeach, every individual holds hundreds of thousands of beliefs and thousands of attitudes but only dozens of values. Rokeach identified 18 instrumental values (ideal states of behavior) and 18 terminal values (ideal states of existence) that appear to be among the most important values held by people. In subsequent years, many researchers undertook studies to identify the underlying factors in Rokeach's list of 36 values. Bearden, Netemeyer, and Mobley (1993) compiled one of the best contemporary surveys of the results of these studies. Their review, which encompasses the years 1962 to 1990, identified the following American values: achievement, activity, collectivism, competence, competitiveness, conformity, culture, democracy, dominance, efficiency, equality, family orientation, freedom, generosity, idealism, imagination, independence, individualism, intelligence, materialism, morality, optimism, patriotism, peace, progress, rationality, responsibility, sociality, and the work ethic.

In the 1980s and 1990s, many marketing studies were conducted that focused on values research. Psychographics involves the construction of a psychological profile of the audience that includes a values and lifestyle component (Arkin, 1992). Mitchell's (1983) Values and Lifestyle Typology divided people into nine categories. The value groupings ranged from poor struggling "survivors" to affluent, spiritually motivated "integrateds." According to Mitchell, survivors do not see an escape from their unhappy existence. Sustainers are young minority Americans who are angry with the system. Like survivors, sustainers are poor. Belongers, emulators, and achievers share in common the fact that they are *outer-directed*. In other words, they respond to how others in society expect them to behave. Belongers, who believe in a strict puritanical code of behavior, aspire to be part of mainstream society. Emulators, however, are upwardly mobile, competitive, and status-conscious. Like sustainers, emulators distrust the system; this distrust is a result of the minority status of many group members. A disproportionate number of achievers are male, white, and Republican. As the label implies, achievers value hard work, success, and material comforts. Mitchell also identified three groups of Americans who are *inner-directed*. Whereas outer-directed individuals try to meet the expectations of others, inner-directed people are more individualistic in their responses. I-am-me's, experientials, and societally conscious Americans comprise the three inner-directed clusters. The young, self-centered, and exhibitionist I-am-me's tend to be insecure, impulsive, inventive, and liberal in orientation. Many young, single females (still dependent on parental support) appear in this cluster. A mature version of the I-am-me orientation, experientials are less egocentric, more adventurous, more liberal in their politics, and more active in political movements, especially women's and environmental causes. The last inner-directed cluster, the societally conscious, represents approximately 14 million Americans. The societally conscious are affluent but less materialistic than achievers. Because they see the need for social reform, many have leadership roles in activist causes and single-issue campaigns, especially concerning environmental issues. Well-educated, they hold intellectual positions in the professions. They tend to support an active role for America on the international scene. At the same time, they stand for cooperation rather than domination, and they support peace movements. The final cluster contains the integrateds, who reflect a mix of outer-directed and inner-directed value and lifestyle orientations. The integrateds are fully mature, self-assured, self-expressive, and actualized individuals according to Maslow's developmental model. It has been said that "they have it all" and they are "above it all" (Grunig as cited in Ferguson, 1994, p. 65).

The majority of social psychologists and anthropologists agree that a finite number of values guide human action. An introductory comment in *Understanding Human Values* (Rokeach, 1979) noted, "In every full-fledged society, every one of Rokeach's 36 values will appear—as will each of the values or themes listed by C. Kluckhohn, F. Kluckhohn, R. F. Bales and Couch, C. Morris, M. Opler, and R. Williams" (p. 17). The majority of researchers also concur that value sets are relatively enduring and unchanging. Shifts in values are much less likely than shifts in beliefs and attitudes. Lipset (1967) observed that no completely new value orientations had appeared to date in the twentieth century, and Williams (1970) concluded that American values had shown little change between 1950 and 1970. A study by Kahle, Poulos, and Sukhdial (1988) also showed stability during a decade in how Americans evaluated the importance of many social values.

Nonetheless, audiences do vary over time in how they rank order values. Williams (1970) and Yankelovich (1981) found that the importance of achievement as a value had declined in the same period that success increased, even if both remained important values. Other studies found that American commitment to equality showed significant erosion in the 1970s (Ball-Rokeach, Rokeach, & Grube, 1984). Since the 1960s, an increasing number of Americans have recognized the importance of environmental values. Research into political values demonstrates the increasing influence of the Christian Right and fundamentalist religions (Badaracco, 1992; Persinos, 1994). The number of Americans valuing honesty and integrity in political candidates grew dramatically after Watergate (Roelofs, 1992). Two surveys of American youth (reported in Easterlin & Crimmins, 1991) confirmed a "modest turning away from the public interest," a "sharp decline in emphasis on personal self-fulfillment," and a "sharp shift toward private materialism." The youths reported a greater tendency to support capitalist institutions and to believe that corporations are doing a good job. Many called themselves "conservative," but relatively few were politically active. D. D. B. Needham, who engaged in a 16-year study of American lifestyles, recently disputed the general wisdom that Americans are returning to traditional values (Winski, 1992).

Shifts also occur in terms of the consistency with which the population at-large adheres to the values (i.e., the number of people at any point in time who believe in the value) or the extent to which the society tolerates conflicts in the values. A study by Prothro and Grigg (1960) found a strain between belief in patriotic values and belief in freedom of speech. Others believe that when a society values achievement, this value comes into conflict with the value of being a caring and compassionate society.

In conclusion, researchers vary in how they choose to label certain values. They sometimes dispute the results of others' attempts to narrow the list of values through factor analysis techniques. They believe that, at different points in time and in different cultural contexts, people vary in how they rank order values and in the extent to which they tolerate conflicts in opposing values. Variations over time and place also occur in the percentage of people who adhere to certain values. Whatever their differences, however, most researchers agree on a core set of relatively unchanging values held by most Americans.

The Role of Values in Communication

The previously discussed findings are significant for advertising, social marketing, and other communication campaigns. Because values remain relatively constant over time and for broad cultural groupings, the campaign designer sometimes disregards shorter term opinion and attitude trends. Instead, the strategist aims to access universal values or the most firmly held beliefs that are common to many audiences. This universal agreement is possible only to the extent that references to the values appear in relatively ambiguous guise. That is, the more one attempts to specify the characteristics of values or to apply them to concrete situations, the higher the likelihood of disagreement and conflict and the lower the chances of achieving consensus among diverse groups. Ambiguity allows many audiences to identify with the values, whereas explicit appeals bring attention to that which divides audiences.

How does the campaign planner access these universally held values? Comprehending the nature of this process allows the student of communication to understand the methods, whether for practical or critical purposes. In the manner described earlier in this chapter, the campaign designer often links more peripheral beliefs, such as taste in politicians, toothpaste, music, and perfume, to more centrally held beliefs about the nature of reality, self-concept, and authority. These peripheral beliefs become gateways, or entry points, to the central value system. Next, the campaign designer uses trigger stimuli to carry the preferred messages. For example, advertisers build triggers into product packaging in the hope that these triggers will be fired at the point of purchase. The cartoon figures who come to life in television advertisements represent, for children, a passage to moments of fantasy and fun with family and friends. In catching a beer can in a Coors silver bullet commercial, a man also obtains a promise of social acceptance, companionship, and sexual fulfilment. The can of beer acts as a trigger symbol, which activates needs and opens the door to the central value system of the viewing audience.

The key to understanding the way in which advertisements use triggers to access our value systems is to understand the nature of signal behavior. Signal behavior implies responding, without conscious thought, to a stimulus. Semanticists define signal behavior as immediate, unthinking, largely automatic and uncritical responses. Hayakawa (1949) used the example of the chimpanzee taught to drive an automobile. The chimpanzee was taught to proceed at green lights and brake at red lights. Differentiating the response of the chimpanzee from the response of the human, however, was the fact that the chimpanzee drove ahead (once the light was green) whether or not the way was obstructed. To the chimpanzee, the green light meant not "Go ahead if all else seems favorable" but simply "Go ahead." The chimpanzee responded automatically and uncritically to the signal, exemplifying signal behavior. The opposite of signal behavior, symbolic behavior, would have involved looking around, assessing the situation, and restarting the car only if other factors in the environment appeared favorable.

The contemporary advertisement encourages signal responses, mostly automatic and uncritical, on the part of viewers. Advertisements contain triggers designed to evoke value-reflexive responses that bypass intermediate filter and gating systems. Much like the hypnotist who, after several sessions with a patient, uses a few cue words to move the patient rapidly into a deep trance state, the advertiser uses verbal and visual cues to gain rapid access to the value system of target audiences. Once a pathway has been established and learned, later access is easy—a fact that raises ethical questions among critics of advertising.

Typically, these visual and verbal cues are embedded in metaphors. Leiss, Kline, and Jhally (1986) contend that metaphor is at the heart of contemporary advertising. Metaphor, they believe, places people, activities, and scenes side by side with products and attempts to "convert this contiguity into a meaningful relationship" (p. 241). For example, a commercial may compare the experience of trying a new brand of coffee (unfamiliar act) to going on a first date with someone (familiar act). In tying the unfamiliar to the familiar, metaphors exploit similarity and difference simultaneously. They create an artificial relationship.

Saussure's (1966) distinction between *syntagmatic* (horizontal) and *para-digmatic* or *associative* (vertical) relationships establishes a foundation for understanding how metaphors work. Syntagmatic relations suggest combinatory possibilities. We read our environment by putting all the elements together to complete a picture. For example, a person's attire is a syntagm or combination of clothing: belt, dress, hat, and shoes. In the same way, a person who orders a meal at a restaurant puts together a syntagm or combination of food choices: Caesar salad, steak, baked potato, asparagus, apple pie, and coffee. By contrast, paradigmatic or associative relations (semioticians use the terms interchangeably) suggest oppositions between elements that are capable of replacing each other. For example, a picture of an Ionic column evokes memories of an earlier experience with a Doric column—a visit to Rome, a photograph from a high school Latin book, or a slide shown in a fine arts class. The Doric column does not exist in the present, except in the person's mind. The brain houses the relationship. Without a previous experience with Doric columns, the relationship will not exist. In the case of the earlier example, each choice that a diner makes from a menu comes from a paradigm of possibilities. From the paradigm of salads, the diner can choose a Caesar, garden, macaroni, or tabouli. Steak, chicken, fish, or pork can be chosen from the paradigm of meats; baked potato, mashed potatoes, or french fries can be chosen from the paradigm of potato dishes; green beans, corn, broccoli, or squash can be chosen from the paradigm of vegetables; Jell-O, pie, or pudding can be chosen from the paradigm of desserts; and milk, juice, or wine can be chosen from the paradigm of drinks.

Metonyms, acting like syntagms, involve combination on a horizontal level, whereas metaphors function in the same oppositional, associative manner as paradigms (Webster, 1980). Applied to television, it can be seen that the Bell Canada advertisement of the father and son playing a board game, while it rains outside, illustrates both metonymic and metaphoric elements. As a metonym, the board game is one of many activities (one part of a greater whole) shared by father and son during a period of many years. The rain also recalls, metonymically, other rainy afternoons and evenings whiled away by father and son engaged in pleasurable activities. As a metaphor, the father stands for love and family security, traditional values universal to most cultures. The higher the level of ambiguity in ethnic types, physical setting, and the game being played, the greater the appeal for large numbers of audience members. The literature on framing of political issues also speaks about the "ability to articulate frames that resonate with broader political values or tendencies within the U.S. culture" (Ryan, Carragee, &

Schwerner, 1998, p. 170). Advertising relies heavily on archetypal metaphors. The archetypal metaphor draws comparisons between light and darkness and other natural forces. It is used to resonate universally held values such as love of home and family. The rain represents basic natural elements, such as cold and stormy weather. The care and love of the boy's father shelters the son from the natural elements. In another television advertisement, a glowing fire and a cup of Maxwell House coffee greet the spouse who returns home late at night, wet and shivering from exposure to rain and cold. Osborne (1967) claims that such metaphors relate to the most basic of human experiences: birth, growth, aging, and death. They appeal to human motivations—love, security, and family. Where audiences are highly diverse, as in the United Nations, archetypal metaphors help to bridge cultural boundaries. References to fire, water, whirlwinds, birth, and death allow individuals of radically different social, economic, religious, philosophical, and political backgrounds to transcend divisive frames of reference (Prosser, 1970). In the same way, advertisers seek to transcend differences and to resonate common chords in viewers. Bachand (1988) noted the frequent appearance of the archetypal metaphor in motorcycle advertisements. A typical advertisement contained a riderless motorcycle set against a cloudy background and a lightning-streaked sky. The advertisement represents the motorcycle as a fantastic apparition that appears against a backdrop of primitive elements.

Fiske (1982) points out that metaphors work paradigmatically for imaginative or surrealistic effect, as in the medium of television:

> Reading soft focus as sentiment involves an imaginative transposition of properties from the plane of feelings to the plane of construction of the signifier. Soft focus is a metaphor for sentiment. A dissolve is a metaphor for the act of memory. Gold buttons in the form of crowns and gold braid are metaphors for the high social status of a general's rank. But these connotations are constructed, rather than true metaphors, in that although they involve the imaginative transposition of properties from one plane to another, they stress the similarity between the planes and minimize the difference. (p. 100)

Fiske (1982) notes that many surreal advertisements exploit differences as much as similarities. Advertisers use a mish-mash of oppositional images and ideas that, when juxtaposed against each other, encourage the reader to make connections. Linked together, the disparate frames tell a story. In the visual language of advertising, events and objects often stand for products:

"Mustangs in the Wild West are a metaphor for Marlboro cigarettes, water-falls and natural greenery are a metaphor for menthol cigarettes. These are clear, manifest metaphors in which both vehicle (mustangs and waterfalls) and tenor (cigarettes) are visually present" (Fiske, 1982, p. 97). The reliance of advertisers on metaphors has spilled over into other programming formats such as rock videos. The format of rock videos is highly compressed—a collage of evocative images. There is a lack of linearity in the images, which appear and disappear at a speed akin to thought processes. Only the words to the songs are syntagmatic, and even these often seem more like discon-tinuous random associations than like logical sequential patterns.

The more obscure the metaphor, the more the readers must use their own experiences to identify similarities between different planes of reality. Perel-man (1982) speaks of the importance of the ambiguity afforded by meta-phorical discourse: "In natural languages, ambiguity—the possibility of multiple interpretations—would be the rule. The language of philosophers, for example, could only without difficulty do without metaphors which are characterized by their lack of clarity" (p. 44). The same principle applies to advertising. Advertisements with the highest potential to penetrate the value systems of viewers or listeners will be those carrying large cargos of nonspe-cific information, designed to activate a network of learned associations. Schwartz (1974) commented that advertisers seek to package stimuli so that it "resonates with information already stored within the individual, and thereby induces the desired learning or behavioral effect" (pp. 24-25). The ambiguity in the signs allows the audience to connect the signifier with core values. The more ambiguous the context in which the cues are embedded, the higher the level of audience involvement in the generation of meaning. The viewer or listener becomes engaged as a participant and not as an observer, thus generating a higher level of investment and commitment.

Ambiguity also enables appeals to conflicting values to coexist in a message. Research has uncovered a trend in American society toward placing less emphasis on doctrinal consistency and tolerating inconsistencies in value profiles. Cross-cultural studies suggest that Americans have a greater tolerance for ambiguity and inconsistencies in values than do people in countries such as Germany (Hofstede, 1980). This ability to tolerate differ-ences is important because of the increasing tendency for conflictive values, such as "freedom" and "equality," to coexist in some societies. Williams (1970) said that mass communication creates "gigantic magnetic fields of common and conflicting items of knowledge, beliefs, and values" (p. 452).

Through reliance on metaphors and ambiguity, advertisers are able to bridge cultural and other differences and avoid focusing attention on value incompatibilities.

Needs and Personality

Maslow's (1954) hierarchy of needs indicates that all people have motives and drives that influence their susceptibility to learning from messages. This staircase of needs includes physiological, safety, love, esteem, and self-actualization factors. At the bottom of the staircase are the physiological, safety, and love needs. The individual must find a way to satisfy these needs before the higher-level needs assume any real importance. A starving man will think only of food. A homeless person will search each day for shelter, giving little thought to matters of esteem or self-actualization. When relationships in a person's life deteriorate, he or she will often find it difficult to engage in work or play. Most health communication campaigns aim to meet the basic safety and health needs of audiences. Advertisers often target the esteem needs of audiences. Self-actualizing needs have to do with creativity, curiosity, independence, ambition, and freedom from restraint. According to Maslow, self-actualizing people are a rare phenomenon. Correspondence schools and the military often appeal to the self-actualizing needs of audiences. They offer the challenge to audiences to "become all that you are capable of being." Successful message design implies that the communicator must know the audience's position on the staircase of needs.

McClelland (1961) and McClelland, Atkinson, Clark, and Lowell (1953) studied achievement, affiliation, and power needs. They found that achievement orientation tends to be higher in the middle class than in the upper or lower classes. High achievement-oriented people set realistic goals, with a calculated risk factor. They prefer and seek tasks that offer a high level of autonomy. They plan ahead, and they want accurate and frequent feedback on their performance. They can accept negative feedback more readily than can those with low achievement needs. Their need for immediate and accurate feedback encourages high achievement-oriented people to seek jobs such as salesperson, architect, or teacher. They tend to avoid managerial jobs that do not offer concrete results. Although they tend to resist authoritarian structures, they like order and discipline. Individuals with a high need for achievement value excellence in performance over monetary or other re-

wards. They choose a competent coworker over a personable one. Comparative studies have found that the United States ranks higher on achievement
orientation than any other country (Hofstedte, 1980). Just as some individuals have high achievement needs, others have high affiliation or power needs.
People with high affiliation needs value friendships and relationships over
achievement and prefer teamwork to individual responsibility. People with
a high need for power seek positions of authority and status that will allow
them to control and influence others.

Personality also mediates how people receive messages. In general, it can
be said that individuals with high self-esteem are more difficult to influence
than individuals with low self-esteem. High-esteem individuals are especially resistant to directive messages that take away their ability to accept or
reject the message (Brockner & Elkind, 1985). Other studies have demonstrated that optimistic messages have a greater influence on high-esteem
individuals, and pessimistic messages have a greater influence on low-esteem
individuals (Leventhal & Perloe, 1962). Individuals with high self-esteem
are less likely to comply with pressures from outside influences than are
individuals with low self-esteem, who tend to seek the approval of others. In
responding to health care messages, low-esteem individuals tend to avoid the
messages, pay little attention, and become tired when forced to attend to the
messages (Bettinghaus & Cody, 1994). Their lack of esteem translates into
lack of confidence that they can cope with the threat to their health (Leventhal
& Trembly, 1968; Nisbett & Gordon, 1967). People with high levels of
anxiety regarding decisions also tend to resist persuasive messages (Nunnally & Bobren, 1959). Rokeach (1960) and associates carried out classical
studies of personality characteristics called "open-mindedness" and "closed-
mindedness." The researchers attached the term *dogmatic* to the closed-
minded individual. They concluded that an open-minded individual tends to
be optimistic about how the world is structured, does not believe that
authorities absolutely determine policies, and tolerates exposure to controversial material. The open-minded person is willing to compare his or her
beliefs to those advocated by others. The highly dogmatic individual, however, tends to be pessimistic about the future of the world, sees problems in
a narrow way, believes in the "absolute correctness" of some authorities, and
rejects the ideas of those who do not agree with these authorities (Bettinghaus
& Cody, 1994). Highly dogmatic individuals place a greater value on messages from trusted sources than do low dogmatics. Also, closed-minded
people find it more difficult to accept messages that conflict with their
existing frames of reference. The open-minded person will examine conflict-

ing beliefs and try to reconcile the beliefs, whereas the closed-minded person will ignore the discrepancies. The open-minded person will pay more attention to new information. Nonetheless, it would be inappropriate to divide audiences into dogmatics and nondogmatics: "Most people have degrees of dogmatism, and only a few fall at the extreme end of the dogmatism scale" (Bettinghaus, 1973, p. 69).

Authoritarian personalities also respond differently from others to persuasion efforts—a fact that is relevant to attempts to persuade against prejudice and intolerance. Following World War II, Adorno, Frenkel-Brunswik, Levinson, and Sanford (1950) developed an instrument that they called the "F-scale." The scale, originally designed to measure degrees of ethnocentrism, seemed to delineate a total personality type. The researchers attached the label "the authoritarian personality" to their findings. Four major factors emerged as characteristics of this personality composite: an authoritarian religious ideology, a suspicious and superstitious worldview, a tendency to submit to authority, and an "alpha-type" fascism. More specific characteristics that appeared to characterize the authoritarian individual were conventionalism, orientation to power, rigidity, conservatism, low degree of tolerance for ambiguity, nationalistic worldview, and an essentially antidemocratic nature. Bettinghaus and Cody (1994) commented on elements of this personality that have implications for persuasion theory:

> People possessing an authoritarian personality tend to be highly reliant on the moral authority of their own reference group, tend to adhere somewhat rigidly to middle-class values, and become preoccupied with the relative power and status of other people, as well as with their own power and status. (p. 163)

They tend to make absolute judgments on values and perceive the world in shades of black and white. Contradictory messages and contrary authorities have little effect on their beliefs. The authoritarian personality differs from the dogmatic in his or her unquestioning deferral to authority, tendency to rely on scapegoats, belief in political conspiracies, and inability to tolerate out-groups and deviants.

Conclusion

This chapter examined the influence of beliefs, attitudes, and values on audiences. Also discussed was the impact of needs and personality on how people receive messages. The communicator who wants to impart knowledge or information, change or reinforce attitudes, or move people to action must consider these variables. Not everyone hears the same messages. Nor does everyone have the same motivation or incentive to act on the messages. A keen understanding of audience psychology lies at the heart of effective communication.

8

The Bases of Source Credibility

Planners make strategic choices when they select some spokespersons and reject others. The credibility of a source can have a dramatic impact on how audiences receive messages. Audiences accept messages from credible sources and reject the same messages from less credible sources. Many factors influence audience perceptions of source credibility: level of expertise, composure, trustworthiness, dynamism, sociability, extroversion, and similarity to audience. How a source uses the media also affects perceptions of communicator credibility. Television makes demands on communicators, to which they must conform if they want to gain acceptance for their messages. The impact of source credibility on communication, the factors that comprise source credibility, and the impact of television on perceptions of source credibility are discussed in this chapter.

Impact of Source Credibility on Communication

Extensive research by scholars such as Hovland, Janis, and Kelley (1953) and McCroskey (1966) found strong support for source credibility concepts. Derived from classical theories of ethos, this research found that more credible sources have a greater initial impact on audiences, whether they speak for political candidates, organizations, products, or concepts. Advertisers clearly recognize the importance of credible sources. One of five television commercials uses celebrities to promote products and services (Cain as cited in Pfau & Parrott, 1993, p. 126). The same is true for children's television. For example, creators of *Sesame Street* undertook testing to determine which television characters should convey different messages to children (Rossi & Freeman, 1989). Health communication campaigns select spokespersons with similarities to the target audiences. As early as 1972, Wilhelmsen and Bret noted that political candidates must demonstrate their capacity to project a saleable image and "charismatic character" before they are seriously considered. The capacity to govern often appears, in the context of American politics, to be secondary: "If he does not look good, he will not be elected" (p. 130). The crisis involving Bill Clinton has led critics to speculate that Clinton's lowered credibility could damage his ability to govern the country. Yankelovich (1991) lists the credibility of sources as one of five critical influences on consciousness-raising in the general public. He cites an example from the 1970s, when public distrust of information from government and the oil companies undermined efforts to convince the public to support a new national energy policy. Convinced that oil companies and the government were collaborating to convince the public of a nonexistent oil shortage, the public rejected information from both sources. Current governments face much the same problem in the environmental arena, in which many Americans suspect that government may be in bed with the big polluters. Similarly, the Red Cross suffered a loss of credibility that persists to this day in the blood donor crisis. In contrast, many other information sources associated with AIDS initiatives continue to enjoy high levels of credibility.

Thus, a knowledge of source credibility theories can enhance the public consciousness-raising process, assist in decision making, and help politicians, bureaucrats, and other organizational spokespersons to understand the bases on which they are being judged. Source credibility studies cannot indicate whether someone is honest or dishonest, expert or not expert. The studies, however, can determine how audiences perceive the person or organization. These audience perceptions can be right or wrong.

According to Aristotle, *ethos* connotes the intelligence, character, and good will demonstrated by a speaker. Ethical proof is one of the three modes of persuasion—an intrinsic type of proof, manifested in the invention, style, arrangement, and delivery of messages. Broadening the concept to include qualities extraneous to the subject matter, Cicero stated that a person's dignity and the actions of his or her life greatly influence the feelings of the audience. Quintilian placed even more emphasis on this concept of personal integrity. Credibility factors, as defined in modern studies, include qualities such as trustworthiness, expertise, status, extroversion, composure, sociability, and similarity to the audience. How sources use different media also has an impact on their credibility.

Source Credibility Factors

The two most important source credibility factors (first proposed by Hovland et al., 1953) are *trustworthiness* and *expertise*. Many factor-analytic studies confirmed their place as the most highly valued factors (O'Keefe, 1990). The trustworthiness factor relates to the extent to which a source is perceived as sincere, safe, family-oriented (in a North American context), honest, hard-working, supportive of laudable causes, socially responsible, willing to take a stand (although it may be personally damaging), or sharing a common fate with the audience. An illustration of this latter point occurred in Canada when an audience member asked the following question of Prime Ministerial candidate Kim Campbell: "A lot of us in this audience eat out of a can of soup. What I want to know is, when we adopt your policies, will you also be eating out of a can of soup?" Audiences trust a source more when they perceive that the source will lose or gain, in the same way that they will lose or gain, by the choices that are made. Audiences will reject messages from sources that appear to be acting only in their self-interest. For this reason, people respond skeptically to commercial and partisan messages. Even children realize and express skepticism, at a very early age, toward commercial messages (Roberts & Maccoby, 1985). Another positive contributor to perceptions of trustworthiness is a source's willingness to take a potentially damaging stand on an issue—a position that is obviously against the person's best interest (Arnold & McCroskey, 1967; Eagley, Wood, & Chaiken, 1981; Walster-Hatfield, Aronson, & Abrahams, 1966). Some politicians gain credibility through their bluntness and willingness to speak out, no matter the cost. Former Louisiana Governor Edwin Edwards acquired this reputation in the 1960s when he confronted the necessity to take a position on the highly flammable issue of busing. He chose to take a moderate stance, which neither the whites nor the blacks appreciated. He was caught in the cross fire, but he stood his ground. Invited to speak at a gathering of black educators, he received advance warning from the head of the association that he should expect the crowd to boo. Despite this fact, Edwards arrived on schedule and presented his viewpoint as he had voiced it prior to the meeting. At the end of the talk, the crowd gave Edwards a standing ovation. Asked afterwards why they had responded so favorably, the head of the Louisiana Educators

Association said, "Well, he may be stupid, but at least he's honest." Edwards also received an invitation to be "King Cotton" at the annual cotton festival. This time, he received a warning from the white organizers of the event. They said that Edwards should expect the crowd to boo and perhaps even throw eggs. In a later interview, the congressman said that he was nervous, but he decided to speak at the event anyway. Again, he presented the same arguments that he had given to the black educators association, and again he received a standing ovation, to the complete surprise of other politicians and the press. People wondered what was happening, but Edwards knew. He said that his credibility derived from his willingness to state his point of view, no matter what the cost (Butler, 1971; Ferguson, 1973). Audiences trusted him to say what he believed. Reardon (1991) offers a caution, however. She says that we admire people for saying what they believe, but we also see them as "boorish" and insensitive if they always speak their minds (p. 12).

Arnold and McCroskey (1967) determined that judgments of trustworthiness and competence tend to be higher when someone gives reluctant testimony. In the same way, "reformed" individuals can increase their credibility by admitting the error of their ways (Bettinghaus & Cody, 1994):

> Patrick Reynolds, who inherited $2.5 million dollars from the R. J. Reynolds Tobacco Company, founded by his grandfather, speaks out against the smoking establishment and actually encourages ex-smokers (or their survivors) to file lawsuits against the industry; J. Robert Oppenheimer worked for years to develop nuclear power, but later cautioned against further development; and Admiral Zumwalt, former naval commander, later campaigned against a number of military developments. (p. 133)

In a similar fashion, Clinton tried to repair his ethos with the American public by speaking at a prayer breakfast of ministers, at which he asked forgiveness of the public, his family, and Monica Lewinsky. He said, "I have sinned." The polls appeared to indicate the success of his actions.

Americans also admire consistency, and they consider those who display consistent behaviors to be more trustworthy. They label public figures who waver in their convictions or change positions on issues as "wishy-washy" or "weak." People accuse them of "flip-flopping" on issues, not having a firm stance. James Baker, a top presidential aide to President Ronald Reagan, once said that Reagan had refused to compromise on a tough budget proposal because the media would have depicted the shift in position as a weakness.

Reagan preferred being depicted as unrealistic to being depicted as weak (Bennett, 1996). Americans do not allow their public figures to learn or to grow with experience, and the media, quick to replay any indications that shifts may be taking place, act as their watchdog.

Family orientation is also important to Americans (Wilhelmsen & Bret, 1972). No president has ever been divorced. Politicians often establish credibility by showing off their wives and children. They play to the fact that North Americans expect their representatives to be family-oriented. Prominently displayed photographs of families on politicians' desks and appearances of family members at political events demonstrate this commitment in a visible way. Many political and corporate campaigns use family values as their organizing concept (Reid, 1988). Some believe, however, that it is more difficult for women to build their credibility on family because they face a no-win situation. They are damned if they give too much attention to their families and damned if they do not.

Trustworthiness may be the most important source credibility factor. No matter how composed, expert, or forceful, a source who is perceived to be dishonest or socially irresponsible will lose the confidence of others. The more personal the issue, the more important becomes the question of trust (Petty & Cacioppo, 1981). Politicians such as Richard Nixon, Gary Hart, and Bill Clinton have learned this lesson at great personal and professional cost. Even when they survive the crisis, they face a difficult future. Acceptability of a source also depends on the source's seeming responsiveness to the needs of audiences (Wilde, 1993).

The advertising and political communication literature also offer some insights in the area of source credibility. Studies have found that the public is more likely to trust advertisements (positive or negative) by independent third-party sponsors (Garramone & Smith, 1984). Impartial sources have more impact than those perceived to have a stake in an issue. Only independents have the credibility to sponsor hard-hitting negative advertisements (Garramone, 1985).

The *expertise* factor relates to the degree to which a source is perceived as qualified, knowledgeable, intelligent, and experienced in relevant areas. As noted earlier, Hovland et al. (1953) were among the first modern communication researchers to discuss the importance of this source credibility factor. Many subsequent researchers, however, have isolated this factor in credibility studies. Status is an extension of the expertise dimension. People who have an impressive educational background, a prestigious occupation, or an association with influential people are believed to possess status. A person's dress also affects perceptions of status. Those who wish to acquire higher status in the eyes of others may arrange to be televised in settings with well-established status symbols such as a flag, a presidential jet, or coats of arms. Appearing in world fora with other international spokespersons can lend an aura of respectability to a national leader or business executive. Through association with status events such as the Olympics, businesses and government leaders enhance their credibility. In good economic times, being photographed in a penthouse office enhances the credibility of an executive on the status dimension. In difficult economic times, however, the same setting can reinforce a negative public perception that corporations are receiving more than their share of "the good life." This consideration has led some organizations (particularly governments) to become wary of glossy publications that appear irresponsible to people who pay high taxes and high prices for consumer goods. Studies (Swenson, Nash, & Roos, 1984) have demonstrated the influence of the expertise and status factors on perceptions of communicator trustworthiness and competence.

McCroskey, Jensen, and Valencia (as cited in Bettinghaus, 1973) identified three additional source credibility factors: extroversion, composure, and sociability. *Extroversion,* sometimes labeled as dynamism, has to do with the extent to which a source is perceived to be forceful, bold, outgoing, active, involved, powerful, healthy, energetic, busy, assertive, progressive, and supportive of change. Every president attempts to set up photo opportunities in which he will be seen jogging, walking, or running. Many voters viewed President Ronald Reagan as "old, tired, and lacking in energy" in the 1984 debate with Walter Mondale (Bettinghaus & Cody, 1994, p. 134). Voters had the same perception of Richard Nixon in the presidential debate with John Kennedy. *Sociability* refers to whether the source is perceived to be likeable and friendly. To convey a sense of their sociability, politicians visit shopping malls and attend groundbreaking ceremonies. They don baseball caps and engage in games of pitch with the children of constituents. They even kiss babies! In the same way, corporation presidents appear at annual Christmas parties or do "walkabouts" at the plant. The Japanese regard this dimension of credibility as particularly important to their chief executive officers, who often have highly accessible offices and assume the role of facilitators in the organization.

The *composure* factor relates to whether we perceive a source to be confident, articulate, and in control—not stumbling or stammering (verbally or nonverbally). Many researchers (McCroskey & Mehrley, 1969; Sereno &

Hawkins, 1967) discuss the importance of this source credibility factor. Former President Gerald Ford learned the impact of the composure dimension when the media began noting every mistake he made after he stumbled, before television cameras, disembarking from an aircraft. On a second occasion, the news showed Ford walking into a helicopter's doors. Meanwhile, *Saturday Night Live* aired a comedy routine that parodied Ford's seeming clumsiness. Chevy Chase, acting out the part of Ford, stumbled over pieces of furniture and became entangled in a telephone cord. The situation deteriorated to the point that, in the presidential debates, a media adviser braced Ford's water glass to the podium to prevent any possibility that the glass could be overturned before a national television audience (Gitlin, 1980). This media depiction of Ford as lacking in composure was an interesting example of the ability of the media to distort reality. Ford was, in fact, an ex-football player noted for his dexterity and physical prowess. The Canadian media was able to undermine the credibility of Prime Minister Joe Clark in much the same way. Many contribute the early demise of Clark's government to the role played by the media. The Conservative government fell after only a few short weeks in office. When an airline lost the prime minister's luggage, the headlines blared, "Joe Clark Loses Luggage." Then they managed to catch Clark almost stepping into an unsheathed bayonet during a welcoming ceremony. Few would dispute the fatal damage that the press did to this mild-mannered Canadian politician. In contrast, minor and temporary lapses in composure can sometimes be a positive factor for an individual, causing others to perceive the person as spontaneous and sincere even if less composed. Being too "smooth" can detract from the safety or trustworthiness dimension, which has a greater weighting with most audiences than the composure dimension. Interpersonal communication theory tells us that we like people who are competent but "human" (Adler & Towne, 1990). Corporations are also discovering that it can be better to admit a mistake or confess a shortcoming than to adhere doggedly to an untenable position (Nakra, 1991).

Many studies in psychology have demonstrated that *similarity* attracts, influencing judgments of credibility (Atkinson, Atkinson, Smith, & Bem, 1990):

> Research all the way back to 1870 supports this conclusion. Over 99 percent of the married couples in the United States are of the same race. Moreover, statistical surveys show that husbands and wives are significantly similar to each other not only in sociological characteristics—such as age, race, religion,

education, and socioeconomic class—but also with respect to psychological characteristics like intelligence and physical characteristics such as height and eye color. (p. 713)

The majority of people respond most favorably to others who are similar in age, gender, social class, personality, group membership, and other factors. Commercial enterprises certainly take advantage of these demographic and psychographic factors when they frame their advertisements. The Dewar's advertisements, which appeared for many years in the *New Yorker* magazine, quite explicitly established reference groups to which readers could relate. The advertisements profiled individuals from different geographic regions of the country, with various vocations and diverse interests. The glue for all the advertisements, however, was their appeal to upper-middle-class Americans. Ashley (1992) claims that contact individuals in public information campaigns must be similar to the target audience to be credible. For example, MTV commercials use rock musicians with varied cultural and ethnic backgrounds and many different styles to appeal to youth of all backgrounds. Some studies (Hass, 1981; Simons, Berkowitz, & Mower, 1970) have demonstrated that perceptions of attitudinal similarity can affect liking, which in turn influences how people react to messages.

Research has demonstrated that the success of political communication strategies often depends on the credibility of the source. For example, negative political advertising will fail when used by "candidates who have not yet established their own positive image" (Garth as quoted in Merritt, 1984, p. 28). Other studies have discovered a "sleeper effect" in which people forget the name and qualifications of a communicator after a time. At that point, the previous influence that source credibility may have had on their judgment of the arguments will disappear, at least until the source reappears. Contemporary researchers have substituted the term *disassociation hypothesis* to describe this phenomenon.

The Language of Television: Effects on Source Credibility[1]

Everyone knows about the ability of the media to encroach upon the lives of public figures. Recent events—the death of Princess Diana and the extensive coverage of Bill Clinton's personal affairs—have demonstrated this point very clearly. Television has another, more subtle way in which it invades the space of public figures, however. That is, media (specifically television) has the capacity to invade the personal space zones of communicators in public situations. The following discussion, which explores the nature of this invasion, has lessons for those who would seek to use television to present or defend their ideas to the public.

The application of Hall's proxemic zones to television's handling of distance is useful in understanding television's capacity to invade the personal space zones of communicators (Ferguson & Ferguson, 1978). According to Hall (1966), the four zones are intimate distance, personal distance, social distance, and public distance. Intimate distance in Western cultures is approximately 6 to 18 in., personal distance is 18 in. to 4 ft, social distance is 4 to 12 ft, and public distance is 12 to 25 ft. Coining the term *optical distance* provides a means to examine communication situations involving television. Optical distance refers to the viewer's perception of the physical distance that would separate him or her from the event if he or she were actually present at the event. Priest and Sawyer (1967) drew a similar kind of distinction between actual and perceived proxemic space. They used the term *phenomenal distance* to indicate the perceived distance between the interactants in an interpersonal communication situation. The distance was a psychic rather than a physical distance.

In the case of television, a close-up head shot of the communicator corresponds to an intimate space arrangement in interpersonal interaction. A medium or waist shot corresponds to personal distance. A medium long shot, showing the full subject, corresponds to social distance. A long shot, in which the subject comprises a relatively small part of the frame, equates to a person communicating at public distance. An observer present at an actual event changes his or her center of attention, from time to time, to look at different aspects of the event. Even when he or she ignores some parts of the setting, the observer still maintains this detail in his or her frame of reference. The media director, however, has to disregard surrounding detail to focus on one aspect of the event. He or she achieves this emphasis through close-up shots of the detail to which he or she wishes to direct attention. Arnheim (1971) explained this point in more depth:

The limitations of a film picture and the limitations of sight cannot be compared because in the actual range of human vision, the limitation simply does not exist. The field of vision is in practice unlimited and infinite. A whole room may be taken as a continuous field of vision, although our eyes cannot survey this room from a single position, for while we are looking at anything our gaze is not fixed but moving. Because our head and eyes move, we visualize the entire room as an unbroken whole. (pp. 68-69)

Television obtains its advantage from the fact that it can offer a ringside seat to observers. For this reason, the television director uses panoramic shots to establish a setting and a series of close shots to record the event. Thus, the communicator in a television event can assume, most of the time, that the camera is observing at close range (Brummett, 1988; Meyrowitz, 1985). Television also offers spectators a sense of togetherness (Katz, Haas, & Gurevitch, 1997). In such a situation, the safest approach may be to behave in a manner suited to intimate or personal space interactions, employing suitable nonverbal and verbal communication techniques.

The history of early films and television illustrates the lag in adaptation to the new media. Performers who made the transition from the stage to films or television frequently made the mistake of overacting. The early motion pictures seem exaggerated to the point of the absurd because the proxemic conventions of theater governed these early productions. Gestures or body movement that had characterized acting for the stage appeared exaggerated, affected, and even ludicrous when transferred to film. The same was true in the early days of television. In the vernacular of the theater, the techniques that had been completely appropriate on stage, when moved into television, gave the impression of a "ham" performance. Early film and television audiences did not react negatively to the exaggeration. As audiences became more trained in the techniques of the new media, however, they expected new levels of expertise in performers and producers.

Like other public speakers, politicians faced the need to adapt when public address moved from the auditorium platform to the television studio. The first televised party convention changed the style of presidential candidate addresses in a dramatic and irreversible way. Speeches became shorter and less emotional to conform to the demands of television. The lengthy speeches that had characterized public speaking for so many centuries seemed boring and out of place. More important, what had seemed in the past like an honest outpouring of emotion looked like acting to the television viewer (Hahn, 1970). In the late 1990s, Nixon's "Checkers" speech is an object of fun, but in the early 1950s, his speech was convincing.

With the advent of television, the optical and audio distance between audience and speaker was collapsed to place the speaker a few feet from the audience. The communicator could no longer know or control the visual content of the communication. The camera's manipulation of the optical space separating the communicator from the audience changed the personal proxemics of the transaction many times during the course of a broadcast.

Nonetheless, television has a certain predictability in its conventions. Close shots are more common than wide shots, and people perceive the major advantage of television to be the ringside seat enjoyed by observers. More often than not, the proxemic zone is intimate or personal, and the style of the communicator must be the same, characterized by "small and natural gestures" (Ranney, 1983, p. 103). As Cater (1981) noted,

> Politicians are struggling to learn the grammar of TV communication and to master the body English so different from that of stump speech. TV has markedly influenced the winnowing process by which some politicians are sorted out as prospects for higher office and others are not. (p. 15)

Just as a communicator may behave inappropriately for the medium in which he or she is operating in terms of the optical distance separating him or her from the audience, the communicator may also behave inappropriately in terms of "audio distance." The term *audio distance* refers to the physical distance that the receiver would have to be from the communicator to receive the message at the same volume without amplification that he or she is receiving it with amplification. Without benefit of voice amplification, the ancient orator had to project in a communication mode suitable to a large audience. His or her style and manner of delivery lacked the quality of intimacy that became possible with electronic media. This shift in the mode of delivery was inevitable because it is not possible to shout intimately. Nonetheless, adaptation to the new medium took time, and designers and users of the new electronic systems frequently overlooked the implications for new techniques of public address. Even now, those who make use of electronic amplification systems sometimes place a microphone in front of the event and a battery of loudspeakers on either side of the event. The end result of such an approach is to give the event a louder voice. The need for a loud voice is an inheritance from preamplification days. Using electronic amplification in a way that exploits the characteristics of the medium entails separating the audience into a number of small groups, each served by a relatively low-powered loudspeaker. With a low volume, a more intimate style of communication becomes possible. Operating in such a situation, people who adopt a low-key or intimate style of delivery have an advantage. Such people are commonly said to have "good microphone technique." In terms of the audio content of the communication event, the communicator will always be operating in the intimate proxemic zone. Also, regardless of the immediate setting for the television address, the audience typically receives the transmission in the intimate territory of their homes. Such a setting for the transaction favors an intimate style of delivery, with a warm, conversational, and well-modulated tone (Ranney, 1983). Television viewers should feel that they are "eavesdropping" on a conversation (Atkinson, 1984, p. 171).

If an intimate nonverbal and delivery style best suit the medium of television, then the language of the communication must conform. Not only the physical elements of the communication but also the content and language style are bound by the demands of intimate or personal address. The stump speaker is a phenomenon of the past because audiences evaluate their efforts with the same cynicism that they apply to television speakers. Not only their speaking style but also their language is histrionic—a relic of the past. Early in the history of television, Postman (1966) made an insightful commentary on the topic:

> It would appear that television's most natural and compelling resource is its ability to communicate ideas and reveal events and people with a sense of intimacy and truthfulness. Perhaps the single most important characteristic shared by such television personalities as Arthur Godfrey, Jack Paar, Dave Galloway, Chet Huntley, David Brinkley, Edward R. Murrow, Eric Severeid, Gary Moore, Arlene Francis, and Mike Wallace is that they are not typical "show business" people. Neither do they appear to be actors in a theatrical sense. They "play" themselves, and when their performances approach the histrionic, as occasionally in the case of Leonard Bernstein, there is a corresponding loss in effectiveness for many viewers. Another way of saying this is that on television, the untheatrical frequently tends to be more believable and more dramatic than the theatrical. This is an aesthetic principle which candidates for office ignore at their peril. (p. 274)

Leonard (1978) said that television creates, as well as records, style. He said that "crybabyism," manifested in Nixon's "Checkers," typified the spirit of the 1950s. In the 1960s, however, Ted Kennedy learned that the public was not so forgiving when he tried to explain the events at Chappaquiddick to a disbelieving public. By the 1960s, television audiences had learned to become critical observers of the new medium. The ubiquitous television commercial had taught the techniques of persuasive communication, and audiences had learned to associate the familiar, repetitive message with the selling of soap powder. When Kennedy appeared in the same context, they made the connection. Commenting on Kennedy's apologia, Farrell (as quoted in Butler, 1972), writing for *Life* magazine in 1969, observed, "First came the incantations to the gods of commerce: Shower to Shower body powder, Kal Kan dog food, Brut cologne, *TV Guide*. Then Ted's face, Ted's grave look, Ted holding the electric rein on 35 million viewers" (p. 287). When television viewers see politicians using the same techniques to market their persona that businesses use to sell dog food, they react with some cynicism. As early as the 1970s, Bagdikian (1971) noted, "Skilled exploiters of television have been voted down on enough occasions to sustain hope. The 'television generation' of the 1960s is characterized by a degree of skepticism about television campaigning bordering on the cynical" (p. 43).

Similarly, television audiences have become educated in the proxemics of the medium. They pass judgment on the actress who is ill adapted to the medium and on the politician who uses a public speaking style to talk to the intimate eye of the television camera. No less than with the actress, the political communicator runs the risk of having his or her actions appear exaggerated and contrived to the viewer who has come to expect a better, more credible performance. The actress moving from the live theater stage to the television studio must take pains to relearn her craft, according to the demands of the medium. The politician also must have a good understanding of the nature of the medium in which he or she works and must behave in a manner appropriate to the medium. The demands on the politician are, in some regards, greater than those on the actress. The actress must adopt a technique appropriate to the medium in which she is working at that moment. The politician, however, is frequently operating in two media simultaneously. At the same time that the politician is delivering a speech to a live auditorium audience, such as a party convention, television is sending the pictures and sound to millions of viewers. Therefore, the politician also becomes a television communicator. Because the two modes of address make conflicting demands on the individual, the person must make a choice as to which audience is primary and which is secondary.

Conclusion

Audience acceptance of messages depends greatly on source credibility. Maximum credibility is granted to those sources perceived as expert, trustworthy, composed, dynamic, sociable, extroverted, and similar to the audi-

ence. Beyond these characteristics, communicators must understand the
language of television if they want the public to accept their messages. In
one of his early films, McLuhan observed that the television medium would
necessitate the emergence of a new kind of communicator—one who is more
flexible, casual, and personable. The styles of Bill Clinton, Ronald Reagan,
and Jimmy Carter reflect this new breed of politician, quite different from
the styles of some of their less popular contemporaries and their predeces-
sors. The new millennium communicators with the greatest source credibility
will doubtless follow in their mold. For those who are charged with the task
of crafting the messages for politicians, advertisers, and governments, the
lesson is no less clear: Communication planners must be knowledgeable in
theories of source credibility.

Note

1. This section of the chapter is an updated version of a 1978 article by Ferguson
and Ferguson.

9

Message Design[1]

Perception, Cognition, and Information Acquisition

Theories relevant to perception, cognition, and information processing and acquisition are discussed in this chapter. Specifically, the chapter explores theories related to penetration of the perceptual screen, attention, comprehension of information, and retention and recall of information. Several major learning paradigms—instrumental, operational, and social learning—are also discussed.

Penetrating the Perceptual Screen

Krugman (1965, 1977) and Langer (1978) concluded that much learning takes place when the mind is at rest—at a time when the individual has a low level of cognitive involvement. Batra and Ray (1983) noted that advertising in particular taps into this subconscious state of audiences. As early as the 1920s, Edward Bernays (the so-called "father of spin") used this strategy to reach consumers. Influenced by his uncle Sigmund Freud, Bernays wrapped "products in a potent symbolic aura, sneaking past the rational defenses of consumers and creeping into their dreams" (Chernow, 1998, p. 5).

The Function of Trigger Signals

Most researchers believe that people react to the symbolic systems of advertising, even if they do not always process the messages at a conscious level (Chesebro, 1984; Salomon, 1987). In fact, modern advertising practices reflect a sophisticated understanding of the way in which humans process information—for example, the repetitiveness and rapid-fire presentation of images on television, the collage of superficially unrelated and often contradictory images evident in many print advertisements, and the use of visual and verbal cues in both print and electronic media intended to evoke mental associations with other ideas and concepts. The human information-processing system assembles information (and attitudes related to the information) in bundles. The activation of these bundles by the firing of trigger signals is analogous to the way in which people store and retrieve computer information by using key words. The key words are reductions, highly compressed metaphorical manifestations of the most important characteristics of the information bundles. In the case of television, advertisers use repetition to plant brand names and images in the minds of viewers. Then they use short, 30-second commercials to evoke recall of these names and images. Larson (1982) noted that the evoked recall process is instantaneous, with "no conscious and time-consuming sifting and weighting of evidence in preparation for a decision" (p. 539). Nor do audiences have the opportunity to rationalize behaviors to achieve cognitive balance when the processes occur without the receiver's active engagement.

Social scientists have had a long-standing interest in the function of trigger signals, cues, and metaphors as devices for accessing cognitive storage systems. Recent increasing interest in artificial intelligence systems has encouraged a closer working relationship between social scientists and physical scientists. The design of fishing lures offers an interesting example of trigger stimuli (Ferguson, 1989):

> Some of the most successful lures seemingly bear very little resemblance to anything that ever swam or hopped, but they are savaged when cast into a pond. Rather than not looking like small fish or frogs, the lures indeed look more like fish and frogs than do fish and frogs, at least in terms of "frogness" or "fishness" as perceived by other fish. The lure designer attempts to isolate the signal characteristic, whether it be the unique marking or the way a lure moves in the water. The designer exaggerates this characteristic and leaves out other irrele-

vant characteristics. The approach is the same as that which the impressionist painter uses to focus attention on what he regards as significant detail.

The Function of Metaphors

Studies suggest that messages that are highly compressed (framed as metaphors) can better penetrate our perceptual screens because they do not come into conflict with existing beliefs and values. The ambiguity enables great freedom in interpreting the messages. For example, the study of advertising is a study of highly compressed codes. Codes have been defined as meaningful systems into which signs are organized. When the codes involve extreme compression of images and ideas, the communication becomes—in essence—metaphorical in nature, and ambiguity characterizes metaphor. This ambiguity encourages personal interpretations of the communication content. Eco (1976) argued that this ambiguity has a positive impact: "Instead of producing pure disorder, it [ambiguity] focuses my attention and urges me to an interpretive effort" (p. 263).

To understand the function of ambiguity in advertising codes, it is necessary to explore the role of the iconic. People process visual and verbal information in fundamentally different ways. In the first case, the image is the starting point, whereas in the second instance the image is the end product of the decoding process. To decode a verbal message, the communication receiver constructs an image from the linguistic cues. The image comes into being when the person assigns meaning to a sequence of words strung together in a particular way. The conventions of language within a particular culture make consensus possible. The level of specificity in a word limits the number of alternative interpretations of a verbal message. Decoding a verbal message typically involves the application of learned linguistic ability more than creativity. As an individual acquires greater familiarity with a particular language and cultural group, the range of meanings that the person will extract from a specific word or term becomes more limited in scope. Acquiring a vocabulary in a given professional area further narrows the choices. A person with little experience of a language or culture, however, may assign little or no meaning to a word or phrase that carries specific content to members of the in-group. Poetry, musical lyrics, and cryptic codes are among the most compressed genres of language. For this reason, they are also the most ambiguous of verbal codes. The meanings attached to poems and songs are as varied as the individuals who interpret the aesthetic codes.

In decoding the iconic content of advertising, the individual starts with the image. All receivers have, as a starting point, the same image. Interpretation of the message does not require facility with the language. Because visual information bypasses linguistic filters, the advertiser can communicate with a much larger and more heterogeneous audience than would otherwise be the case. The more successful a medium is in garnering a mass audience, the more diverse will be the perceptions of the audience. The process by which individuals assign meaning to visual messages is a highly creative one, with an immense range of possible interpretations of any given message. To narrow the range of alternatives, the advertiser uses trigger symbols (also discussed in Chapter 10) to evoke reference to commonly held values. In this manner, the advertiser associates the company's product inferentially with these core values.

The ambiguity in the iconic content of the advertisement allows a large diverse audience to assign meaning to the message, whereas the triggers elicit common value responses and facilitate a certain level of consensus on interpretation of the message. Leiss, Kline, and Jhally (1986) agree that visual imagery can support high levels of ambiguity. They speak of the "indeterminancy of the associations" and the applicability of symbolic qualities to a wide variety of product types: "The openness of the product image to varying permutations and interpretations means that both advertisers and consumers can experiment freely with the meanings—which may be constructed differently by each, to be sure—in a particular ad campaign" (p. 245). Higher levels of ambiguity result when the emphasis shifts from "textual to pictorial information, the carefully considered indeterminancy of the advertisement's open codes of interpretation, and the abstract quality of the product's symbolic attributes" (p. 246). Leiss et al. view text as a key to decoding the visual. They note that early advertisers used written text to state their messages in an explicit fashion. Beginning in the 1920s, however, the relationship became a complementary one, with the text explaining the visual. In the period following World War II (particularly since the 1960s),

> The functions of text moved away from explaining the visual and toward a more cryptic form, where text appeared as a kind of "key" to the visual. In all, the effect was to make the commercial message more ambiguous; a "reading" of it depended on relating elements of the ad's internal structure to each other, as well as drawing in references to the external world. (p. 151)

Bachand (1988) likewise noted the importance of ambiguity in advertisements appearing in the print media. This ambiguity, he said, facilitates the shift in meaning from one semantic field to another.

Novel and Value-Congruent Stimuli,

Novel or unintelligible stimuli can more easily penetrate our perceptual screen because the screen has few, if any, means for establishing the relevance of the stimuli (Wilde, 1993). These stimuli do not clearly confirm or contradict the existing values of the message recipient. Similarly, stimuli that are congruent with existing belief, attitude, and value systems can more easily penetrate the perceptual screen.

Selective Exposure, Perception, and Attention

People selectively expose themselves to information with which they basically agree. The Democrat tunes into political messages about Democrats. The Republican changes channels when a Democrat begins to speak. Toyota owners read Toyota advertisements, and Ford owners read Ford materials. The term *selective attention* refers to the fact that people see what they want to see and expect to see. People who are hungry see signs about food, and people who are looking for a partner notice other people. In the same way, people interpret information on the basis of past experience. *Selective perception* is governed by "family background, physical and personality characteristics, cultural differences, organizational affiliation and position, professional experience, and other factors" (Garnett, 1992, p. 23).

What captures the attention of audiences and the media? Many studies have demonstrated that the following elements function to gain attention: proximity or immediacy, concreteness, the vital, suspense, repetition, familiarity, simplicity, novelty, conflict, activity, repetition, visual and vivid content, elite personalities, messages with affective content, and humor.

Audiences attend to messages that appear close at hand, personally relevant, and important to their lives in physical and psychological terms. They attend to messages with strong motivational appeals (Andrews & Shimp, 1990). Typically, audiences care more about domestic than foreign affairs. They are more interested in the events of next year than those 10 years from now, a fact that creates particular challenges for those involved in environmental causes or health communication campaigns. The women who care most about women's issues are those most at risk (Yankelovich, 1991). Youth have a sense of immortality, and those who smoke do not worry about whether they will get cancer in 30 or 40 years. They are more concerned about whether the use of cigarettes will have an impact on their appearance (skin problems) or popularity (loss of friends and dates) in the next month.

Raising public consciousness on environmental and budget issues is difficult because the "causes, consequences, and terminology" applied to the problems are vague, complex, and difficult to understand (Yankelovich, 1991, p. 78). Therefore, the most effective messages convey a sense of immediacy, especially when the messages target young audiences in areas such as health and safety. Translating abstract concepts into concrete realities can create an awareness of what an issue means to the audience (Bransford & McCarrell, 1974). For example, a community's plans to spend a million dollars on a new town hall probably means little to the average person unless a critic explains that the million dollars represents two new snow plows and a fire engine, which will no longer be affordable. Losing 400 people each hour to lung cancer has more meaning if one equates the loss to the crash of 24 fully loaded jumbo jets each day. The most effective messages transform numbers into experiences and portray the consequences of decisions in terms of audience impact.

References to elements in the immediate environment of the audience capture attention. The media typically cover an event on the day of its occurrence or not at all. This characteristic of the news leads political figures to engage in questionably ethical practices, such as withholding unfavorable press releases until the current edition is on the street. A late Sunday morning release is a favorite time for those who do not want the news to reach the public before Monday evening. When Ford announced Nixon's pardon, he did so on a Sunday morning in the hopes that fewer newspapers would carry the story. A weekend press conference draws fewer reporters than a weekday conference. Even when newspapers carry the stories, they frequently fail to make critical comment on the stories due to the short time lines. For their part, organizations wager that the news item will lose some of its immediacy (and consequently its appeal) given an adequate lapse of time between the event and the analysis of the event (Jamieson & Campbell, 1988).

Personalizing ideas and concepts enhances the possibility that the audiences will recognize and accept the relevance of the ideas to their lives. Organizations that seek sponsorship of children in developing countries use this technique effectively. They ask for people to adopt one specific child. They send photographs and letters from the child to the donor to create a strong personal connection between the two. When animal rights groups lobby for legislation to protect animals, they personalize the plight of the animals with photographs. For example, a student speaker brings a stuffed animal to class, her last treasured present from a friend who committed suicide in high school.

This leads to another attention factor: the use of visuals. Highly visual material attracts audiences, as does the sensational and the bizarre. If pro-lifers position themselves before an abortion clinic and thrust baby gifts at women entering the clinic, the television stations will certainly report the event. The picture of a young widow, at the grave side of her husband killed in military action, will receive preference over less emotional depictions. Images of starving children in Somalia and the bleeding victims of an automobile accident have the stark dramatic quality that television demands. Studies have determined that bright colors and loud sounds catch the attention of audiences (Taylor & Thompson, 1982).

Humor can be an attention-getting factor, especially in an interpersonal situation (Johnston, 1994). Researchers also acknowledge its limitations, however. Although humor can improve a dull message, it has no impact on an interesting message (Gruner, 1967, 1970; Sternthal & Craig, 1973).

People pay more attention to appeals with an affective dimension (Ray, 1977). The use of messages with a positive emotional appeal (e.g., an attractive spokesperson, visual images, beautiful art, and popular songs) can be especially effective. A "warm and touching" situation can capture the attention of an audience who believe that they have nothing new to learn from a message (Monahan, 1995, p. 85). These kinds of appeals can establish the mood for audiences to attend to—and learn from—the message.

Repetition captures attention. A news commentator recently remarked that when Russian skaters perform new tricks in their skating programs, they perform them more than once. The first time, no one reacts; the second time, the audience applauds. Speakers throughout history have used this attention-getting device to their advantage. In 1940, Winston Churchill delivered the following emotionally stirring words, punctuated by the use of repetition:

> We shall not flag or fail. We shall go on to the end, we shall fight in France, we
> shall fight on the seas and oceans, we shall fight with growing confidence and
> growing strength in the air, we shall defend our Island, whatever the cost may

be, we shall fight on the beaches, we shall fight on the landing grounds, we
shall fight in the fields and in the streets, we shall fight in the hills; we shall
never surrender.

In June 1963, President John Kennedy also made effective use of repetition
in the speech that he delivered at the wall that separated East and West Berlin:

> There are many people in the world who really don't understand or say they
> don't, what is the great issue between the Free World and the Communist world.
> Let them come to Berlin. There are some who say that communism is the wave
> of the future. Let them come to Berlin. And there are some who say in Europe
> and elsewhere we can work with the Communists. Let them come to Berlin.
> And there are even a few who say that it's true that communism is an evil system,
> but it permits us to make economic progress. Laot sie nach Berlin kommen. Let
> them come to Berlin!

Martin Luther King used similar techniques in his powerful, emotionally
compelling speech "I Have a Dream," delivered shortly before his death to
200,000 demonstrators in Washington, D.C. The repetition of phrases "I have
a dream," "Let freedom ring," and "Go back to . . ." echoed through the
entirety of his speech.

The familiar and the simple draw audiences. Zajonc (1980) determined
that people like familiar stimuli (nonsensical or meaningful) more than
unfamiliar stimuli. Perhaps for this reason, the content of political messages
is typically "simple, familiar, and idealistic" (Bennett, 1996):

> Political messages generally begin with a key phrase, idea, or theme that creates
> a convenient way for people to think about a political object—be it an issue, an
> event, or even a person. For example, Franklin Roosevelt appealed to the hopes
> of the masses by using the simple term "New Deal" to refer to his complex
> patchwork of untried economic programs. Borrowing these characteristics of
> simplicity and idealism, John Kennedy added the power of familiarity when he
> presented his programs to the people under the title of "New Frontier." Ronald
> Reagan used "New Federalism" to label his efforts to dismantle Roosevelt's
> New Deal, Kennedy's New Frontier, and Johnson's Great Society. (p. 82)

Also, journalists sometimes lack the expertise to write about complex issues (Bennett, 1996). The profession stresses the importance of being a generalist, moving from issue to issue. Coverage of political campaigns demonstrates these same preferences for simplicity of presentation. The primaries assist the media in arriving at a manageable number of competitors, typically two or three front-runners. In the end, there is a winner and a loser (Nimmo & Combs, 1990). This example also depicts the preference of media for activity—things in motion and happenings. The media thrives on public debate over opposing points of view. Scandal, fraud, and corruption, which involve conflict and controversy, provide fodder for the media mill.

Although references to familiar people, places, and events grab the attention of audiences, holding that attention requires going beyond what they know—offering new information and novel insights. Campaign designers warn that, in the case of overexposed issues such as antidrug or antismoking, organizers need to explain what is new in the campaign (Backer, Rogers, & Sopory, 1992). Novelty of size, either unusually small or unusually large, also captures audience attention, and comparisons that involve strong contrasts gain the attention of audiences. The presence of a celebrity increases the chances that the media will cover an event or issue and that the audience will pay attention to the message (Baldwin, 1989).

When interest groups do not have the right kind of activities to capture news coverage, they stage media events to draw attention to their causes (Dayan & Katz, 1992; Saxer, 1993). It was noted previously that the media does not like to report the historical context of issues. Instead, the media tends to cover stories characterized by action, sensationalism, conflict, highly visual events, immediacy, personalization, and novelty—coverage that will draw large audiences. Interest groups respond to the situation by creating pseudoevents that meet media demands. An anniversary celebration, peace walk, candlelight vigil, and a visit to a political constituency all qualify as pseudoevents, created to obtain positive media coverage for the group or individual. Other political happenings that qualify as pseudoevents, according to Boorstin's (1961) definition, include the presidential debate, the press conference, the fireside chat, and the analysis of other pseudoevents. The characteristics of these artificially generated events include the fact that they are (a) planned, packaged, and staged for news coverage; (b) designed to be enjoyable; and (c) characterized by drama. An interesting example of a pseudoevent that demonstrates all these characteristics took place in Kansas

City (Jamieson & Campbell, 1988). An antiabortion group arrived at a large local hospital with small white caskets. They asked the hospital administrators to turn over aborted fetuses so that they could bury the fetuses. Prior to arriving at the hospital, they notified the news media of their intentions. The event met all the criteria for a newsworthy event. The angry encounter between shocked hospital administrators and pro-lifers had strong dramatic appeal. The small white caskets for individual fetuses personalized the issue. The event was novel and highly visual. The setting was also conducive to media coverage: The hospital was close to television stations; the encounter took place in daylight outside hospital doors; the early afternoon time allowed the station to film and edit the coverage before news hour; a local group staged the event at a local setting; and finally, the event fit neatly into a 99-second news clip. Thus, the appearance of the event on the evening news was predictable. According to Jamieson and Campbell, a well-staged event such as this "invites coverage from a particular point of view" (p. 103).

The previous discussion considered the importance of external factors of attention in gaining audience attention and media coverage. Messages that do not contain external factors of attention will probably go unnoticed.

Comprehension of Information

How messages are framed can influence an audience's ability to learn from the message. Some studies have indicated that people pay more attention to the first message in a series of messages. Clear, simple language makes a message more understandable and compelling (Stuyck, 1990). Large amounts of technical language in televised messages result in decreased levels of audience satisfaction, comprehension, and recall (Jackson, 1992). Some of the most effective messages on AIDS, for example, present the hard facts in a "simple and straightforward manner" (Baggaley, 1988). Audiences tend to react negatively to complex messages. Those who wish to ensure that the media do not carry their messages, however, sometimes use the opposite strategy. In a report titled "Politics and the Oval Office," the Institute for Contemporary Studies suggested that President Reagan should "overwhelm media representatives with technical data," thus circumventing the possibility that media could complain about lack of access to information (Jamieson & Campbell, 1988, pp. 99-100). Incomprehensible messages are typically loaded with "legal terminology, technical jargon, slang, complex sentences, statistical terms, and evidence" (Bettinghaus & Cody, 1994, p. 63). Früh

(1980; also cited in Windahl & Signitzer, 1992) identified many textual factors that influence comprehension of written texts: the graphic structure (e.g., paragraphing and use of upper- or lowercase letters), word frequency, length of sentences, number of clauses in sentences, variety in sentence structure, and the frequency of common versus uncommon words. Früh argued that readers will put only a certain amount of energy into decoding text. They will reject excessive complexity or excessive repetition of thoughts and words.

For these and other reasons, the press demonstrates a preference for issues that are simple, easy to verify, and nontechnical. The media typically searches for statements that are "uneditable, dramatic, concise, and synoptic" (Jamieson & Campbell, 1988, p. 96)—the generic press line. Novak (1982) observed that it is necessary in preparing messages for television to avoid " 'dead' spots, 'wooden' lines, 'excess verbage' " (p. 21). Characters and scenes change rapidly, and bite-sized works best.

Retention and Recall of Information

The term *selective retention* refers to the phenomenon whereby people forget much of what they perceive. The quantity of information that must be processed by the average person, on a daily basis, means that large amounts are dumped into the subconscious storehouse. What people retain at a conscious level will frequently be information that meshes with existing values and beliefs (Cannell & MacDonald, 1956). The smoker will not recall the specifics of antismoking literature. The environmental activist will probably not note or remember the details of an article that suggests the atmospheric problem is improving. People maintain their equilibrium by filtering out dissonant or uncomfortable information (Festinger, 1957). Factors that have been found to mediate people's responses to dissonant information are the extent to which people are well-informed on the issues, the extent to which they have partisan affiliations, the strength of their convictions, and their educational level.

Studies have demonstrated that people retain visual information better than verbal information (Alesandrini, 1983; Childers & Houston, 1984; Horton & Mills, 1984; Lutz & Lutz, 1977; MacInnis & Price, 1987). Standing (1973) demonstrated that subjects can remember pictorial advertisements, even after a long period of time. This ability of people to recall pictures more easily than words is known as "pictorial superiority effect." By the same token, words that represent concrete objects (a university diploma or a fashion model) elicit better recall from subjects than words that represent abstract concepts (education or beauty) (Paivio, 1971). Larger visuals in print illustrations produce more learning than do smaller visuals (Kosslyn, 1981). Other studies have found that audiences have better recall of television and radio messages than of newspaper and magazine messages (Brieger, 1990).

Some argue that the effect of humor on message comprehension is "equivocal" (Johnston, 1994), whereas others claim that humor can make a message memorable (Bettinghaus & Cody, 1994). In the commercial sphere, repetition can increase consumer learning and establish new products and brands in the marketplace (Bettinghaus & Cody, 1994). Some studies have demonstrated that shorter television commercials (15 seconds vs. 30 seconds and 30 seconds vs. 60 seconds) generate "as much as two thirds or more of the recall of the longer versions, but at less cost" (Pfau & Parrott, 1993, p. 112).

Currently, it is controversial whether the use of highly emotional techniques can help people to learn and recall a message. Reeves, Newhagen, Maibach, Basil, and Kurz (1991) argued that such techniques result in less attention from audiences. Others have found that viewers demonstrate better recall of messages that have negative rather than positive emotional content (Newhagen & Reeves, 1991). This effect is likely because audiences process positive content in a much less thoughtful way than they process negative message content. Positive content enters the consciousness through peripheral routes (Petty & Cacioppo, 1986). For these reasons, positive emotional states tend to decay rapidly (Monahan, 1995; see also Frijda, 1988). In the experience of politicians, negative advertising is more informative than other types of advertising (Garramone, Atkin, Pinkleton, & Cole, 1990). Political consultants state that people do not like negative advertising, but they remember the advertisements. Despite the general finding that people retain negative better than positive message content, Flora and Maibach (1990) found that those most likely to remember positive messages are low-involvement audiences.

Some studies show that an individual will better recall the first message in a series of messages. Others believe that the need and readiness to learn from a message mediates the effects of a message on both recall and learning (Cacioppo, Petty, & Morris, 1983). In the following section, these ideas are considered in more detail.

Learning Theories: Instrumental, Operational, and Social Learning

In the previous section, the results of studies related to perception, cognition, and retention of information were discussed. In this section, I discuss several major theories of learning: instrumental and operant learning as well as social learning and modeling theories.

Instrumental (operant) learning refers to a situation in which someone obtains a reward or reinforcement for acquiring a learned behavior. In Skinnerian terms, a monkey gains access to a banana when it punches the right button on a machine as reinforcement. In the case of people, an individual who donates to a veterans' organization receives a personalized key chain, and a young person who participates in a sobriety campaign receives a certificate for displaying socially responsible behavior. Information campaign designers and others who seek to influence behavior use rewards to reinforce desirable behaviors. Some people are satisfied with *intrinsic* rewards —the satisfaction of doing a job well or adopting healthy behaviors. Others want *extrinsic* rewards—money, thanks, or praise. Stressing the advantages or future rewards that can be derived from adopting a particular attitude or behavior increases the chances that people will learn from the message. People seem to learn better from positive reinforcements than from negative, although they learn from both (Hilgard, 1956). The shorter the time interval between response and reward, the greater the likelihood that the individual will repeat the behavior in the future. In the same way, fear appeals based on distant future consequences have little effect on young people. The rewards appear too remote in time to be effective.

Conditioned learning (associated with John B. Watson) refers to a situation in which an animal learns to associate the ringing of a bell (unfamiliar stimulus) with the presence of food (familiar and desired stimulus) or a young person learns to associate cigarette usage (unfamiliar stimulus) with popularity (familiar and desired stimulus). The campaign designer who wishes to dissuade youth from smoking has the choice of disassociating the two stimuli or substituting a more healthy stimulus for the cigarettes. In this situation, an information campaign designer can (a) attempt to demonstrate that students who smoke are not popular or (b) substitute involvement in sports for cigarette smoking as a way to become popular. Advertisers often try to sell a new kind of automobile, soap, or brand of jeans (unfamiliar stimulus) by evoking an association with beautiful women or attractive men (familiar and desired stimulus). They try to connect people with products, and Olympic athletes become symbols for athletic equipment, orange juice, and cereal. The advertiser hopes that the audience will make the association between the successful athlete and the company's product.

Academics have recognized the work of Bandura (1977, 1994) and associates as groundbreaking in the area of social learning and modeling. Bandura demonstrated that children will emulate violent behaviors observed on television when they do not perceive sanctions to be attached to the behaviors. The surgeon general of the United States recognized the validity of Bandura's model when he declared that televised violence is related to antisocial behavior in youth. In recent years, researchers have applied Bandura's social learning and modeling theories to many different phenomena, including the design of information campaigns. Principles relevant to the application of social learning and modeling theories to message design include the following. First, messages should specify the exact nature of the behaviors to be displayed (Barber, Bradshaw, & Walsh, 1989). Second, messages should encourage people to find a visible means to show their commitment to these behaviors (Mogielnicki et al., 1986). Finally, the timing of the message should enable people to apply and practice the behaviors at a close future date. For maximum effectiveness, campaign designers can encourage early adopters to wear a button or make a speech to support the new behavior. This type of behavior display encourages others to follow suit—for example, "voluntary seat belt wearing doubled in parts of France where seat belt users were encouraged to put a bumper sticker on their car that said: 'I wear my seat belt. How about you?' " (Wilde, 1993, p. 990).

Designers of the North Karelia project (a highly successful health care campaign that targeted a community with high levels of cardiovascular disease) applied modeling theory to their campaign design. Acting as positive role models, team members appeared in posters and print advertisements that promoted healthy heart behaviors. Project planners also established a 10-person television studio panel to discuss their feelings of resistance to quitting smoking, problems experienced when they attempted to quit, and achievements. By the end of the 7 weeks of televised discussions, 8 of 10 panelists, representing many different demographic groups, had stopped smoking, as had thousands of viewers who had identified with and learned from the experiences of the panelists. The North Karelia project also encouraged participants to wear the logo of the project—two red hearts. Using the same strategy, the Stanford Heart Disease Prevention Program distributed red heart-shaped magnets to hold tip sheets on refrigerator doors, an appropriate location for information on nutritional habits. This latter example involved an adaptation of the point-of-sale display advertising used in commercial marketing. Even the heart-shaped logo reflected commercial marketing strategies, adapted for social marketing purposes (Backer et al., 1992).

In general, people learn best from active involvement and participation. Therefore, ministers often ask members of their congregation to recommit their lives to God in a very public fashion. The parishioners' movement to the front of the church is an act of engagement. It is also an act of commitment. Encouraging people to state a point of view involves them so that they care about the outcome of a debate. People become attached to viewpoints that they articulate. Acquiring skills, whether riding a bicycle, driving a car, or learning how to play tennis, requires practice. The same is true for acquisition of knowledge and attitudes. Information campaigns, which impart new ideas and ways of behaving, often elicit active participation from audiences (Bettinghaus, 1973). Practicing the behaviors increases the chances that they will become habitual. Just as repetition gains audience attention, repeated stimuli also increase the chances that the audience will learn from the message. Because television personalities and other public figures can be negative role models, in the same way that they can be positive models, many argue that television personalities should not display inappropriate behaviors, such as drinking and smoking, from which youth can learn the wrong behaviors.

Conclusion

In this chapter, I examined the ways in which people learn. The classical philosophical question asks the following: If no one sees or hears a tree fall in the forest, has the tree fallen? The communicator can ask the same question about learning: "If no one is listening and no one understands, has communication taken place?" Some researchers, such as Garnett (1992), answer "no": "Public administrators fail to communicate if their message is not even heard or read by the intended audience" (p. 22). Garnett noted that people stop listening when they perceive the message to be irrelevant or the source to be unknowledgeable or untrustworthy. Those not listening often include those most in need of information: "potential AIDS victims or gay bashers, teenage unwed mothers, crack addicts, and employees who habitually abuse office hours" (p. 22). Campaign designers want to ensure that people hear, attend to, comprehend, and remember the messages that they distribute. A knowledge of learning theories can enhance this possibility.

Note

1. Many of the topics discussed in this chapter appeared in Ferguson (1988).

10

Message Design

Theories of Persuasion

A classical model of persuasion, the Elaboration Likelihood Model, differentiates between persuasive efforts that stimulate conscious processing of messages and those that work on the unconscious mind (Petty & Cacioppo, 1986). The model reflects research by Krugman (1965, 1977) and Langer (1978), who spoke of a continuum of awareness in how people process messages. This awareness can range from "mindless" to "mindful" thought: "Mindful message processing assumes that receivers will be active in making distinctions, assigning meanings, and creating categories, while mindless processing relies on distinctions and meanings previously developed . . . or on triggering emotion" (Pfau & Parrott, 1993, p. 175). That is, triggers in the message content (often visual) transport the audience to an earlier experience and evoke an emotional reaction to that experience.

Persuasion can use either approach. That is, it can stimulate conscious or unconscious engagement of audiences in processing messages. The typical advertisement seeks to bypass conscious thought process. Because few distinctions exist between products, advertisers cannot appeal, ethically, to logical thinking. Therefore, they seek to create emotional responses to products based on packaging and presentation. Information campaigns, however, generally seek to stimulate active consideration of message content.

Strategies that ask audiences to engage in active thinking processes are considered in this chapter. Specifically, the following discussion considers the persuasion literature on the development of message content, the organization of content, and strategies for achieving change.

Message Content

In this section, I discuss the results of persuasion studies under the following headings: supporting materials, one-sided versus two-sided arguments, explicit versus implicit conclusions, visual content, negative content, emotional appeals, fear appeals, creativity and humor, and reference group appeals.

Supporting Materials

Studies have determined that some kinds of supporting materials are more effective than others in effecting attitude change. Examples, illustrations, and case histories have a greater impact than statistical or other data summaries (Taylor & Thompson, 1982). Argument by example is the most difficult type of argument to refute. Koballa (1986) concluded that attitudes formed on the basis of examples and case histories were more stable over time than attitudes stimulated by data summaries. Publicizing the case of a celebrity with a manic depressive disorder or a first lady with alcohol dependency can have a greater impact on the public than the most pretentious statistics. Similarly, specificity in messages is persuasive. To say that computers can be dangerous is much less convincing than to say that a computer virus can cause the failure of monitoring systems in hospitals, the collapse of a subway system, and disaster for those who rely on air traffic control systems.

One-Sided Versus Two-Sided Argumentation

Research has found that two-sided arguments are more effective than one-sided arguments in gaining audience acceptance of a message (Jackson & Allen, 1987). That is, the most persuasive messages present both points of view but refute the opposing arguments. Well-educated audiences and audiences who hold contrary points of view, in particular, respond better to messages that acknowledge both points of view before stating a biassed perspective. An audience with a preexisting knowledge of the subject area also has a greater need for two-sided argumentation (Hovland, Janis, & Kelley, 1953). Providing support to this conclusion was an analysis of trends in smoking among Americans. This study demonstrated that the greatest reduction in cigarette smoking took place in the United States between 1967 and 1970, a period in which broadcast media was mandated to give equal time to cigarette advertisements and public service advertisements. No decline in smoking rates occurred during the period of time in which the government completely banned cigarette commercials from the airwaves.

Anticipating that the audience may come into contact with opposing views at some future date, the persuader can choose to "inoculate" the audience against the contrary views (Hovland et al., 1953; McGuire, 1961). Many situations offer appropriate opportunities for inoculation (Reardon, 1991):

> Political candidates can effectively forewarn voters of tactics their opponents might employ to damage their credibility. Corporations planning huge layoffs, rate hikes, relocation, or other major changes can offset some of the shock and anger of employees and customers if the need for such changes is introduced prior to the action. (pp. 54-55)

Some health communication campaigns also employ inoculation strategies. For example, a study in Helsinki, Finland, found that a social inoculation campaign against tobacco advertisements influenced the attitudes of fourth- and sixth-grade children for a period of time after the campaign (Haukkala, Uutela, Vartianen, Burton, & Johnson, 1994). As in other situations in which people disagree on a topic, the most effective inoculation occurs when the communicator combines supportive and refutational arguments (Tannenbaum, Macaulay, & Norris, 1966). That is, the communicator prepares the listener with counterarguments in case the listener has to defend his or her position at some future date. When audiences hold compatible views, however, the communicator can proceed to reinforce those beliefs without the need to address opposing points of view (Hovland et al., 1953).

Explicit Versus Implicit Conclusions

Some studies have examined whether sources should include explicit conclusions and recommendations or let the audience draw their own con- clusions. The majority of studies have suggested that messages (especially in fear-arousing situations) should specify how the audience should think or act in response to the message (Cope & Richardson, 1972; Fine, 1957; Leventhal, Watts, & Pagano, 1967). Some studies, however, have found that factors such as intelligence, education, previous acquaintanceship and in-

volvement with the topic, and self-esteem can mediate how audiences respond to specific suggestions (Cacioppo, Petty, & Morris, 1983; Hovland &
Mandell, 1952).

Visual and Vivid Content

Visuals can act as a powerful persuader. For example, some researchers
have determined that visuals can have a positive impact on belief in a
particular brand of product and expressed intention to purchase the product
(Mitchell & Olson, 1981). In fact, the larger and more concrete the visual,
the more positive the response (Rossiter & Percy, 1983). Sometimes "vivid"
stimuli have a stronger impact on attitudes than does "pallid" information
because they evoke more emotion and they are more concrete in their
imagery. Nonetheless, Taylor and Thompson's (1982) review of 50 studies,
which had tested the effectiveness of vivid stimuli, suggested inconclusive
results.

Positive Versus Negative Content

Commercial advertisers tend to design messages with positive content
(Monahan, 1995). Political campaign consultants, however, argue that emotional messages with negative content have a greater ability to persuade than
more rational messages with positive content: "People are more apt to vote
against than for something; it is easier to appeal to emotion than to logic.
Negative ads are a form of gossip, and word-of-mouth publicity multiplies
the message" (Nugent, 1987, p. 49). Others argue that negative advertising
can be more informative and credible than its positive counterpart: "The
superior informativeness of negative political advertising suggests that it can
be especially useful to voters in developing their images of candidates, and
in differentiating between those candidate images" (Garramone, Atkin,
Pinkleton, & Cole, 1990, p. 301). Advocates claim that some negative political advertisements provide accurate, substantive information about candidate
qualities, positions, and performance that force candidates to respond to the
issues (Johnson-Cartee & Copeland, 1991).

Critics, however, claim that negative advertising creates negative feelings
toward both the sponsor and the competitor (Merritt, 1984; Naisbitt, 1961).
A dramatic example illustrating this point occurred in Canada in the 1990s.
The Conservative Party of Canada designed an attack advertisement to take
votes away from the Liberal candidate for prime minister, Jean Chretien.

Paralysis on one side of his lower face causes Chretien to talk out of only one side of his mouth, an unfortunate characteristic for a politician. Playing on this disability, the Conservatives aired a negative campaign advertisement that depicted the Quebec politician as retarded and dishonest. The day after the initial broadcast of the advertisement, the Conservative Party received hundreds of telephone calls from irate Canadians, including many Conservatives. Some volunteers called to say that they did not want to be associated with a party that would sponsor such a political commercial. In fast retreat, the Conservatives pulled the advertisement. The damage was done, however. When the votes were counted at the end of the campaign, the Conservatives were not even able to qualify as an opposition party. They won only a handful of seats, despite the fact that they had won the last election with an impressive majority. Although there were many reasons for the defeat, Canadians viewed the poor judgment exercised in airing the negative advertisement as typical of what the Conservatives had come to represent.

Garramone (1985) discussed the kind of boomerang effect that can occur with negative political advertising when voters perceive that they are being put under undue pressure to vote a particular way. The public becomes cynical toward the political process and distrustful of those who are conducting the negative campaign. This type of reaction is most likely when the candidate has not yet established a favorable image with the public (Merritt, 1984). This was the case in Canada when Kim Campbell's party attempted to use the negative political advertisement against the much more popular Jean Chretien. Despite the risks, American politicians have made negative advertising a part of their political history (Johnson-Cartee & Copeland, 1991).

Emotional Appeals

Some believe that the use of highly emotional techniques can be enough on its own, even without negative content, to elicit unwanted and irrational responses (Baggaley, 1988; Zielske & Henry, 1980). Moreover, people tend to resent a paternalistic or lecturing tone (Stephenson, 1967). Others, however, argue that a certain level of emotional engagement is necessary if people are to think about a topic at all. They believe that people are more receptive to messages with an affective dimension (Reeves, Newhagen, Maibach, Basil, & Kurz, 1991). Such appeals encourage people to consider important social topics. If an individual feels threatened by the content of a message, however, he or she may not respond with greater receptivity. In fact, the individual may block subsequent messages (Forest, Clark, Mills, & Isen, 1979).

Fear Appeals

Empirical studies have demonstrated the limitations of fear appeals. The majority of leading campaign researchers and designers cited in Backer, Rogers, and Sopory (1992) do not believe that strong fear appeals work. They observe that strong fear appeals (based on threat of injury or death) lead to defensive avoidance of the message. Appeals that predict social embarrassment or rejection tend to be more effective with teenagers. Teenagers fear that friends and parents will learn about their undesirable behaviors. Appeals based on less consequential, but high-probability, outcomes have more effect than appeals based on more serious, but less likely, outcomes (Atkin, 1992). Wilde (1993) summarized the view of many when he said that "mild or intermediate fear appeals can be useful, provided that the audience has the immediate opportunity to take the advocated action so that the induced state of anxiety will effectively be reduced" (p. 987). Despite these cautions, two meta-analytic studies of fear appeal research have demonstrated that when a communicator does succeed at inducing fear, the persuasive effectiveness of the message is greater than it would be otherwise (Boster & Mongeau, 1984; Sutton, 1982). Boster and Mongeau's review of the literature suggests that strong fear appeals may not work because the designers of experimental research into the effectiveness of fear appeals rarely succeed at creating strong fear in audiences, and they question the ethics of trying to induce high levels of fear in a laboratory situation. OKeefe (1990) explains that it may be necessary to tone down a message to produce high levels of fear, if audiences are unlikely to pay attention to highly gruesome messages. Boster and Mongeau argue that different audiences react in different ways to fear appeals, depending on age, levels of existing anxiety, and other factors. Increasing the fear level of already anxious personalities only serves to intensify their resistance to change (Janis & Feshbach, 1954). Arkin (1992) noted that fear appeals may be more effective at achieving short-term than long-term results. Meyerowitz and Chaiken (1987) suggest that it is better, in framing fear appeals, to emphasize what the audience will lose rather than what they will gain. Nonetheless, the messages must also assure the audience that they can escape the negative consequences if they follow the advice given in the message (Petty & Cacioppo, 1981).

Creativity and Humor

To succeed, public service announcements and advertising messages should be unique and entertaining. The benefits of humor are more questionable. Occasionally, humor produces a positive residual effect; that is, the "affect generated by the humor can place the persuadee in a favorable frame of mind for the receipt of the persuasive message" (Johnston, 1994, p. 132). Also, humor can prompt the audiences to yield to simple requests (trying a new brand of coffee or subscribing to a newspaper). Perry and colleagues (1997, p. 36) demonstrated that "overall, the more humorous the commercial, the greater the benefit for the product advertiser," unless the sponsored program has humorous content. In the latter instance, the commercial must be more humorous than the program to be effective.

Despite these findings, comparison tests have shown that humorous appeals do not produce any more attitude change than nonhumorous appeals (Johnston, 1994). Moreover, humor rarely persuades people to change serious behaviors, such as alcohol or other drug use, smoking, and reckless driving habits (Bettinghaus & Cody, 1994). Despite rave reviews, the Alka Seltzer campaign of the late 1960s and early 1970s failed to sell the product (Pfau & Parrott, 1973). Humor can even decrease the credibility of a source (Bryant, Brown, Silberberg, & Elliott, 1981; Munn & Gruner, 1981). Paradoxically, advertising companies that win awards for creativity and humor often go out of business (Ogilvy, 1985). Commercials that rely on a gag or punch line wear out faster than those with a narrative approach (Bettinghaus & Cody, 1994). Repetition of humorous messages offends audiences and consumes valuable air time or copy space. Effective use of humor in mass media contexts depends on its relevance to the persuasive goal and its suitability to the audience (whether the audience can appreciate the humor).

Reference Group Appeals

The term *reference group* refers to a group to which someone belongs or to which the person aspires to belong (Patton & Giffin, 1981). Dewar's advertisements, which appeared for years on the back cover of the *New Yorker* magazine, illustrate the use of this technique. Each week, the magazine featured a different person who had ties to different reference groups. The reference groups reflected varying regions of the country, ages, occupations, hobbies, and interests. The common factor was that all the individuals in the advertisements qualified as "yuppies" (upwardly mobile, relatively young, highly successful men and women) and, of course, all drank Dewar's. Similarly, information campaign designers can associate their products with credible sources from various reference groups. This approach works particularly well with youth.

Organization of Messages

The organization of messages also affects their persuasive impact on audiences. The following discussion considers the relevance of different patterns of organization, climactic versus anticlimactic ordering of arguments, and primacy versus recency effects.

Psychological Ordering of Information

Monroe (1945) presented one of the best accepted patterns of organization for persuasive messages: (a) attention, (b) need, (c) satisfaction, (d) visualization, and (e) action. To engage in successful persuasion, the source must obtain the audience's attention, convince the audience that a need or problem exists, suggest solutions that can satisfy the need, help the audience to visualize a future with or without the solutions, and outline specific steps of action. Monroe's motivated sequence is only marginally different from Dewey's (1933) reflective-thinking pattern, which substituted an evaluation step for the action step at the end of the sequence. In the spirit of inoculation theory, the evaluation step anticipates objections to the proposed solutions.

Primacy Versus Recency Effects

Primacy-recency studies examine the advantages of presenting first or last in a persuasive situation (e.g., a debate) or the advantages of placing an appeal at the beginning or the end of a persuasive statement. In general, research findings are mixed. Conflicting and inconclusive results have characterized this field of study from its beginnings (Cromwell, 1950; Ehrensberger, 1945; Hovland, Harvey, & Sherif, 1957; Jersild, 1928; Lund, 1925). The current wisdom tells us that there is no general advantage to either position. Nonetheless, in some specific circumstances, one may be more advantageous than the other to the persuader. For example, if audience members are not committed (i.e., if they have unstructured attitudes), they will be more favorable toward the first speaker and more swayed by appeals placed early in the discourse. In other words, the primacy effect dominates. The primacy effect also dominates when the audience is initially disposed to accept the arguments of a favorable source. Rosnow and Robinson (1967) further concluded that a primacy effect is most likely in any situation in which the issues are relatively unimportant, the topic is interesting and familiar, and the issue is controversial. If the topic is interesting and controversial, the listener will comprehend better and retain more information from the early part of the presentation (before the fatigue factor begins to operate). There is little cost attached to a quick judgment. A primacy effect is also most likely to occur when a person's character is in question (Lind, 1982). Recency effects, however, are more likely if the topic is less interesting, the issues are important but noncontroversial, and the topic is unfamiliar. If the subject matter is not interesting, the audience may not pay as much attention in the beginning. Even so, they may persevere if the issues are important. If the topic is unfamiliar, they may withhold judgment until they know more about the subject. The differences in effects are small, however, and other factors such as the strength of the argumentation can eliminate the advantage of presenting in one order or another (Rosnow & Robinson, 1967).

Climactic Versus Anticlimactic Ordering of Arguments

A second category of studies has to do with the question of where to put the best or strongest arguments versus the weaker arguments (climactic versus anticlimactic ordering of arguments). That is, should the strongest arguments be placed at the beginning, the middle, or the end of persuasive discourse? Climax order implies putting the strongest arguments at the end of the discourse. Anticlimax order implies putting the strongest arguments at the beginning. In this sense, the research into climactic versus anticlimactic ordering of arguments fits under the broader mantle of primacy-recency research. In response to these questions, researchers have concluded that little advantage adheres to either ordering (Gilkinson, Paulson, & Sikkink, 1954; Sponberg, 1946). Some researchers, however, advise that those seeking to persuade should use climax order, unless they think the audience will stop paying attention. They also suggest that designers of messages should avoid placing the strongest arguments in the middle of the discourse (Bettinghaus & Cody, 1994). Jackson and Allen (1987) found evidence to confirm the idea of placing supporting arguments before refutational arguments or interweaving the two.

Message Strategies

The following strategic considerations relate to identifying target audiences, judging the latitude of acceptability of a message, making strategic decisions on timing, committing to the long term, violating expectations, employing repetition, increasing the relevance of messages through associations with news content, and considering cross-cultural factors.

Identifying Target Audiences

Deciding on appropriate target audiences is critical to the success of an information campaign. Campaigns tailor their messages to specific audiences and cultures—those with the greatest need for (and interest in) the information. Sending an AIDS brochure to 17 million people is a waste of resources. Culbertson (1994) discussed the necessity to "pinpoint" audiences—geographically, media-wise, and topic-wise. In reaching these audiences, communicators must also consider the influence of opinion leaders, those held in high esteem by others. Opinion leaders tend to respond more to messages originating outside rather than inside the social system. They also tend to be more cosmopolitan in their attitudes and more predisposed to accept change and innovations (Rogers & Shoemaker, 1971).

Judging Latitude of Acceptability

Initial audience attitudes toward the message have a significant impact on the potential to achieve attitudinal or behavioral changes. Campaigns also work best if the audience does not have to surrender any pleasurable habits, as in the case of seat belt campaigns (Ashley, 1992). Moreover, the message is likely to have the greatest impact on those with unstructured attitudes. Wilde (1993) argued that advocated change should not exceed the recipients' latitude of acceptability:

> Within these limits, the greater the advocated change, the greater the persuasive effect will be. For example, highway postings of 100 km/hour had more effect on decreasing speed of travelers than did highway postings of 80 km/hour on a six-lane highway in Vienna. If, however, the advocated change exceeds the latitude of acceptability, no actual change will occur; or worse still, the message may produce *reactance,* that is, a "boomerang" effect. (p. 987)

Without a knowledge of these limits, the campaign designer should advocate a series of small, incremental changes over an extended period of time.

Many researchers have studied the relationship between discrepancy (distance between the receiver's initial views of the subject and the persuader's position) and persuasiveness. The evidence on this point does not appear to be conclusive because early studies found large discrepancies to be associated with greater persuasive results (Hovland & Pritzker, 1957). Other studies (Hovland, Harvey, & Sherif, 1957), however, reported a reduction in persuasive effect, in some circumstances, as the gap between audience and source position increased. O'Keefe (1990) proposes (as do other sources that he cites) that persuasive effect increases up to a certain level of discrepancy and then declines. In other words, there is a "latitude of acceptability," similar to Wilde's (1993) argument, beyond which no persuader can reach. Not unexpectedly, some studies have found that high-credibility sources can advocate more discrepant positions than low-credibility sources, with positive results (Aronson, Turner, & Carlsmith, 1963; Bochner & Insko, 1966). Another variable relates to the previous involvement of the audience with the subject. Highly involved subjects have a smaller latitude of acceptability (Freedman, 1964).

Making Strategic Decisions on Timing

People respond differentially to two types of innovations or changes: incremental and preventative. *Incremental* refers to an innovation that will offer desired returns from an investment in the near future (e.g., increased yield from planting a new kind of crop). *Preventative* innovations, however, keep an unwanted event from occurring at a much later point in time (e.g., an unwanted pregnancy, cancer, and AIDS). It is not easy to convince audiences to adopt preventative innovations because the events are in the distant future, if they occur at all. Moreover, the innovation may not prevent the person from getting the condition, even if he or she adopts the prescribed behaviors. Acceptance of innovations tends to follow an S-shaped curve over time (Backer et al., 1992):

At first the number of adopters of the new idea are relatively few per unit of time. Then, when about 15% or 20-25% of the members of a system adopt, the rate of adoption "takes off" and the number of adopters per unit of time begins to increase rapidly. (p. 9)

Those who propose innovations must try to achieve this "critical mass." After this point is reached, the diffusion of the innovation will become self-sustaining. This theory suggests that organizations should invest greater resources in the early stages of campaigns to create this momentum. When early adopters share their new ideas with friends and family members, they contribute to building the critical mass. Moreover, persuasion theory indicates that people often change themselves when they attempt to change others (Reardon, 1991).

Communicators try to reach audiences in places and at times when they will be prepared to listen. For example, messages on condom use can reach many viewers at 6 p.m., but not everyone will feel comfortable receiving the message at that time. Targeted viewers may be more inclined to listen to the message at 10 p.m., when their parents are not around.

Committing to the Long-Term: The Importance of Duration

The most effective campaigns take place during a long period of time. Research has found that the time required to respond to persuasive efforts varies for all individuals. For example, Rogers and Shoemaker (1971) categorized people into the following groups: (a) innovators or the first to adopt an innovation (often fringe members of the social system), (b) early adopters (higher-status individuals who are well integrated into the system), (c) early majority (individuals of average status who use the mass media more than their counterparts in the system), (d) late majority (low-status individuals who are particularly responsive to interpersonal communication from peers), and (e) laggards (highly traditional members of the system, the last to be persuaded). Differences in response time imply that campaign designers should be prepared to run long-term campaigns for maximum effectiveness.

Violating Expectations

Studies (Hunt, Smith, & Kernan, 1985; Settle & Golden, 1974) have demonstrated that advertisements that admit that some features of a product are not superior (whereas others are) are more credible and persuasive than those that claim superiority for all features of a product. The relevance of similar findings for source credibility was discussed in Chapter 8. People tend to believe sources who take a stance against their own best interest.

Using Repetition to Effect Change

Repeated exposure to a message also increases the likelihood that attitudes and behaviors will change. Some studies have found a positive association between degree of exposure to antismoking messages and stopping (or reducing) smoking (Ben-Sira, 1982). Most researchers agree that the single airing of a campaign spot will do little to effect attitude or behavior change. Any given message changes the attitudes and behavior of a relatively small number of audience members. The effects of well-designed messages in broadly aired campaigns repeated over time, however, can be significant (Wilde, 1993). Audiences tend to like familiar products, people, and materials. Good commercials increase in effectiveness until they reach a "wear-out" threshold (Bettinghaus & Cody, 1994). Too frequent airing of a message can result in listener fatigue. Research has demonstrated that the optimum number of repetitions is three (for review of classic research, see Bettinghaus & Cody, 1994; see also Schultz, 1990). Nonetheless, the introduction of variations on a message can extend its life (Weiss, 1966).

Increasing Relevance of Messages Through Associations With News Content

For maximum effectiveness, public communication campaigns should embed campaign messages within larger media portrayals of relevant social issues. Weaving information on a health-related topic into the news can also increase the effectiveness of the message (Ettema, Brown, & Luepker, 1983). For example, the inclusion of information on the role of alcohol in accidents, driver age, sex, and seat belt usage can be an effective way to inform the public on health risks and prevention strategies. Similarly, politicians learned long ago that blurring the line between commercials and news can increase the impact of their messages. To accomplish this end, they place advertisements adjacent to television news and public affairs programming (Jamieson & Campbell, 1988). Sometimes, the commercials include actual news footage; at other times, the advertisements resemble news items. The use of handheld cameras and natural lighting convey a sense of the spontaneous and immediate. In slice-of-life commercials, politicians mingle with the public to convey this same impression of news coverage. The camera eavesdrops on their conversations with constituents, family, and friends.

Considering Cross-Cultural Factors

The communicator must consider cross-cultural implications in the choice of certain symbols and colors for particular ethnic groups. For example, the Chinese consider the color blue to be funereal. Logo designers for a Mexican bank added a top hat to a stylized eagle so that Mexicans would not perceive the logo as too American. A study of hygiene instruction in Egypt demonstrated that Egyptians viewed a red "X," used in social marketing campaigns, as a symbol of death (Garland, 1982). Different countries handle the same topic in different ways. For example, an American newspaper advertisement displayed the explicit warning "Don't go out without your rubbers" beside the spilled contents of a woman's purse, including a condom. By contrast, a Trinidad advertisement showed a man and his girlfriend sitting on a park bench. The accompanying text spelled out: "You're safer with one partner. Avoid AIDS." France and Sweden take a low-key, factual approach to their safe sex messages, whereas the Japanese employ a "discreet and euphemistic" style (Magdenko, Disman, & Raphael, n.d.). Culture also mediates how people respond to attempts to persuade. For example, Americans tend to accept higher levels of negativity in advertisements than do Canadians.

Conclusion

People resist change and innovations. Psychologist Kurt Lewin (1951) noted that to "unfreeze" behavior, one must increase the magnitude of the "driving force" and decrease the magnitude of the "restraining force." Consumers who wish to stop drinking confront many forces that encourage them to continue their behavior: drinking by role models and celebrities, availability of alcohol at social and work gatherings, peer influence, positive portrayals of drinking in television shows and films, and alcohol advertisements. For this reason, a knowledge of persuasion theories can be important to the information campaign designer, who attempts to raise awareness and effect positive changes in attitude and behavior. This chapter has emphasized the ways in which persuaders can achieve their aims by stimulating active thought processes. Topics examined dealt with message content, organization of messages, and strategies for achieving attitudinal and behavioral changes.

11

Choosing the Channel

Lessons Learned

This chapter examines the findings of research into appropriate media for communication campaigns. More specifically, it looks at how people use the media, media successes at raising awareness and influencing attitudes and behavior, limitations on conclusions that can be reached, and strategies for effective use of the media. Finally, the chapter examines agenda-setting theories.

How People Use the Media

Many studies have attempted to discover how people use different media. Some have found that people depend less on television for information than for surveillance of the environment or for parasocial and interpersonal purposes. Recent studies indicate that, despite dwindling readerships, newspapers remain America's "premier source of public affairs information" (Robinson & Levy, 1996, p. 135). At the same time, specialized cable programs such as the *MacNeil-Lehrer Report* and channels such as C-SPAN have begun to rival newspapers and news magazines as suppliers of long-term political knowledge. Usage patterns vary for different media, depending on subject matter and demographic affiliations. For example, studies indicate that people prefer television to newspapers for general information (Roper,

1985; Roper as cited in Reagan & Collins, 1987, p. 560). For an increasing number of people, television is the dominant medium from which they acquire their daily news. The young, elderly, poor, and people with disabilities are the heaviest viewers (Comstock, Chaffee, Katzman, McCombs, & Roberts, 1978)—a point that has relevance for organizations aiming to reach at-risk viewers. People also trust television more than they trust other media, both in general and in specific situations involving health-related information. University students rely on television as their primary source of information on health-related topics such as AIDS (McDermott, Hawkins, Moore, & Cittadino, 1987). Interviews with black smokers revealed that they had heard of the health risks of smoking mostly from television, followed by radio, newspapers, magazines, local newsletters and bulletins, and other sources (Cernada et al., 1989/1990).

Some viewers use television and radio to help solve their problems. A classic study by Herzog (1944) found that 41% of radio soap listeners said that the serials had helped them to learn how to deal with their problems. A case study that examined the depiction of alcoholism on *All My Children* concluded that health educators can "enlarge and deepen" health messages by working with the entertainment media to tell stories (DeFoe & Breed, 1991). Health communication researchers argue that television can provide prosocial role models that influence attitudes and behaviors and educate people on topics such as cardiac conditions, diabetes, and chronic bronchial asthma. Entertainment formats such as soap opera and drama can help to reach viewers who use television primarily for interpersonal and diversionary purposes (Montgomery, 1990).

Media Successes at Raising Awareness and Influencing Attitudes and Behavior

For many years, researchers have investigated the ability of media to raise awareness and influence attitudes and behavior on health care issues. The majority of researchers agree that television, used properly and in conjunction with other means such as interpersonal communication, can be an effective medium for transmitting information and for influencing attitudes. Raising the consciousness of the public on specific issues (i.e., creating awareness and concern) relies on publicity, best accomplished by mass media including television (Yankelovich, 1991). The following discussion provides details of some such findings.

The AIDS crisis spawned many studies that explored the effectiveness of television in increasing awareness and knowledge and modifying attitudes and behaviors. A survey of 1,006 individuals (aged 16-54) demonstrated that a televised public health and education campaign had played a positive role in increasing their knowledge of AIDS (Wober, 1988). Interviews with 505 randomly selected University of Wisconsin undergraduate students found that knowledge levels and risk-reduction behaviors improved as a consequence of exposure and attention to mass media messages (Dunwoody & Neuwirth, 1988). Following the discovery of a link between aspirin use and Reye's syndrome, the media played a central role in effecting changes in consumer purchasing habits. In Houston, Texas, a media campaign on child abuse resulted in significant increases in reporting of abuse cases (Friedrich, 1977). Deaths from intrauterine devices (IUDs) ceased only after widespread publicity in the news media. Scientific publications and drug package inserts had not persuaded doctors to remove IUDs from pregnant patients (Cates, Grimes, Ory, & Tyler, 1977).

Some antismoking campaigns also provide convincing evidence of media effects. Data from the first 28 weeks of an antismoking print and broadcast campaign showed that 10 times more requests for information came from communities that had received the print and broadcast messages than from communities that had not received the information (Cummings, Sciandra, David, & Rimer, 1989). In another instance, researchers followed a group of 5,458 elementary school students for 4 years. Some of these students received antismoking messages from their schools and from radio and television, whereas others received only the school messages. Findings supported the effectiveness of mass media interventions aimed at high-risk youth used to supplement school prevention programs (Flynn et al., 1992). Also, survey data confirmed that approximately 10,000 adult smokers had quit for at least 6 months by the conclusion of a Finnish antismoking program (McAlister, 1980). Other recent studies also have demonstrated the value of the media exposure in promoting specific social norms and raising the salience of smoking as an issue (Wallack & Sciandra, 1990/1991).

In Norway, researchers evaluated the effectiveness of a national media health education campaign designed to effect lifestyle changes. Interviews with 878 individuals indicated that 22% reported changes in one or more habits, 33% said they were exercising more, and 25% reported that they had reduced or quit smoking (Sogaard & Fonnebo, 1992). Other studies have found that carefully designed television messages can result in improved eating habits, greater numbers of requests for specific medical tests, reduced cardiovascular risk behaviors, and lowered incidence of smoking (Solomon, 1982). Studies have demonstrated that even kindergarten-age children can process and remember health-related information presented on television (Faber, 1984).

Research into the effectiveness of television in carrying messages about mental health has demonstrated increased information levels, more favorable attitudes, and changed beliefs regarding mental illness following television documentaries (Medvene & Bridge, 1990). Most researchers accept that television plays a critical role as an educational medium in developing countries.

Limitations on the Effectiveness of Media: Influential Variables

Despite generally positive results, some studies have found limited public acceptance of the mass media for certain types of messages. A survey of 588 American college students, for example, determined that students believed mass media sources to be less acceptable than interpersonal and institutional sources (Cline & Engel, 1991). People tend to use media channels in conjunction with other sources, such as doctors, friends, and family (Johnson & Meishoke, 1992). Some researchers believe that people would be more willing to select media as an information source if the media generated greater amounts of usable information. Other researchers have concluded that mass media do not provide the most cost-effective means of reaching target publics.

Individual variables influence receptivity to messages. One study found that whites, females, younger adolescents, and those who did not intend to smoke in the future were most likely to respond to an offer in an antismoking broadcast (Bauman, Padgett, & Koch, 1989). A second study determined that high-risk groups (i.e., heavy smokers) had less exposure to—and lower recall of—antismoking messages than median-risk groups (Ben-Sira, 1982). Australian researchers uncovered a connection between media exposure and social attitudes. Those who exposed themselves to media programs on AIDS tended to have less fear of those with same-sex orientations, less fear of death, and lower levels of social conservatism (Ross & Carson, 1988). People vary greatly in how they receive messages about AIDS (Dickinson, 1990). The ability to process the information and motivation to learn can be significant predictors of learning and knowledge levels (Rosser, Flora, Chaffee,

& Farquhar, 1990). The latter study did not find that socioeconomic status, education, or income predicted the frequency with which people would attend to media messages. Language acculteration, however, does predict exposure to media messages (Ruiz, Marks, & Richardson, 1992).

Other researchers argue that there is little evidence to support implementation of mass media programs to modify health behaviors (Redman, Spencer, & Sanson-Fisher, 1990). Although media have some impact on agenda setting with regard to health care issues, they have little capacity to alter behavior (Peterson, Jeffrey, Bridgwater, & Dawson, 1984). An effort in Australia to increase public knowledge of Pap smears, change attitudes, and change behavioral patterns succeeded, to some extent, in the first two categories but failed in the third (Shelley, 1991). Some argue that the pervasiveness of negative influences in the social environment (e.g., tobacco advertisements and commercials for alcoholic beverages) limits the potential of television to effect meaningful social change. These critics believe it is necessary to effect dramatic structural and systemic changes before television can become more effective (Wallack, 1983).

Improving the Effectiveness of the Media

To minimize the problems discussed previously, health professionals often (a) use multiple sources to reach their audiences, (b) integrate their campaigns into larger community interventions, and (c) rely on the principle of immediacy in reaching audiences.

Although large-scale campaigns use broadcast media, they also employ newspapers, magazines, radio, and other media. Hofstetter, Schultze, and Mulvihill (1992) found that exposure to multiple media sources increased the likelihood that people would report health-related concerns, interests, and behaviors. Warnecke, Langenberg, Wong, Flay, and Cook (1992) found that responses to televised segments from the American Lung Association's manual *Freedom From Smoking in 20 Days* were most pronounced for those who registered for the program, watched television programs, and read their manual on a daily basis. The most successful interventions relied on both printed and televised materials. Wewers, Ahijevych, and Page (1991) obtained similar results when they evaluated the effectiveness of a smoking-cessation campaign that used printed and televised materials.

The North Karelia project, begun in Finland in 1972 to combat high levels of cardiovascular disease in the population, combined a television component with one-to-one interpersonal communication and extensive collaboration among project staff and supermarkets, bread companies, and other businesses (Backer, Rogers, & Sopory, 1992). The Finnish project also combined television counseling sessions with self-help groups. Soumerai, Ross-Degnan, and Kahn (1992) explained the media's success at educating the public on the linkage between aspirin products and Reye's syndrome as follows:

> In the past, media-only health education campaigns have been relatively unsuccessful in achieving long-term changes in complex health behaviors. . . . Media warnings about the hazards of common products can successfully change consumer behaviors when: the illness is devastating; the behavioral message is simple; acceptable and inexpensive alternatives are available; and the campaign is comprehensive, involving multiple professional groups to reinforce direct consumer appeals. (p. 178)

One of the most publicized and long-term studies, the Stanford Heart Disease Prevention program, targeted selected residents of three California towns who were at higher than average risk for cardiovascular disease. The project employed a combination of mass communication (e.g., television, radio, newspapers, and print media distributed through mass media) and interpersonal communication (e.g., small group aerobic classes and smoking-cessation classes). Efforts to educate the public also employed a mix of media and interpersonal components (contests, correspondence courses, and special activities for Spanish-language radio, newspapers, and mass media-distributed print media). The Stanford program encouraged networking through opinion leaders.

At the end of the program, researchers concluded that media interventions had resulted in significant risk reduction. Under some conditions, greater and longer lasting change characterized the groups that had received both face-to-face and mass media instruction (Meyer, Nash, & McAlister, 1980; Schooler, Flora, & Farquhar, 1993). Joining media and people can be a successful strategy in achieving attitude change. Ashley (1992) argued that media prepares the soil for someone else to seed. In other words, personal contact must follow media exposure. Although the previous discussion has emphasized television, many people believe that radio is underused (Ashley, 1992).

The integration of media-based campaigns into larger community or institution-based interventions produces the greatest behavioral change

(Arkin, 1992). A "media-plus-community" approach helped an antidrinking campaign to remain for a long time on the public policy agenda and to garner support for related public policies (Casswell, Ransom, & Gilmore, 1990).

The principle of immediacy should influence choices of media for carrying messages. This principle relates to the idea that audiences should be able to display the newly adopted behaviors soon after receiving the persuasive or informative message. Using this pattern of reasoning, television is a low-immediacy channel for messages that recommend workplace safety or driving with headlights on in the rain. Audiences have no immediate opportunity to display the behaviors. Television is a high-immediacy medium for alcohol advertisements, however, because many people have the opportunity to drink in environments with television sets (pubs and homes). Similarly, countertop advertising has high immediacy for consumers who visit stores to purchase cigarettes or food (Wilde, 1993).

Agenda Setting

Agenda setting refers to the ability of the mass media to direct attention to specific issues. Cohen (1963) noted, "The press may not be successful much of the time in telling people what to think, but it is stunningly successful in telling its readers what to think about" (p. 4). Rogers and Dearing (1988) discussed three kinds of agenda setting: public agenda setting, media agenda setting, and policy agenda setting. They concluded that a relationship exists among the three varieties of agenda setting. That is, media have a direct, often powerful influence on both the public and the policy agendas. The public agenda, in turn, has an effect on the policy agenda. Researchers ask the following questions about agenda setting: Who sets the media's agenda? How does the media prime audiences through agenda setting? and What variables mediate the agenda-setting process?

Who Sets the Media's Agenda?

Newspapers play a key role in the early weeks of campaigns, whereas television becomes more important closer to the election date (Shaw & McCombs, 1977). Early studies of intermedia agenda setting found that wire services tend to standardize the content of client newspapers (McCombs & Shaw, 1976). Other newspapers can also act as agenda setters. For example, the *New York Times* acted as an agenda setter for the *Washington Post* and

Los Angeles Times on the drug issue (Reese & Danielian, 1989). During several years of tracking foreign affairs issues in the Canadian press, I noted that the *New York Times* also influences the agenda of major Canadian newspapers such as the *Globe and Mail.* Political advertising influences both newspaper and television agendas. Although advertising has a greater influence on newspaper agendas, newspapers set television agendas (Roberts & McCombs, 1994).

Weaver's (1994) study of an American election demonstrated "grassroots" agenda setting. Many candidates in the 1992 election chose to reach the public through talk shows and tabloid programs, electronic town hall meetings, toll-free telephone numbers, and computer bulletin boards. The public was able to question the candidates directly, without intermediate filters. As the campaign progressed, it was clear that the candidates, their advisers, journalists, pollsters, academics, and other interested citizens were discussing the issues that had surfaced first in the nontraditional media. The mainstream media were also addressing these same issues. The highest turnout of voters in a presidential election since 1968 (nearly 56% of the voting population) added credence to the possibility that new media had made a difference in levels of voter engagement. No other presidential election in this century had seen such a voter turnout. Of 142 participants in a 1992 panel, none said that they had learned about the candidates from news commentators, analysts, or pundits. Instead, they mentioned television talk shows, early morning shows, and shows sponsored by the candidates (Sandell, Mattley, Evarts, Lengel, & Ziyati, 1993). After actively seeking the opinions of voters on the significant issues, some radio and television stations and newspapers let these issues drive their election coverage (Roberts & McCombs, 1994). Some of this coverage focused on possible solutions to the problems raised by voters.

Researchers and social critics have expressed concern regarding the fact that many groups seek to manipulate the media's agenda. Organizations are often willing to wager that a news item will lose some of its appeal or impact given an adequate lapse of time between the event and the analysis of the event. Also, organizations may withhold unfavorable news releases until the appearance of the current edition. A late Sunday morning release is a favorite time for those who do not want the news to reach the public before Monday evening. When Ford announced Nixon's pardon, he did so on a Sunday morning hoping that fewer newspapers would carry the story (Jamieson & Campbell, 1988). A weekend press conference draws fewer reporters than a weekday conference. The reverse of this situation occurs when an organization releases news at a time when large numbers of people are available to receive the information. Many groups plan their events for times when the media can easily cover them (e.g., prime time for live television coverage). Political parties plan their conventions so that chosen leaders make their acceptance speeches at peak viewing times. They learned their lesson when George McGovern delivered his acceptance speech for the Democratic nomination in the wee hours of the morning, when only a small viewing audience remained awake to hear it. Information released in the opening week of the fall television season reaches optimum numbers of the viewing public.

How Does the Media Prime Audiences and Frame Issues?

Media also influence the standards by which the public judges governments and corporations. Media "prime" the public to evaluate the performance of politicians and others on the issues to which it accords importance (Iyengar & Kinder, 1987). If employment issues are front-page news, the public judges its leaders by how well they manage these concerns. If, however, health care issues capture headlines, these issues become the standard by which the public judges the performance of politicians and bureaucrats. Thus, the media prime audiences to alter the centrality of issues to which they accord importance. Preparing for one of his election campaigns, Governor Nelson Rockefeller learned that his opponents had significantly more favorable ratings for every issue except one, concerning the construction of roads and highways, which less than 5% of the electorate considered to be important. With no other options, Rockefeller told his advertising agency, "Make that an issue": "Over the next few months, voters in New York state were deluged by advertising which glorified that state's highway system. . . . By the end of the campaign, roads and highways became the most important issue and Mr. Rockefeller was reelected" (Reid, 1988, p. 137).

If issues remain on the media agenda for a sufficiently long period of time, the public begins to judge their leaders on how they perform on these issues. Thus, priming assumes that the media have a direct and significant influence on how people perceive their leaders and issues.

Some researchers suggest that we should take care in drawing too heavy a line between the media's potential to tell us "what to think about" and "what to think." They believe that agenda setting can also lead to action—that people do more than think about the issues that are on the media agenda.

> Sender → Expert interpreter →
>
> Television commentator → Opinion leader
>
> → Opinion Leader → Receiver

Figure 11.1. Influence Diagram
SOURCE: Reprinted with permission from Ferguson, 1994.

They attend more meetings, write more letters, sign more petitions, and vote in more elections. They must feel a sense of efficacy, however. They must believe that their votes and actions can make a difference: "Agenda setting can lead to either political involvement or alienation of citizens, depending on whether it is mainly top-down or bottom-up and whether real issues or pseudo issues are emphasized" (Weaver, 1994, p. 354).

Research on framing of issues also assumes that the media have a significant impact on stories: "Framing analysis recognizes that the media can impart a certain perspective or 'spin' to the issues that they cover and this, in turn, might influence public attitudes on an issue" (Wimmer & Dominick, 1997, pp. 356-357). News stories can emphasize a particular story line or establish the criteria by which people assign responsibility for social problems (Rhee, 1997). Politicians often complain that the media interpret and reframe everything that they say. Figure 11.1 illustrates this multistep influence process that can involve many stages of interaction, including expert interpreters, television commentators, several stages of opinion leaders, and the public.

Limitations on the Public's Willingness to Accept Media Agendas

Some studies demonstrate the limits of the public's willingness to accept media agendas. These limits grow out of characteristics of issues, audiences, context, and journalistic practices.

Issue Characteristics

Some issues are obtrusive, incapable of being ignored, whereas other issues are unobtrusive, with little impact on our daily lives. People pay more attention to some issues than to others. The issues that someone recognizes as most important to the community or nation (issues on the public agenda) may differ from the issues that are most significant on a personal level (issues on one's private agenda) (McCombs, 1978). Where choices must be made, the voters will give greater priority to the issues on their private agenda. The scandals faced by Bill Clinton illustrate this point. The public cared less about Clinton's affairs with Jennifer Flowers and Monica Lewinsky than they cared about jobs and eliminating the deficit. The opposition's repeated attempts to prime the public to judge President Clinton on issues of morality failed. "Issue fatigue" occurs when the public wearies of hearing and reading about an issue, especially when its ranking on the public or media agendas fails to correspond to its ranking on people's private agendas (Ferguson, 1994). At some point, the public says "enough." On other occasions, issue fatigue grows out of a feeling of impotency, a sense that no answer will satisfy all interested parties or meet the standards set for a solution. It is possible that the public is neither apathetic nor uncaring, but people lose faith in their own ability, and in the competency of others, to generate answers to some problems. Where problems exist for long periods of time (e.g., issues of separation in Canada, land disputes in the Middle East, and the war of Protestants against Catholics in Northern Ireland), people begin to feel that no event or person will make a difference. The media continues to cover the topics, but the public loses interest.

Audience Characteristics

Audience characteristics can set limits on the media's efforts to set the public agenda on issues. For example, some studies have demonstrated that the media agenda has a greater influence on people who are interested in the issues (McCombs, 1994; Weaver, 1994). Knowledge of the issues can also influence receptiveness to agenda-setting influences (Weaver, 1994). Another influential variable is the need for orientation (Wanta & Hu, 1994). Some studies have found that better educated audiences tend to agree more with the issue agendas of newspapers, whereas the less educated agree more with the issue agendas of television. Another variable is the level of political involvement (Williams & Semlak, 1978).

Context

The impact of agenda setting varies according to "the campaign context, the length of time being considered, and the kind of effects being studied"

(Weaver, 1994, p. 348). McCombs and Shaw (1972) concluded that agenda-setting influences become more pronounced in election periods, when voters pay more attention to political news than at other times. In the heat of political elections, opinions become more consistent.

Journalistic Practices

Some researchers have noted that cultural, institutional, and organizational factors also influence the media agenda (Reese, 1991). Moreover, journalistic traditions, practices, and values have a strong impact on the agenda (McCombs, 1994). Every media establishment faces deadlines, and every reporter, editor, and producer must adhere to these deadlines. Media are biassed toward early release of information, and stale news is no news. Therefore, if an organization releases controversial information shortly before media deadlines, the initial coverage of the event or issue will probably be uncritical. Faced with such time restraints, media cannot do more than publish the basic facts. Editorial coverage or commentaries follow later if the item maintains its newsworthiness and if a more current event does not bump it from the media agenda.

Providing prepackaged materials to the media also increases the chance that the media will air the organization's viewpoint. Reporters working on tight deadlines make only minor changes to press kit materials. Similarly, layout editors often fill last-minute news holes with materials prepared by public relations personnel (Saxer, 1993). Gatekeeping studies have analyzed the characteristics of press releases and video news releases (style and content variables) that allow them to pass through the journalistic gate. Studies have found that the news releases most likely to pass through the gate are short and simply written, deal with localized financial matters, and include a hometown photo (Wimmer & Dominick, 1997). McCombs (1994) explained as follows:

> Even the largest and best national newspapers with their huge staffs of reporters and editors, newspapers such as the *New York Times* and *Washington Post,* obtain over half of their daily material from press releases, press conferences, and other routine channels created by governmental agencies, corporations, and interest groups. Only a small proportion of the news results from the initiative and innovation of the news organizations. (p. 11)

Many authors have addressed the phenomenon of pack journalism, the tendency of reporters to follow each other in "packs" (Timothy Crouse first described the phenomenon in *The Boys on the Bus* [1972]). If the United Press International or the Associated Press lists an event in its daily calendar, the media will be afraid not to cover the event. If a respected journalist or an elite medium covers an issue, other media will follow. Reporters traveling in packs borrow quotations from each other and compare perceptions in writing their stories. They check with pack leaders to define the lead story or issue for the day.

Journalists also respond to commercial imperatives. Survival requires that media consider what "sells." Therefore, the stories that ultimately find their way onto the agenda are predictable in their characteristics. Highly visual material attracts media audiences, as does the sensational and the bizarre—executions, survival stories, and the occult. For example, if pro-lifers position themselves before an abortion clinic and thrust baby gifts at women entering the clinic, the event will almost certainly receive media attention. The picture of a young widow, at the grave side of her husband killed in military action, has a highly personal and dramatic quality. Images of starving children in Somalia and the bleeding victims of an airline crash have the stark dramatic quality that television demands. The media are drawn to stories that expose human weaknesses and foibles—scandal, fraud, and corruption. Similarly, news feeds on the controversial. There is a tendency in the press to prefer issues that are simple, easy to verify, and nontechnical—a fact that works against interest groups that are trying to educate the public on complex issues with complicated histories. There is also a tendency to avoid issues that require interpretation and analysis—more time-consuming exercises for the journalist. Because journalists pride themselves on being generalists, many lack the in-depth knowledge to deal with such issues in a satisfactory way.

The presence of a celebrity also increases the chances that media will cover an event, and incumbents in office have an advantage over those who aspire to office. Exclusive interviews with influential figures guarantee media coverage. Information leaked from high places will be media worthy. Because news organizations require ongoing good relations with people in positions of power, they tend to accommodate these individuals in return for continued access (Picard, 1991).

Technical requirements influence news coverage. Photographers and television camera crews require adequate light, proper facilities to accommodate sound and video equipment, and a good vantage point for filming or witness-ing events. An organization that wishes to receive live media coverage must plan its event so that daytime conditions guarantee optimum light levels. The presence of these conditions contributes to the likelihood that a media organization will choose to cover the organization's event. Pattakos (1992) observed that activist groups take advantage of many media opportunities, including letter writing, sit-ins, marches and demonstrations, prayer vigils, seminars and lectures, and the writing and distribution of printed materials. He observed that some extreme and highly questionable attention-getting strategies include violence and subversion—for example, bombing abortion clinics, pounding nails and spikes into trees scheduled for harvesting, har-assing employees, stealing animals from research laboratories, and placing dead fish in safety deposit boxes in protest of bank policies.

Conclusion

The findings of research into appropriate media for communication cam-paigns were discussed in this chapter. Specifically, I have examined some success stories, pointed to limitations on conclusions that can be reached, suggested strategies for improving the effectiveness of the media, and dis-cussed in the literature on agenda setting. Many factors make it difficult for researchers to identify influential variables in media effects. Peoples' use of media varies. Also, communities vary in their attitudinal and behavioral norms, casting doubt on the findings of some studies. Drop-out rates are high in some studies. Most important, so many variables exist in the larger social environment that it is difficult to isolate cause-effect relationships. Nonethe-less, reasonably compelling evidence supports the conclusion that, used in conjunction with interpersonal and organizational sources, media can be effective in conveying information, influencing attitudes, and, less fre-quently, changing behaviors. Moreover, a combination of different media works best.

The largest body of research, relevant to channel effectiveness, has been derived from evaluation of information and advertising campaigns. Much of the commercial research is not available for public or academic consumption.

PART
IV

Strategic Approaches

12

Strategic Approaches to
Planning for Issues Management

I deally, the strategic communication plan will include an issues management component, which identifies all the organization's issues. Support plans also address the management of individual issues. Strategic approaches to issues management emerge from an understanding of the following questions: (a) Does the organization own the issue? (b) In the case of multiple stakeholders, who shares ownership of the issue? (c) What is the probability that the issue will have a significant impact on the organization? (d) What variables influence controllability of the issue? and (e) How can the organization help the public to reach "social judgment" on issues?

Ownership of the Issue: Sole or Shared?

Questions of ownership relate to the issue's bearing on the organization's mandate or mission. Therefore, the strategic planner must ask "Does the issue fall within the mandate and mission of the organization?" To have the authority and legitimacy to make a difference, an organization must own some critical dimension of an issue. In other words, it must have some control over the issue. Even in the absence of such authority, however, bureaucrats, politicians, or business executives may be tempted to respond, especially in a politically charged environment, when confronted with public cries for action. In such situations, it is important for the organization to determine the aspects of the issue that it owns and those that it does not own.

The Seattle-First National Bank (Seafirst) experienced this problem first-hand soon after it became trustee for the Washington Public Power Supply System's (WPPSS) Project 3 bonds, designated to build a new nuclear plant. When WPPSS experienced huge cost overruns, the company passed the costs on to consumers. Angry consumers obtained legislation that required a vote to approve any further financing of nuclear power plants. Caught in the middle between consumers and bondholders, Seafirst Bank had to file a lawsuit to overturn the legislation. Had they not acted, they would have been vulnerable to a lawsuit by angry bondholders. The consumers responded with an Irate Ratepayers campaign to encourage Seafirst customers to close their accounts. The bank faced an issue that they did not create: They became a scapegoat for anger that consumers felt against a third party. They were not responsible for the cost overruns at WPPSS, and they had no mandate to correct the problem. An aggressive media relations campaign educated customers, employees, journalists, bondholders, and utility consumers on the fact that Seafirst did not own this issue. As a consequence, there was a dramatic turnaround of public opinion, with minimal negative consequences for the bank (Howard & Matthews, 1985).

Another excellent example to illustrate this point occurred in Canada in 1990. A dispute over ownership of sacred Mohawk burial grounds (designated for development as a golf course in Oka, Quebec) escalated into a face-off between Mohawks, the Quebec police, and ultimately the Canadian army. Confusion over ownership of the issues made management of the crisis extremely difficult. The confusion existed at all levels of government (federal, provincial, and municipal) and between the two main governing councils at Kanehsatake. The debate over ownership of the issues extended to factions within these councils, Mohawks on other reserves and those who lived in Oka, and the First Nations Assembly (which represented the Indian community throughout Canada). Additional ambiguities concerning leadership related to the matriarchal nature of Mohawk society. Soon after army troops had reopened the Mercier Bridge at Chateauguay, the women of Kahnawake staged the largest demonstration of the summer. In a show of support for the last holdouts at the Oka pines, they blocked a single-lane highway leading to the bridge. A spokesperson for the women made the following statement: "We feel this is our time to point out to the country, the world, that women in Kahnawake are serious. . . . It has not come across enough that we brought up the men to do what they are doing" (MacLeod,

1993). Two weeks later, other women led a march to the Kahnawake Long-house to issue an eviction notice to the army and the police. One commentator observed, "The army had only negotiated with the men. Now they are made to realize that the women are a real political force in the community" (MacLeod, 1993). In brief, disputes over claims to leadership made it extremely difficult for the federal or provincial governments to identify appropriate negotiators to represent the native position (Roth, 1990). In fact, no one native position existed.

The army had the clearest mandate of any stakeholder in the events at Oka. Cogden (1990) emphasized the importance of this point to their operations:

> People must realize that the military are not policymakers. We had nothing to do with the policy that was going on. . . . I think people in Canada still don't know what the issue [was]. . . . I mean, was it a law and order issue? Was it a native issue? I don't think people really know. . . . But we knew—for us, it was a very clear issue. It was a legal issue—we were tasked legally through the province of Quebec. . . . It was a simple law and order issue. It was not a native issue; it was not a federal-provincial issue. (pp. 127, 134)

A member of the Canadian Armed Forces stated, "From our perspective, we were not dealing with other issues. . . . We had our mandate and we stuck to our mandate and did our mandate, and our mandate was legal" (Anonymous, 1990, pp. 140-141). Nonetheless, senior army officials often had to explain federal policies or policy reversals, even though they had no authority to influence the decisions. Second Lieutenant Dave Scanlon (1990) said that Army spokespersons sometimes complained, off the record, that they were "left holding the bag" (p. 84). In other words, they were forced to assume ownership of issues that they lacked the jurisdiction to resolve.

The more clear-cut the ownership of issues, the easier the job of the issues management team. The more blurred and fuzzy the lines of ownership, the more difficult the task. A major task for politicians and bureaucrats is to clarify questions of ownership for the larger public, to act on those that fall within the mandate and mission of the organization, and to educate the public on lack of jurisdiction in areas in which there is no mandate. Robinson (1990) observed, "Communicational situations are by definition messy situations . . . trying to unravel who's in charge of what; who is to be made accountable for what" (p. 173).

Where debates over ownership take place within the boundaries of the organization (e.g., within different branches of a government department), issues management becomes still more difficult. For instance, the Canadian Department of the Solicitor General has a Correctional Services branch and a Parole Board branch. When murders occur at halfway houses, debates often erupt over which branch of the department failed to protect the public. The two branches sometimes play a game of "hot potato," passing ownership of the issue back and forth between each other. The Correctional Services branch claims that the Parole Board erred in releasing the offender too soon, and the Parole Board alleges that Correctional Services failed to provide proper supervision of the parolee. This same kind of situation developed at Oka with the army and Quebec police. When a controversy arose over the disarming of native peacekeepers (the Mohawk equivalent of the local police), both the army and the Quebec police rejected responsibility for the decision. Faced with criticism, the two peacekeeping contingents, which should have been working together, took turns accusing each other (MacLeod, 1993).

When the media carry these kinds of debates over ownership, top executives and politicians (who represent the larger organization and not regional or business units) face a no-win situation. Thus, those at the highest levels of the organization, rather than those with more limited interests, should be in control. A strategic planning team should represent this larger viewpoint and ensure coordination of messages and response strategies.

Who Shares Responsibility for Managing the Issue?

When an organization does accept full or limited responsibility for an issue, it must then decide to what extent that ownership is shared by other units under its administration or by other organizations. In other words, who are the other stakeholders in the issues? The recall of a defective product by a corporation may raise issues that are owned by several different business units: design, manufacturing, legal, and others. Within government, it is not uncommon for multiple departments to have a stake in the same issue.

The term *stakeholder* refers to "any individual or group who can affect or is affected by the actions, decisions, policies, practices, or goals of the organization" (Freeman, 1984, p. 25) or "groups of individuals whose interests coincide in one or more ways with the organization" (Brody, 1988, p. 81). Stakeholders in an issue may be defined by a region (e.g., community, city, state, and nation), by an ethnic or racial grouping, by political orientation, or by other demographic or psychographic factors. To identify stake-holders, it is useful to examine the dimensions of an issue. Issues tend to belong to the following portfolios: political, social and cultural, legal and criminal, human rights, technological, ecological, regulatory, public health, and public safety. Because these categories relate to areas of social concern, they also describe the social institutions that have evolved to meet these concerns. Governments institutionalize these areas of concern in the form of departments or agencies—for example, the Environmental Protection Agency (ecological concerns), the Department of Health and Human Services (public health and social concerns), and the Department of the Interior (cultural concerns). A Washington executive described how the issues of concern to his organization clustered into groups that related to House and Senate committees as follows (Lusterman, 1988):

> Members of my staff follow their issues into the House, the Senate, executive branch agencies—wherever they lead. And their bundles of issues change very little because they relate to congressional committees. Tax and trade issues, for example, center in the House Ways and Means Committee and the Senate Finance Committee. . . . The same with the Public Works Committee and the Environmental Committees. The committee structure on the Hill dictates the issues assignments. (p. 3)

By identifying the dimensions of an issue, an issues management team can identify the range of institutions, special publics, and interest groups with a stake in the issue (i.e., audiences for communication). For example, issues pertaining to animal rights have the following dimensions:

- Political—animal rights groups, governments, associations of hunters, and funding agencies for animal-based medical research
- Social and cultural—native organizations
- Economic—Department of Revenue, fashion industry, regional and municipal chambers of commerce, business lobby, and tourism industry
- Technological—research councils, cosmetic industry, and medical research groups
- Ecological—groups that promote the cause of threatened species

Analysis of the tobacco issue also demonstrates the usefulness of the stakeholder identification tool. An adviser for a government department faced with managing such an issue could arrive at the following stakeholder analysis:

- Political—state governments, surgeon general, tobacco lobby, and antismoking lobby

- Health—Department of Health and Human Services, health care industry, medical researchers, and heart and lung associations

- Economic—insurance companies and tobacco companies

- Ecological—Environmental Protection Agency

- Legal and criminal—Department of Justice and state and local police associations

- Social—boards of education, local schools, and youth organizations

In the case of Oka (discussed previously), the Canadian government's decision to accept partial ownership of the issues implied the need for various stakeholders within its jurisdiction to become involved: the legal and criminal dimension (Justice Canada and the Department of the Solicitor General, which includes the Royal Canadian Mounted Police), the social and cultural dimension (Department of Indian and Northern Affairs), the political dimension (the prime minister's office), the public safety dimension (Department of National Defence), and the ecological dimension (Department of the Environment). As the crisis progressed, Health Canada and the Human Rights Commission became stakeholders when the provincial police stopped the movement of food and medical supplies into reserves at Kanehsatake and Kahnawake. To manage the issues at Oka, the government of Canada also had to interact with stakeholders in other jurisdictions and organizations: the legal and criminal dimension (Justice Department of Quebec), the social and cultural dimension (Quebec Native Affairs Ministry, other native societies, and some multicultural groups), the political dimension (the premier of Quebec, his cabinet, the Iroquois Confederacy, the First Nations Assembly of Canada, the band councils across Canada, the Longhouse governments, governing bodies on other Mohawk reserves that are currently negotiating land claims disputes, and the international community), the public safety dimension (Surete du Quebec, the Oka police force, and native peacekeepers), the ecological dimension (native groups across Canada that demonstrate against clear-cut forestry practices, building of dams, and other environmental issues), the public health dimension (Quebec Ministry of Health), and the human rights dimension (Quebec Human Rights Commission and the United Nations Human Rights Commission).

The trend toward "boundaryless" organizations has made questions of ownership increasingly complicated. The solutions do not reside in one place with one organization. Therefore, organizations must be able to identify others with whom they can work to find solutions and manage issues with multiple dimensions. In general terms, it can be said that the greater the number of dimensions to an issue, the greater the number of stakeholders. The greater the number of stakeholders in an issue, the more complex and difficult the issue will be to manage.

Characteristics of the Issue

Having answered the questions related to ownership and shared responsibility, the organization must next ask *What is the probability that the issue could have a significant impact on the organization?* The limited resources of the organization translate into a necessity to address some issues through monitoring and communication activities and to ignore other issues. From the relevant environment, the organization seeks to identify its most critical issues—those with the potential to affect its bottom line or even its survival (Lauzen, 1995). The organization must address these issues in a direct, transparent way. Many organizations establish criteria for identifying the potential impact of issues on the organization. Xerox, for example, reported using the following classification scheme (Brown, 1970, p. 33):

High priority—"Those issues on which we need to be well-informed in order to provide knowledgeable counsel or take specific action"

Nice to know—"Those issues which are interesting but neither critical nor urgent enough to warrant spending a disproportionate amount of time and resources on"

Questionable—"Those unidentified or unframed issues that will become important as soon as something happens or somebody elevates them"

Likewise, PPG Industries classified issues according to their potential impact (Brown, 1970, p. 33):

Priority A—"Issue is of such critical impact on PPG as to warrant executive management action, including periodic review of the issue and personal participation in implementing plans to manage the issue"

TABLE 12.1 Calculating Issue Priority

Issue	Impact (1-10)	Probability of Occurrence	Impact × Probability	Ranking of Issue
A	8.8	0.3	2.64	4
B	6.7	0.7	4.69	1
C	4.4	0.9	3.96	2
D	3.8	0.8	3.04	3
E	2.1	0.5	1.05	5

SOURCE: Reprinted with permission from Ferguson (1994, p. 57).

Priority B—"Issue is of such critical impact on PPG as to warrant division general manager or staff department executive involvement"

Priority C—"Issue has potential impact so as to warrant government and public affairs department surveillance, assessment, and reporting"

Some analysts assign weights to the impact and probability of occurrence of issues. They rate issues such as A, B, C, D, and E on a scale of 1 to 10 in terms of probable impact on the organization. After attaining a score for each issue, they rate the likelihood (on a scale of 0.0 to 1.0) that the scenario will materialize. To obtain an overall ranking for the issue, they multiply the predicted impact of the issue by the probability of occurrence. Impact can relate to bottom line, image, or internal morale (Meng, 1992). Table 12.1 illustrates this kind of calculation. To add a time factor into these considerations, the analyst adds another column to the tabulation and assigns a weight to alternative dates on which issues might have an impact. Earlier dates have a greater weight. Analysts consult with others to classify issues.

Such formulas can be problematic, however, because criteria for determining impact are difficult to specify. Moreover, a relatively low-impact issue with a high probability of occurrence could conceivably be weighted the same as a medium-impact issue with a moderate probability of occurrence or a high-impact issue with a low probability of occurrence. No matter how high the likelihood of occurrence, a low-impact issue may be of limited interest to the organization. A high-impact issue with low probability of occurrence, however, may have such potentially serious ramifications that the organization cannot ignore the threat. Assume that an environmental agency wants to determine the comparative ranking of three potential issues: elimination of parking spaces for long-term employees, a shooting incident by a disgruntled employee, and a pollution issue. The parking issue has a high probability of occurrence (0.8) but the decision is likely to have a low impact on the organization (2.0). The shooting incident has a low probability of occurrence (0.2) but an extremely high impact (8.0). The pollution issue has a moderate chance of occurrence (0.4) and a medium impact (4.0). All three issues rank at approximately the same level, despite the widely varying profiles of the issues.

The following discussion provides a basis for analyzing characteristics of issues in a more qualitative fashion. Factors considered are genealogy and family ties, salience, value potency, maturity, likely life span, reproductive capability, and field of influence (Ferguson, 1994).

Genealogy and Family Ties

Understanding the history of an issue—its roots, linkages to other issues, and the debates surrounding the issue—can be important. Some issues, especially religious and sovereignty questions (e.g., the conflicts in Northern Ireland, the Middle East, and Eastern Europe), have a long and checkered history. Others (e.g., debates over capital punishment, gun control, and abortion) have dominated the American issue landscape during the past century. Still other issues have a comparatively brief, but sometimes highly emotional, history. Privacy issues surrounding the information highway have emerged only during the past decade, as have issues related to cloning and advanced biogenetic engineering. Some issues have ties to others in the same family of issues. Privacy concerns are in the same handbag as freedom to information, and cloning is in the same family of issues as many other biogenetic engineering issues.

Salience

Salience has to do with the visibility of an issue. Issues such as abortion maintain a fairly high level of activity over time. Other issues emerge only briefly and under certain conditions. For example, the issue of homelessness appears and disappears from the media agenda. It wanes and then reemerges after an unpredictable length of time (Musto, 1993). What kinds of activities tend to push more passive, inactive issues such as homelessness into moments of prominence? Events such as the death of a homeless person on a city street can drive an issue. Celebrities or elite personalities can propel an issue into prominence. For example, the appearance of Melanie Griffith at a food bank, tears in her eyes and arms laden with groceries, has inevitable media appeal. The issue of homelessness received a temporary boost when Prince Charles arranged to meet a former schoolmate, now homeless, at a shelter. Advocacy groups can push the issues to the front page, and systemic influences can also drive media coverage. For example, press on South African apartheid issues achieved a high level of predictability for many years, with annual flurries of media coverage marking the anniversary of the Soweto uprising, Mandela's birthday, commonwealth meetings, and human rights events. Similarly, legal issues wend their way through the system in a time-ordered way. An analyst can forecast their appearance at certain times—pretrial hearing, trial, sentencing, and appeals. An analyst can create activity calendars. Understanding the rise and fall of issues on the media agenda can be important to the public relations practitioner (Dyer, 1996).

Value Potency

Important values are at the heart of the most threatening issues. Pension and employment issues, employee safety, and quality-of-life work programs connect with values such as material comfort, the work ethic, consideration of others, and worth of the individual. When companies engage in insider trading, they violate the value of honesty. When businessmen take more than their due in profits, they trespass against the values of social responsibility and generosity.

Some issues connect more closely to first-order values than others. Corporate and political campaigns tend to use family values as an "organizing concept" (Reid, 1988, p. 138). The abortion issue is so value laden that public figures regard it as an issue to avoid. Pro-life groups identify the abortion issue with the first-order value of right to life, whereas pro-choice groups tie the issue to individual determinism. Because right to life has a higher ordering than individual determinism on the absolute scale of priorities, the task of the pro-choice groups is more difficult. Even in cultures that place a strong emphasis on individual determinism, pro-choice groups find their attempts to persuade easier when they are able to relate the rights of the woman to life-and-death concerns. For this reason, some pro-choice groups put images of coat hangers on T-shirts to remind women that the abortion issue is not just about the lives of unborn children. In this way, they appeal to a higher-order value than simply the right to self-determination. Similarly, when activist groups argue against corporate positions on environmental issues such as toxic waste and protection of the ozone layer, they connect their arguments with right-to-life concerns, quality-of-life concerns, and social responsibility. This focus on first- and second-order values is a change from the 1970s, when environmental campaigns used the slogan "Keep America Beautiful." Lady Byrd Johnson appealed to the lower-order values of cleanliness and beauty. Some issues connect indirectly to a first-order value through a series of associated connections. For example, women in conflict with the law may connect justice issues with core family values.

Maturity of the Issue

In general, decision makers have little interest in fledgling issues. Until an advocacy group adopts an issue or the media or general public take an interest in the issue, top-level executives and politicians will not pay much attention to the issue. Therefore, strategic planners track the progress of the issue through the public policy cycle. They assume that the more advanced the issue on the public policy continuum, the higher the likelihood that the issue will have garnered support and the lower the likelihood that the organization will be able to influence its future development (Getz, 1991). The most common stages through which an issue progresses are as follows (Ferguson, 1994):

Emergence phase. A gap between organizational performance and public expectations generates visible public discontent. People begin to discuss the issue and form opinions on the topic. These opinions surface in informal conversations and less mainstream media (e.g., community newspapers, association meetings, and alternative and ethnic media) and sometimes in radio talk shows or television documentaries, movies, and sit-coms. Business firms and government departments begin to show interest in issues that relate to their jurisdiction. References to the issues appear occasionally in speeches and statements to the press. Policymakers are most likely to have a knowledge gap on issues that are narrow in focus, complex, political in nature, and just beginning their journey on the policy continuum.

Organizational phase. At some point, people with common attitudes and opinions form activist groups to promote their point of view. Their representatives begin to organize petitions and lobby legislators for action on the issue. This quest for media coverage becomes more strategic than at earlier stages of protest. Some interest groups become part of broader social movements that seek to effect systemic changes. For example, human rights activists, arguing against government support for the East Timor regime, eventually joined forces with environmentalists, who had other complaints. The environmentalists had more money, organizational capabilities, and influence than the human rights activists. Joining the two causes was a sensible action.

Legislative phase. Formal negotiations begin. One or more politicians adopt the group's issue and introduce it into the formal policy process. Now on the public policy agenda, the issue enters a new stage in its development. Groups with opposing points of view become more vocal as the legislative phase proceeds. At the same time, the media places the issue higher on its agenda. Legislators accord more prominence to the issue in speeches and press conferences.

Implementation phase. Finally, the government oversees the implementation of the new rules and policies. Negotiations take place between government and business regarding enforcement standards and timetables, sometimes making this final stage adversarial in character.

Issues progress at different rates through the public policy cycle. Some explode into full-blown crises that do not follow the normal issue-development cycle. For example, the bombing of the Pan American aircraft over Lockerbie, Scotland, the tragic deaths of American astronauts aboard the *Challenger* spacecraft, and the Swissair and TWA crashes created issues that demanded immediate attention. Sometimes, issues progress to later stages of the public policy cycle, then encounter resistance, endure attacks by opposition forces, suffer defeat, or lose some of their momentum and return to an earlier stage to begin the cycle again. Identifying an issue's position on the public policy continuum enables planners to identify the maturity of the issue and, by extension, its status as a potential threat to the organization.

Reproductive Capabilities

Issues sometimes spawn new issues that assume an independent life. For example, the issue of clean water can stimulate a new or renewed debate over the use of chlorine to kill bacteria, the dangers of acid rain, the practices of environmental polluters, appropriate penalties for offenders, the role of government in protecting the environment, the difficulties of preserving the health of urban dwellers, the cost of new water purification systems, or a host of other issues. A debate over whether rehabilitation works can raise issues related to the comforts of life in prison, the economic viability of the current prison system, or the merits of treating native offenders in a different manner from others (e.g., healing lodges for native offenders). Also, the treatment of bears and elephants in circuses may lead to discussion over whether individuals should be able to purchase wild animals as pets, the sale of animal organs for transplants, or the endangerment of elephants in some developing countries. Sometimes, a single incident that receives publicity can motivate a larger public discussion on issues that may not have come to the public's attention for some time. The death of Diana, Princess of Wales, stimulated renewed public debate over the place of the monarchy in modern British society—a debate that ultimately motivated Queen Elizabeth and Prince Charles to find new and unfamiliar ways of interacting with people. In the year following Diana's untimely death, Queen Elizabeth was photographed chatting with a pink-haired rock singer who has an earring in her nose. Such a photography opportunity would have been rejected, with vigorous protest, a year earlier. Prince Charles took his sons to a Vancouver high school, where young girls swooned openly over Prince William, and the boys accepted T-shirts and other favors from their young hosts. The death of Diana was not the first event to stimulate agitated public discussion over the role of the monarchy. The burning of Windsor castle, a few years earlier, had less emotional content but raised equally serious issues: the question of whether British royals should pay taxes and foot the bill for restoration of Windsor castle. Some issues have the potential to create many spin-off issues.

Field of Influence

The term *field of influence* refers to both the range of the issue's influence and the linkages between issues (Ferguson, 1994). The range of an issue refers to the geographical areas in which the issue has generated notice. That is, is the issue of local, state, regional, national, or international interest? Planners tailor their communication strategies for specific audiences. Second, with what other issues does the issue interact? Ecological issues are inevitably played against economic issues, native rights issues, and many other areas of public concern. When wildlife conservationists try to enforce laws against poaching in developing countries or Greenpeace tries to thwart the seal hunt in Newfoundland, they address cultural, economic, and sovereignty issues that reach far beyond the ecological. The issue of gun control interacts with the debate over the right of government to intervene in the affairs of private citizens, and the issue of capital punishment plays into the larger debate over government's inability to control crime levels in America. Euthanasia issues interact with AIDS and abortion issues. In Western countries, campaigns for CFC-free products now have a high level of public acceptance, but when moved into the international arena, the issue interacts with unemployment and economic issues.

Longevity

Some issues persist for long periods of time. Others have a fleeting, but sometimes electric, history. Yeric and Todd (1989) speak of transitory issues that capture the headlines but have little lasting impact. The longevity of an issue is determined by the following influences (Ferguson, 1994):

- The seeming inability of competing parties to reach a workable compromise can keep an issue alive indefinitely.

- The sensational content of an issue (i.e., its potential to be dramatized) can sustain an issue for long periods of time.

- The attractiveness of an issue to opposition stakeholders can keep the issue indefinitely before the public.

- Interest groups may find it useful to keep a specific issue alive because other issues in which they have a larger stake depend on the issue for enhanced visibility.

- Issues with strong value potency can persist for indefinite periods of time.

The salience of an issue (discussed earlier) is not necessarily an indicator of the issue's longevity. Issues such as capital punishment maintain a low profile over time but never disappear from the issue landscape. Other issues are nothing more than a blip on the radar screen.

Controllability of the Issue

Chase (1984) discussed the importance of considering the controllability of issues. Controlling the development of an issue implies the possibility of negotiating changes in people's attitudes and stances on the issues. The more salient the issue, however, the more difficult it is to negotiate changes in public attitudes. An issue that receives much media attention will be more difficult to manage because compromises require public shifts on the part of parties with opposing points of view. In a society that values strength of conviction, those who appear to waver in conviction can suffer long-term damage to image. Rather than appearing flexible, moderate, and open to new points of view, the individual or organization that effects a public shift in position is labeled "weak-kneed," "wishy-washy," or "indecisive." They are said to "flip-flop" on issues. Former President Reagan once indicated that he would rather be perceived as wrong than weak (Jamieson & Campbell,

1988). Also, the more prominent the issue, the greater the number of different viewpoints on the issue and the more complex the process of achieving consensus.

The More Central the Beliefs Housed in the Issue, the More Difficult It Is to Effect Changes in Position on the Issue

The ability to control an issue implies the ability to influence public opinion. Central beliefs will be more resistant to change, and attitudes on issues connected to these central beliefs will tend to resist manipulation. See Chapter 7 for further discussion of this point.

The Larger the Field of Influence, the Less Controllable the Issue

It can be argued that local issues are more controllable than state issues, state issues are more controllable than national issues, and national issues are more controllable than international issues. Beck (as quoted in Yeric & Todd, 1983) found that no state issues garnered the same attention as national issues: "It seems safe to conclude, therefore, that state public opinion involves a much smaller segment of the citizenry than does national public opinion" (p. 198). The extension of an issue's field of influence into other issue zones can also complicate the issue management process. The larger the array of issues to be considered, the higher the likelihood that the issues will connect with diverse (and often conflicting) belief systems. The possibility that some of these beliefs will have connections with more centrally placed beliefs also grows in likelihood.

The Greater the Number of Dimensions to the Issue (Social, Political, Technological, Economic, and Legal), the Less Controllable Is the Issue

Investment issues, for example, have strong economic and legal dimensions, but unless the investment issues take on social and political aspects (e.g., the Japanese purchase extensive agricultural holdings in the United States), the issues will not be so difficult to manage. The potency of environmental issues grows partially out of the multiple dimensions of such issues, which activate a plethora of concerns that touch almost every area of our lives.

The More an Issue Is Event-Driven, the Less Controllable the Issue

Managing an issue implies being able to plan ahead—to predict the time at which the issue will impact. The events that serve to activate many issues, however, are difficult to foresee (e.g., terrorist attacks and shooting sprees at elementary schools). Although the initial events are not predictable, the follow-up stages are predictable (trial and sentencing of offenders). The most highly erratic issues, not unexpectedly, relate to health and environmental concerns.

The Greater the Power Capability of the Stakeholders That Oppose an Organizational Stance, the Less Controllable the Issue

The term *power capability* refers to the property of an individual or group that enables the party to be politically influential (Adams, 1967). To be taken seriously, an individual or group must be able to demonstrate a viable power capability. The power capability of stakeholders can be derived from budget, membership, paid staff, or volume of business conducted. Resources can translate into more consultants, staff, and media opportunities (Davis, 1995). Not everyone's opinion exerts the same influence in the policy process. Some opinions (e.g., the views of experts) count more than others (Yankelovich, 1991). To assess the power capability of the opposition stakeholder, the organization must ask whether the interest group is *institutionalized* (a large relatively stable membership and long-standing informal access to government), *quasi-institutionalized* (a shorter collective history and more formal relationship to government), or *emergent* (membership that does not have a coherent articulated structure or well-defined political influence). Institutionalized groups have a greater power capability than quasi-institutionalized, and quasi-institutionalized groups have a greater capability than emergent groups to mount a threat. Organizations such as the Media Research and Action Project assist marginalized groups to use news as a political resource (Ryan, Carragee, & Schwerner, 1998).

Within a North American context, access to the media is one of the strongest capabilities of which an advocacy group can boast. Media access can make the weakest of adversaries powerful. By mobilizing others with similar complaints to place pressure on their local authorities or political representatives, a single broadcast can have a substantial impact on public opinion. Investigatory television shows often champion the rights of those least able to defend themselves. As discussed earlier, access to the media can be derived from one of many different influences: newsworthiness of the issue, newsworthiness of stakeholders in the issue, popular support for the advocacy position, economic resources of stakeholders, and technical skills. The presence of any one of these factors can overcome other organizational weaknesses, such as size, levels of funding, and staffing shortages.

Some issues have inherent media appeal—for example, the endangerment of dolphins, the plight of children in developing countries, and the criminal activities of the "travelers" (an eccentric Irish community in Murphy, South Carolina, inhabited by people who allegedly have made their living for more than a century by traveling around the United States committing fraud and scams). Groups associated with these issues have a natural ability to access the media. The newsworthiness of stakeholders also increases the chances that an issue will receive media attention. The causes of Jane Fonda, Jack Nicholson, and Elizabeth Taylor can easily gain visibility in the media. Meryl Streep's efforts to pressure Alar to withdraw a pesticide from the market kept the issue of food safety on the front pages for weeks and "sent waves through the business community" (Rose, 1991, p. 29). Large grassroots membership can also constitute a power capability for advocacy groups. Other groups are well funded, with professional staffs that include attorneys, public relations and issue specialists, and lobbyists. A power capability, based on financial assets, commands the attention of the establishment in the same way as newsworthiness or celebrity and popular support: "Resource-rich sources enjoy certain advantages that place them in a much stronger position to bargain with reporters and to manage the news than resource-poor groups" (Goldenberg, 1975, p. 145). For those without money, more than 30 centers in the United States provide the technical skills that activists require to challenge the system. The Midwest Academy claims to have trained more than 20,000 people in more than 900 organizations (Pattakos, 1992).

The credibility of stakeholders can also influence the level of controllability of an issue. The higher the level of credibility of the opposition stakeholders, the more substantial the threat. Many advocacy groups have learned how to make the system work for them: "Ralph Nader and other public interest lawyers have become respected celebrities, often interviewed for response statements, photographed in suits and ties and sitting squarely behind desks or in front of bookshelves, embodying solid expertise and mainstream reliability" (Gitlin, 1980, p. 284). Television recently featured the rise through politics of Al Gore, from his days as a congressman arguing for action on the "Greenhouse effect" to his current tenure as vice president. The documentary discussed the difference in credibility that Gore brought to this cause in the 1980s as opposed to the present day. Credibility depends on factors such as the status of the individual, expertise, sociability, dynamism or extroversion, trustworthiness, similarity, and composure. (See Chapter 8 for a detailed discussion of these factors.) Classical studies in communication have demonstrated that credibility has an effect on relatively mundane, nonpolitical decisions that we make in our everyday life (e.g., whether to follow someone across the street against a red light) and on political decisions (whether to accept the point of view of a speaker or vote for a particular candidate) (Lefkowitz, Blake, & Mouton, 1955).

Conversely, the weaker the power capability and credibility of the organization, the less controllable the issue. Strategic planners must ask the following: What is the power capability of the organization to manage a particular issue? In terms of human resources? Financial resources? Levels of access to the media? Public or interest group support? Capacity to organize the support? (Ferguson, 1994). The same factors that constitute a power capability for the opposition group can be a power capability for the organization.

The Greater the Number of Stakeholders in the Issue, the Less Controllable the Issue

When the responsibility for managing an issue is shared, involving more than one business or government department, the problems in reconciling the interests of the different parties grow in magnitude. The necessity to assign accountability brings different organizations or units into conflict. Members of these organizations can interpret the same issue in different ways, depending on their individual perspectives and personal commitments. The negotiations surrounding the North American Free Trade Agreement illustrate this point. Prior to the onset of free trade negotiations, the government could assure logging and other interests that it would place their interests first. Once the negotiations were in progress, however, the administration had to be more discrete in its assurances. At the same time that the government had the ongoing responsibility to assure its commercial stakeholders that their concerns were high on its agenda, the negotiating team also had to assure Mexicans and Canadians that the team was negotiating in good faith, placing the mutual concerns of the three countries first on the agenda.

Much of the current difficulty in managing issues arises from the number of single-issue groups that coalesce around the groups or persons who adopt their issue (Badaracco, 1992). Yeric and Todd (1989) observed the following:

> There are increasing signs that the American political system has indeed broken down into narrowly focused publics. Providing evidence of this trend is the growth of single-issue groups known as *political action committees* (PACs). Unlike interest groups, which traditionally have been partners in the political system with the political parties, these groups have a narrow focus. Each one is engaged in projecting *its* issue and *its* concern as the most important of the day: The task of the PAC is to mold opinion in its favor. PACs direct their attention to policymakers at all levels of government; in 1985 there were over 14,000 officially registered national PACs. . . . Single-issue politics makes the decision maker's job more difficult because the citizens' use of selective perception allows them to choose the "most important" issue without having to compromise, bargain, or negotiate with other groups. (p. 237)

The More Polarized the Stakeholders, the Less Controllable the Issue

In instances in which large numbers of the population have aligned themselves on opposite ends of a continuum on a specific issue, as has occurred with issues related to abortion and capital punishment, the people responsible for managing the issue will find their task a difficult one. Those who are most susceptible to persuasion are the stakeholders with moderate views—the undecided. It is unlikely that those strongly for or against will change their attitudes. If the information does not fit well within their existing value system, individuals will filter out or distort the information. Saul Alinsky (as quoted in Pattakos, 1992), admonished would-be activists: "Pick the target, personalize it, and polarize it" (p. 114).

Heath (1988) noted,

> A successful communication campaign begins by being part of effective strategic planning to consider which policy issues will yield to communication efforts and which ones will not. Because of the hostility and rigidity of opinions surrounding some issues, some communication efforts will not succeed and therefore are not cost-effective. The planning process must consider when it is

better to change company mission, philosophy, or operations than to wage a
communication campaign. (p. 171)

Before an organization rejects an issue as "strategically uncontrollable," the
issues management team should ask whether there are "other stakeholders
(suppliers, customers, or potential sources of new products) whose mutual
interest and participation could make an issue controllable" (Stoffels, 1982,
p. 11). Also, some elements of an issue may be controllable, whereas others
are not.

Helping the Public to Reach
Social Judgment on Issues

According to Yankelovich (1991), an individual moves through three stages
in reaching what he terms "public judgment" on an issue. Stage 1 involves
responding to consciousness-raising activities that create awareness and
concern. The public learns about the issue, attaches meaning to information
received about the issue, and develops a readiness to respond. The media
drives this stage. Sometimes, Stage 1 develops very slowly, but at other times
events (e.g., the drug-related death of a rock star, poor scores by American
students on achievement tests, or a flagging economy) expedite the consciousness-raising process. To encourage people to reach public judgment
on issues, the media must offer a range of choices to the public at the
consciousness-raising stage.

At Stage 2, the individual confronts the need for change—a change in
attitudes or behavior. The person must become actively involved, on an
internal level, in accepting the need to change. Whereas the media can
facilitate and hasten the consciousness-raising stage, the time required for
"working through" depends on the emotional significance of the anticipated
change to the person. Some issues require minutes to work through; others
require centuries, as conflicts in the Middle East, Northern Ireland, and North
Africa demonstrate. Facilitating public judgment on such contentious issues
can be extremely difficult, and often policymakers choose to deal with other
elite experts instead of the general public. An effective consciousness-raising
stage can expedite the working-through stage, whereby audiences come to
accept the need for attitudinal or behavioral changes. In the case of AIDS,
the media have presented the public with many agonizingly difficult choices
related to distribution of needles and condoms, testing in the workplace, and

insurance costs. The public is currently enmeshed in trying to work through these options and make decisions. The media facilitate such a task when they present the available choices, identify their likely consequences, and keep the issue on the media agenda sufficiently long for the public to understand the options. Jumping from one issue to another confounds the public's efforts to reach judgment on the issues.

Achieving resolution at Stage 3 may require negotiation, compromise, and the acceptance of majority opinion. To reach resolution on a personal level, an individual must recognize where he or she stands "cognitively, emotionally, and morally" on an issue (Yankelovich, 1991, p. 65). Cognitive resolution entails clarifying thinking, reconciling inconsistencies, recognizing the relationship between different aspects of issues, and understanding the likely consequences of different choices. Emotional resolution implies confronting ambivalent feelings, accommodating unwelcome realities, and reconciling strongly held values in conflict. Moral resolution means putting ethical obligations ahead of personal needs and wishes. At this point, the individual will have come to "public judgment."

Yankelovich (1991) proposed the following guidelines for leaders who want to encourage "considered judgments"—that is, "stable, coherent, and responsible judgments on issues" (p. 160):

1. Identify and address the public's "starting point."
2. Do not rely on experts to present issues to the public; they speak a different language (full of jargon and bureaucratese).
3. Identify and address the public's pet preoccupations before considering any other facets of the issue.
4. Let the public know that someone is listening—and cares.
5. Limit the number of issues to which people must attend to no more than two or three.
6. Give people choices to consider.
7. Highlight the value components in choices.
8. Help the public to move beyond the "say-yes-to-everything" form of procrastination.
9. When two conflicting values reside in an issue, try to preserve some element of each value in the proposed solution to the problem.
10. Allow sufficient time for the public to work through an issue and reach public judgment.

Conclusion

To survive and succeed, organizations must manage their critical policy issues. The strategic communication plan includes an issues management component, which identifies priority issues. Also, communicators write support plans for the management of many different individual issues. Strategic approaches to issues management emerge from an understanding of the variables discussed in this chapter: questions of ownership, the impact of the issue on the organization, the organization's power to control and defuse the threat, and ways to help the public to reach social judgment on issues.

13

Planning Cooperative Strategies

Partnering, Consulting, and Negotiating

English author Samuel Johnson once observed, "Marriage has many pains, but celibacy has no pleasures." Despite the difficulties and pains of partnerships, many organizations have decided that it is far worse to "go it alone" in today's environment. Terms such as strategic alliances, joint ventures, partnerships, mergers, acquisitions, boundaryless and borderless organizations, and integrated marketing communications pepper the current literature. Whereas organizations once preserved their place among competitors by guarding information and following a policy of containment, many now attain their competitive edge by sharing resources, combining assets, and partnering on projects of mutual interest. Business, industry, governments, voluntary organizations, and universities are combining resources to accomplish together what they can no longer do on their own. Advertising, public relations, and marketing executives are consulting and cooperating. As Woodrow Wilson, 28th president of the United States, once observed, "We should not only use all the brains we have, but all that we can borrow." Trends toward partnering and sharing of resources and the implications of these trends for communication strategies are examined in this chapter.

Trends Toward Partnering
and Sharing of Resources

Within the business world, an increasing number of organizations have substituted horizontal networks (technology-sharing, ownership, and development networks) for vertical hierarchies. Multifunctional work teams and partnerships composed of customers, suppliers, and even competitors are commonplace in leading-edge organizations. In 1997, two studios collaborated to produce *Titanic*. MGM recently partnered with the catalog division of Neiman Marcus to market its clothing line. In 1998, Chrysler and GM pooled their resources to produce and market an electric bicycle. Delta and Continental buy seats on each others' flights in markets unable to support the operation of more than one airline. The New Breton Corporation (Nova Scotia, Canada) engages in a yearly planning exercise that is public. Any interested party can attend the meeting at which annual corporate goals and preferred means to achieve those goals are determined. In the automobile industry, the "big three" American manufacturers have established supply alliances with their Japanese counterparts—GM with Isuzu, Ford with Mazda and Nissan, and Chrysler with Mitsubishi. Many major firms view themselves as a "web of subcontractors" (Peters, 1990, pp. 13, 16). Business and government are joining forces to address concerns that span the public and private sector (e.g., drugs in the workplace, housing for seniors, environmental programs, and products and services for disabled individuals). Health Canada partnered with more than 40 private and voluntary sector organizations in its "Really Me" antidrug campaign, and the "Just Say No" campaign in the United States generated similar partnerships. Some organizations have optimized scarce resources by integrating the efforts of their promotional, marketing communications, and advertising departments. Accordingly, a new area of studies has emerged called integrated marketing communications (IMC). Programs in IMC introduce students to business, communication, and marketing concepts so that they are prepared to cross functional lines in the organization.

Companies are increasingly going outside their organizational boundaries to get specialized expertise, add people in peak periods, and obtain fresh views. Alliance partners, consultants, third-party contractors, and freelance firms complement the internal resources of organizations (Sonnenberg, 1992). All the previous efforts represent a trend toward creating organizations without boundaries or walls. One of the best examples to illustrate the concept of the boundaryless organization is Galoob Toys, a San Francisco firm that employs 115 people. Its business is built on relationships: "It farms out manufacturing and packaging to a dozen contractors, uses outside distributors without ever taking delivery from the manufacturers, and sells its accounts deliverables to a manufacturing company" (Keen, 1991, p. 6). Such transactional processes alter the concept of "organization." At one time, an organization was the place at which communications were most concentrated (e.g., within the confines of a building or a plant). This sort of distinction no longer applies. For example, the travel agent who books hotels, car rentals, insurance policies, and sight-seeing tours for customers interacts far more frequently with employees of other organizations and with customers than with other agency workers. Similarly, companies such as MCI are nothing more than networks and switchboards—quasi-firms born out of electronic linkages that tightly couple the operations of the "metabusinesses." In such situations, as in so many others, it is almost impossible to determine where the boundary of one organization ends and the next begins (Ferguson & Ferguson, 1988).

For a partnership or an alliance to work, organizational members must have compatible objectives and perceive complementary needs. Moreover, they must be willing to share risks (Lewis, 1990). Cooperation rather than competition characterizes successful partnerships. The old approaches to controlling and owning information no longer apply, and many have discovered that the best way to compete may be to understand and work with the organization's many constituencies—competitors, clients and customers, suppliers, all levels of government, and other stakeholders. Increasingly, information has become a shared commodity, leaky and difficult to contain; and organizations that fail to make the adjustment to this new sharing environment face the possibility of extinction or, in the case of government, rejection (Cleveland, 1985). Most progressive organizations have decided that "cocooning" is an inappropriate response to the demands of a global information society (Ferguson, 1994).

Building Consultation Strategies Into One's Plan

Consultative strategies imply the need to reach out to partners and constituencies, to initiate discussions, and to build coalitions. Whereas negotiation places an emphasis on mutual persuasion processes, consultation focuses on involvement in decision-making processes. Appropriate levels of consulta-

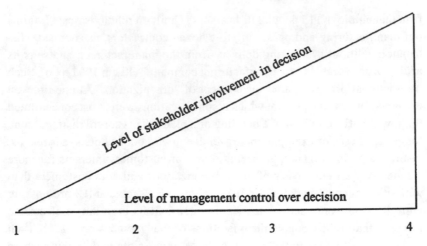

1. Management makes decision and acts on it.
2. Management seeks input from stakeholders, makes decision, and acts on it.
3. Management consults with stakeholdrs and acts on joint decision.
4. Mnagement seeks instruction on course of action from stakeholders and acts on their instructions.

Figure 13.1. Stakeholder Involvement Continuum

SOURCE: Reproduced with permission from Ferguson, 1998a, p. 203, Copyright © 1998 by the International Communication Association.

tion can help to eliminate the need for negotiation (i.e., resolution of conflicts). An increasing number of public, private, and nonprofit organizations have accepted the importance of consultation. In recent years, many have built consultation strategies into their communication plans.

Consultation methods can range from formal written submissions and public hearings to more interactive measures, such as workshops and advisory committees. A characterizing feature of consultation is that the ultimate decision on how much power to hand over to stakeholders remains with the decision maker. Figure 13.1, which draws its logic from Tannenbaum and Schmidt (1958), presents a normative model of consultation that suggests the range of possibilities for stakeholder involvement in organizational decision making. The model assumes the existence of an organizational culture that places a value on appropriate levels of stakeholder participation in decision-making processes.

Management's decision to consult or not to consult will depend on situational, organizational, and stakeholder variables. Situational variables include the nature of the problem (e.g., a threat to the safety of the population) and perceived level of urgency (the immediacy of the threat). Organizational variables include the availability of resources (human and financial) and the will to carry out the consultation process. Consulting with large numbers of stakeholders is a costly and time-consuming process, unlikely to be undertaken on low-impact issues or decisions of a minor nature. Stakeholder interest in, knowledge of, and support for the issues are other significant factors. It could be speculated that issues that rank high on the private agendas of stakeholders (e.g., health care or pensions) necessitate higher levels of consultation than issues that are low on private agendas. Moreover, consulting the general public on highly technical issues (e.g., trade initiatives) is often inappropriate. Finally, a popular initiative requires less consultation than a more controversial one.

At Position 1 on the stakeholder involvement continuum, management makes a unilateral decision and acts on it. In crisis situations, public relations and legal advisers often encourage an immediate management response, reserving the right to consult at a later point in time. At the other extreme, minimal or no consultation can also be appropriate for many types of routine decisions in which stakeholders have low levels of interest. In crisis situations, organizations may limit their internal consultation process to upper management, legal advisers, high-level public relations advisers, and scientific or technical experts (as required).

At Position 2 on the stakeholder involvement continuum, management invites stakeholder input before deciding on a course of action. Management has the option of limiting consultations to elite opinion leaders or experts on the topic or engaging larger numbers of stakeholders. Although the general public may not have the knowledge to contribute a viewpoint on highly technical matters, interest groups or professional organizations may have gathered large amounts of information on the topic. Organizations tend to assume a Position 2 stance when (a) they do not perceive the need for immediate action or (b) they want to buy time to work out an acceptable course of action. The suggestion box and the restaurant questionnaire offer vehicles for leisurely change and good customer relations. Governments, however, often establish commissions of inquiry to buy time to develop policy. In such a way, they demonstrate a commitment to act but postpone binding decisions to a later date.

A Position 3 approach suggests that management perceives the issue to be sufficiently salient to warrant larger scale involvement of stakeholders. For example, a state government decides to consult with seniors on decisions related to subsidized housing. The bureaucracy commits itself to arriving at a mutually agreeable solution through processes of consultation with opinion leaders and the general population of stakeholders. Partnering contracts sometimes result from such consultations. At Position 3, management grants stakeholders a higher level of decision-making power than they accord at Position 1 or Position 2 on the continuum. Position 4 implies that the organization has granted full decision-making power to stakeholders. Governments that call for a referendum or plebiscite assume this position. Private sector organizations rarely move to Position 4 on the stakeholder involvement continuum.

A contingency approach to stakeholder involvement assumes that no one option or position on the continuum is appropriate all the time—a stance that would be credible to public relations practitioners. Many different variables (organizational, stakeholder, and situational) influence decisions on when and how much to involve stakeholders. No one position holds inherent merit over the others; for example, no one would suggest that we should turn decisions on criminal law over to the most obvious stakeholders—the criminals. Arkin (1992) cautions that advocacy groups should be "distant partners" in a public information campaign. She notes that these groups can advance an issue through creating controversy; at some point, however, this function becomes counterproductive. It is the place of program evaluators to judge the appropriateness of positions assumed by the organization. The extent to which public relations specialists participate in the consultation process will vary at different positions on the continuum. They are likely to play an advisory role at all points, however.

Negotiation Strategies

Many believe that organizations should initiate dialogue with publics, build understanding and relationships, and manage conflict—in other words, collaborate and negotiate with publics (Dozier, Grunig, & Grunig, 1995; Plowman et al., 1995; Vasquez, 1996). These representations should enable mutual persuasion processes to occur. According to the negotiation literature, the best solutions are *integrative agreements* (those that reconcile the interests of parties in conflict to achieve high joint benefit) as opposed to *compromise agreements* (characterized by concessions that result in both parties moving to middle ground but with lower joint benefits). Within an organizational context, Serini (1993) concluded that public relations practitioners have the greatest power to effect changes when they have the opportunity, time, and credibility to negotiate. Planning failures stem from a lack of (a) perception of the need to negotiate, (b) ability to negotiate and accommodate diverse interests, (c) sufficient penalties and incentives to be used for that purpose, and (d) trust (Benveniste, 1989). A communication plan specifies requirements for negotiation.

Conclusion

The preceding discussion addressed the dominant characteristic of twentieth-century organizations—the trend toward sharing of resources and cooperative endeavors. Transposed into communication terms, the trend implies public information campaigns that engage grassroots, government, and business organizations in efforts to improve the health and well-being of citizens. It suggests the need to pool resources (advertising, marketing communications, and public relations) and establish opportunities for people with diverse areas of expertise, knowledge, and skills to contribute to the direction of organizations. Finally, the trend implies the importance of planning together to resolve and manage issues that cannot be decided by one organization or one group within the organization.

References

Adams, R. (1967). Political power and social structures. In C. Veliz (Ed.), *The politics of conformity* (pp. 15-42). Oxford, UK: Oxford University Press.

Adler, R. B., & Towne, N. (1990). *Looking out, looking in.* New York: Holt, Rinehart & Winston.

Adorno, T. W., Frenkel-Brunswik, E., Levinson, D. J., & Sanford, R. N. (1950). *The authoritarian personality.* New York: Harper & Brothers.

Alesandrini, K. L. (1983). Strategies that influence memory for advertising communication. In R. J. Harris (Ed.), *Information processing research in advertising* (pp. 65-82). Hillsdale, NJ: Lawrence Erlbaum.

Allport, G. W., Vernon, P. E., & Lindzey, G. (1950). *A study of values: A scale for measuring the dominant interests in personality.* Boston: Houghton Mifflin.

Andrews, J. C., & Shimp, T. P. (1990). Effects of involvement, argument strength, and source characteristics on central and peripheral processing of advertising. *Psychology and Marketing, 7*(3), 195-214.

Andriole, S. J. (1985). Software tools for high order corporate crisis management. In S. J. Andriole (Ed.), *Corporate crisis management* (pp. 259-278). Princeton, NJ: Petrocelli.

Anonymous. (1990, November). *Post-Oka Communications Symposium* [Speech]. Symposium conducted by the Department of National Defence, National Defence Headquarters, Ottawa, Ontario.

Arkin, E. B. (1992). Interview. In T. E. Backer, E. M. Rogers, & P. Sopory (Eds.), *Designing health communication campaigns: What works?* (pp. 36-40). Newbury Park, CA: Sage.

Arnheim, R. (1971). Film and reality. In A. Kirschner & L. Kirschner (Eds.), *Film: Readings in the mass media* (pp. 68-74). New York: Odyssey.

Arnold, W. E., & McCroskey, J. C. (1967). The credibility of reluctant testimony. *Central States Speech Journal, 18*(2), 97-103.

Aronson, E., Turner, J. A., & Carlsmith, J. M. (1963). Communicator credibility and communication discrepancy as determinants of opinion change. *Journal of Abnormal and Social Psychology, 67,* 31-36.

Ashley, W. J. (1992). Interview. In T. E. Backer, E. M. Rogers, & P. Sopory (Eds.), *Designing health communication campaigns: What works?* Newbury Park, CA: Sage.

Atkin, C. K. (1992). Interview. In T. E. Backer, E. M. Rogers, & P. Sopory (Eds.), *Designing health communication campaigns: What works?* (pp. 46-50). New-bury Park, CA: Sage.

Atkinson, M. (1984). *Our master's voices: The language and body language of politics.* London: Methuen.

Atkinson, R. L., Atkinson, R. C., Smith, E. E., & Bem, D. J. (1990). *Introduction to psychology* (10th ed.). San Diego: Harcourt Brace Jovanovich.

Bachand, D. (1988). The marketing of ideas: Advertising and road safety. *International Journal of Research in Marketing, 4*(4), 291-309.

Backer, T. E., Rogers, E. M., & Sopory, P. (Eds.). (1992). *Designing health communication campaigns: What works?* Newbury Park, CA: Sage.

Badaracco, C. (1992). Religious lobbyists in the public square. *Public Relations Quarterly, 37,* 30-36.

Bagdikian, B. H. (1971). *The information machines: Their impact on men and the media.* New York: Harper & Row.

Baggaley, J. P. (1988). Perceived effectiveness of international AIDS campaigns. *Health Education Research, 3,* 7-17.

Baldwin, H. (1989). *How to create effective TV commercials* (2nd ed.). Lincolnwood, IL: National Textbook.

Ball-Rokeach, S. J., Rokeach, M., & Grube, J. W. (1984). *The great American values test.* New York: Free Press.

Bandura, A. (1977). *Social learning theory.* Englewood Cliffs, NJ: Prentice Hall.

Bandura, A. (1994). Social cognitive theory of mass communication. In J. Bryant & D. Zillmann (Eds.), *Media effects: Advances in theory and research.* Hillsdale, NJ: Lawrence Erlbaum.

Barber, J. G., Bradshaw, R., & Walsh, C. (1989). Reducing alcohol consumption through television advertising. *Journal of Consulting and Clinical Psychology, 57,* 613-618.

Batra, R., & Ray, M. L. (1983). Advertising situations: The implications of differential involvement and accompanying affect responses. In R. J. Harris (Ed.), *Information processing research in advertising* (pp. 127-151). Hillsdale, NJ: Lawrence Erlbaum.

Baugniet, R. N. (1984). Crisis communications management: Forewarned is fore-armed. *Emergency Planning Digest, 11*(4), 6-7.

Bauman, K. E., Padgett, C. A., & Koch, G. G. (1989). A media-based campaign to encourage personal communication among adolescents about not smoking cigarettes: Participation, selection and consequences. *Health Education Research, 4,* 35-44.

Bearden, W. O., Netemeyer, R. G., & Mobley, M. F. (1993). *Handbook of marketing scales.* Newbury Park, CA: Sage.

Bennett, W. L. (1996). *News: The politics of illusion* (3rd ed.). White Plains, NY: Longman.

Ben-Sira, Z. (1982). The health promoting function of mass media and reference groups: Motivating or reinforcing of behavior change. *Social Science and Medicine, 16*(7), 825-834.

Benveniste, G. (1989). *Mastering the politics of planning: Crafting credible plans and policies that make a difference.* San Francisco: Jossey-Bass.

Bergeron, P. G. (1989). *Modern management in Canada: Concepts and practices.* Scarborough, ON: Nelson Canada.

Best, J. (1973). *Public opinion: Micro and macro.* Homewood, IL: Dorsey.

Bettinghaus, E. P. (1973). *Persuasive communication* (2nd ed.). New York: Holt, Rinehart & Winston.

Bettinghaus, E. P., and Cody, M. J. (1994). *Persuasive communication* (5th ed.). Fort Worth, TX: Harcourt Brace College.

Bochner, S., & Insko, C. A. (1966). Communicator discrepancy, source credibility, and opinion change. *Journal of Personality and Social Psychology, 4*(6), 614-621.

Boorstin, D. J. (1961). *The image: A guide to pseudo events in America.* New York: Atheneum.

Boster, F. J., & Mongeau, P. (1984). Fear-arousing persuasive messages. In R. N. Bostrom & B. H. Westley (Eds.), *Communication yearbook 8* (pp. 330-375). Beverly Hills, CA: Sage.

Bouchard, A. (1992). Freak explosion jolts Baie des Ha! Ha! *Public Relations Journal, 48*(10), 42-44.

Bransford, J., & McCarrell, N. (1974). A sketch of a cognitive approach to comprehension. In W. B. Weimar & D. S. Palermo (Eds.), *Cognition and the symbolic processes.* Hillsdale, NJ: Lawrence Erlbaum.

Brieger, W. (1990). Mass media and health communication in rural Nigeria. *Health Policy and Planning, 5,* 77-81.

Brockner, J., & Elkind, M. (1985). Self-esteem and reactance: Further evidence of attitudinal and motivational consequences. *Journal of Experimental Social Psychology, 21*(4), 346-361.

Brody, E. W. (1988). *Public relations programming and production.* New York: Praeger.

Brody, E. W., & Stone, G. C. (1989). *Public relations research.* New York: Praeger.

Brooker, R. E., Jr. (1991). Orchestrating the planning process. *Journal of Business Strategy, 12*(4), 4-9.

Broom, G. M., & Dozier, D. M. (1990). *Using research in public relations: Applications to program management.* Englewood Cliffs, NJ: Prentice Hall.

Brown, J. K. (1970). *This business of issues: Coping with the company's environments.* New York: Conference Board.

Brummett, B. (1988). The homology hypothesis: Pornography on the VCR. *Critical Studies in Mass Communication, 5*(3), 202-216.

Bryant, J., Brown, D., Silberberg, A. R., & Elliott, S. M. (1981). Effects of humorous illustrations in college textbooks. *Human Communication Research, 8,* 43-57.

Bryson, J. M. (1988). A strategic planning process for public and non-profit organizations. *Long Range Planning, 21,* 75-81.

Burkhart, P. J., & Reuss, S. (1993). *Successful strategic planning.* Newbury Park, CA: Sage.

Butler, S. D. (1971). *Edwin Edwards: A study in ethos.* Unpublished master's thesis, University of Houston, Houston, TX.

Butler, S. D. (1972). The apologia, 1971 genre. *Southern Speech Communication Journal, 37*(3), 281-289.

Cacioppo, J. T., Petty, R. E., & Morris, K. J. (1983). Effects of need for cognition on message evaluation, recall, and persuasion. *Journal of Personality and Social Psychology, 45*(4), 805-818.

Cain, C. (1986, August 17). Advertisers flock to famous faces. *Sioux Falls Argus Leader,* pp. 1E, 2E.

Cannell, C., & MacDonald, J. (1956). The impact of health news on attitudes and behavior. *Journalism Quarterly, 33,* 315-323.

Casswell, S., Ransom, R., & Gilmore, L. (1990). Evaluation of a mass media campaign for the primary prevention of alcohol-related problems. *Health Promotion International, 5,* 9-17.

Cater, D. (1981). Television and thinking people. In R. P. Adler (Ed.), *Understanding television: Essays on television as a social and political force* (pp. 11-18). New York: Praeger.

Cates, W., Jr., Grimes, D. A., Ory, H. W., & Tyler, C. W., Jr. (1977). Publicity and the public health: The elimination of IUD-related abortion deaths. *Family Planning Perspectives, 9*(3), 138-140.

Cernada, G. P., Darity, W. A., Chen, T. T. L., Winder, A. E., Benn, S., Jackson, R., & Tolbert, J. (1989/1990). Mass media usage among black smokers: A first look. *International Quarterly of Community Health Education, 10*(4), 347-364.

Chase, W. H. (1984). *Issues management: Origins of the future.* Stamford, CT: Issue Action.

Chernow, R. (1998, August 16). First among flacks. In *New York Times Book Review* (p. 5) [Book review of *The father of spin: Edward L. Bernays and the birth of public relations* by L. Tye]. New York: Crown.

Chesebro, J. W. (1984). The media reality: Epistemological functions of media in cultural systems. *Critical Studies in Mass Communication, 1*(2), 111-130.

Childers, T. L., & Houston, M. J. (1984). Conditions for a picture-superiority effect on consumer memory. *Journal of Consumer Research, 11*(2), 643-654.

Churchill, W. (1940, June 4). We shall fight on the beaches [Speech]. In *Complete speeches of Winston Churchill.* http://www.winstonchurchill.org/beaches.htm.

Cleveland, H. (1985). The twilight of hierarchy: Speculations on the global information society. *Public Administration Review, 45,* 185-195.

Cogden, D. (1990, November). *Post-Oka Communications Symposium* [Transcript]. Symposium conducted by the Department of National Defence, National Defence Headquarters, Ottawa, Ontario.

Cohen, B. C. (1963). *The press and foreign policy.* Princeton, NJ: Princeton University Press.

Comstock, G., Chaffee, S., Katzman, N., McCombs, M., & Roberts, D. (1978). *Television and human behavior.* New York: Columbia University Press.

Coombs, W. T., & Holliday, S. J. (1996). Communication and attributions in a crisis: An experimental study in crisis communication. *Journal of Public Relations Research, 8*(4), 279-295.

Cooper, D. A. (1992). CEO must weigh legal and public relations approaches. *Public Relations Journal, 48,* 39-40.

Cope, F., & Richardson, D. (1972). The effects of reassuring recommendations in a fear-arousing speech. *Speech Monographs, 39,* 148-150.

Correctional Services of Canada. (1990, August). *Mission of the Correctional Service of Canada.* Ottawa, Ontario: Minister of Supply and Services Canada.

Cromwell, H. (1950). The relative effect on audience attitude of the first versus the second argumentative speech of a series. *Speech Monographs, 17,* 105-122.

Crouse, T. (1972). *The boys on the bus: Riding with the campaign press corps.* New York: Random House.

Culbertson, H. M. (1994). Working with the press between elections. In G. H. Stempel, III (Ed.), *The practice of political communication* (pp. 117-133). Englewood Cliffs, NJ: Prentice Hall.

Cummings, K. M., Sciandra, R., Davis, S., & Rimer, B. (1989). Response to anti-smoking campaign aimed at mothers with young children. *Health Education Research, 4*(4), 429-437.

Cutlip, S. M., Center, A. H., & Broom, G. M. (1994). *Effective public relations* (7th ed.). Englewood Cliffs, NJ: Prentice Hall.

Davis, S. (1995). The role of communication and symbolism in interest group competition: The case of the Siskiyou national forest, 1983-1992. *Political Communication Journal, 12,* 27-42.

Dayan, D., & Katz, E. (1992). *Media events.* Cambridge, MA: Harvard University Press.

DeFleur, M. L., & Dennis, E. E. (1985). *Understanding mass communication.* Boston: Houghton Mifflin.

DeFoe, J. R., & Breed, W. (1991, August). *Consulting with media for health education: Some new directions.* Paper presented at the annual meeting of the American Psychological Association, San Francisco.

Dewey, J. (1933). *How we think.* Boston: Heath.

Dickinson, R. (1990). Beyond the moral panic: AIDS, the mass media and mass communication research. *Communications, 15*(1/2), 21-36.

Downs, A. (1967). *Inside bureaucracy.* Boston: Little, Brown.

Dozier, D. M., & Ehling, W. P. (1992). Evaluation of public relations programs: What the literature tells us about their effects. In J. E. Grunig (Ed.), *Excellence in public relations and communication management* (pp. 159-184). Hillsdale, NJ: Lawrence Erlbaum.

Dozier, D. M., Grunig, L. A., & Grunig, J. E. (1995). *Manager's guide to excellence in public relations and communication management.* Hillsdale, NJ: Lawrence Erlbaum.

Dozier, D. M., & Repper, F. C. (1992). Research firms and public relations practices. In J. E. Grunig (Ed.), *Excellence in public relations and communication management* (pp. 185-215). Hillsdale, NJ: Lawrence Erlbaum.

Dunwoody, S., & Neuwirth, K. (1988, July). *The impact of information on AIDS risk judgments and behavioral change among young adults.* Paper presented at the annual meeting of the Association for Education in Journalism and Mass Communication, Portland, OR.

Dutton, J. E., Stumpf, S. A., & Wagner, D. (1990). Diagnosing strategic issues and managerial investment of resources. In P. Shrivastava & R. Lam (Eds.), *Advances in strategic management* (Vol. 6, pp. 143-167). Greenwich, CT: JAI.

Dyer, S. C. (1996). Descriptive modeling for public relations scanning: A practitioner's perspective. *Journal of Public Relations Research, 8*(3), 137-150.

Eagley, A. H., Wood, W., & Chaiken, S. (1981). An attribution analysis of persuasion. In J. H. Harvey, W. Ickes, & R. F. Kidd (Eds.), *New directions in attribution research* (Vol. 3, pp. 37-62). Hillsdale, NJ: Lawrence Erlbaum.

Easterlin, R. A., & Crimmins, E. M. (1991). Private materialism, personal self-fulfillment, family life, and public interest: The nature, effects, and causes of recent changes in the values of American youth. *Public Opinion Quarterly, 55*(4), 499-533.

Eco, U. (1976). *A theory of semiotics.* Bloomington: Indiana University Press.

Ehrensberger, R. (1945). An experimental study of the relative effectiveness of certain forms of emphasis on public speaking. *Speech Monographs, 12,* 94-111.

Ettema, J. S., Brown, J. W., & Leupker, R. V. (1983). Knowledge-gap effects in a health information campaign. *Public Opinion Quarterly, 47*(4), 516-527.

Faber, R. J. (1984). The effectiveness of health disclosures within children's television commercials. *Journal of Broadcasting, 28*(4), 463-476.

Fearn-Banks, K. (1996). *Crisis communications: A casebook approach.* Mahwah, NJ: Lawrence Erlbaum.

Ferguson, S. (1989, May). *Presentation to Government of Canada communicators.* Seminar on strategic planning, University of Ottawa, Ottawa, Ontario, Canada.

Ferguson, S., & Ferguson, S. D. (1978). Proxemics and television: The politician's dilemma. *Canadian Journal of Communication, 4*(4), 26-35.

Ferguson, S. D. (1973). A study of the good will speaking of a U.S. congressman. *Southern Speech Communication Journal, 38*(3), 235-243.

Ferguson, S. D. (1988). Advertising effectiveness as a consequence of congruence with information processing models. *Recherches Semiotique/Semiotic Inquiry, 8*(3), 319-337.

Ferguson, S. D. (1993). Strategic planning for issues management: The communicator as environmental analyst. *Canadian Journal of Communication, 18,* 33-50.

Ferguson, S. D. (1994). *Mastering the public opinion challenge.* Burr Ridge, IL: Irwin.

Ferguson, S. D. (1998a). Constructing a theoretical framework for evaluating public relations programs and activities. In M. E. Roloff (Ed.), *Communication yearbook 21* (pp. 190-229). Thousand Oaks, CA: Sage.

Ferguson, S. D. (1998b, May). *Performance indicators in communication.* Presentation to the Conference on Performance Measurement for Government, sponsored by International Quality and Productivity Center, Ottawa, Ontario, Canada.

Ferguson, S. D., & Ferguson, S. (1988). The systems school. In S. D. Ferguson & S. Ferguson (Eds.), *Organizational communication* (pp. 38-60). Rochelle Park, NJ: Transaction Publishing.

Festinger, L. (1957). *A theory of cognitive dissonance.* Stanford, CA: Stanford University Press.

Fine, B. J. (1957). Conclusion-drawing, communicator credibility, and anxiety as factors in opinion change. *Journal of Abnormal and Social Psychology, 54*(4), 369-374.

Fink, S. (1986). *Crisis management: Planning for the inevitable.* New York: American Management Association.

Fiske, J. (1982). *Introduction to communication studies.* London: Methuen.

Flesch, R. (1948). A new readability yardstick. *Journal of Applied Psychology, 32*(2), 221-233.

Flora, J. A., & Maibach, E. W. (1990). Cognitive responses to AIDS information: The effects of issue involvement and message appeal. *Communication Research, 17,* 759-774.

Flynn, B. S., Worden, J. K., Secker-Walker, R. H., Badger, G. J., Geller, B. M., & Costanza, M. C. (1992). Prevention of cigarette smoking through mass media intervention and school programs. *American Journal of Public Health, 82*(6), 827-834.

Forest, D., Clark, M. S., Mills, J., & Isen, A. M. (1979). Helping as a function of feeling state and nature of the helping behavior. *Motivation and Emotion, 3,* 161-169.

Freedman, J. L. (1964). Involvement, discrepancy, and change. *Journal of Abnormal and Social Psychology, 69*(3), 290-295.

Freeman, R. E. (1984). *Strategic management: A stakeholder approach.* Boston: Pitman.

Friedrich, W. N. (1977). Evaluation of a media campaign's effect on reporting patterns of child abuse. *Perceptual and Motor Skills, 45,* 161-162.

Frijda, N. (1988). The laws of emotion. *American Psychologist, 43*(5), 349-358.

Früh, W. (1980). *Lesen, verstehen, urteilen: Untersuchungen über den zusammenhang von textgestaltung.* Freiberg: Verlag Karl Alber.

Fry, E. (1977). Fry's readability graph: Clarifications, validity, and extension to level 17. *Journal of Reading, 21*(3), 242-252.

Garland, K. (1982). The use of short term feedback in the preparation of technical and instructional illustration. In *Research in illustration: Conference proceedings, Part III* (pp. 63-80). Brighton, UK: Brighton Polytechnic.

Garnett, J. L. (1992). *Communicating for results in government: A strategic approach for public managers.* San Francisco: Jossey-Bass.

Garramone, G. M. (1985). Motivation and selective attention to political information formats. *Journalism Quarterly, 62,* 37-44.

Garramone, G. M., Atkin, C. K., Pinkleton, B. E., & Cole, R. T. (1990). Effects of negative political advertising on the political process. *Journal of Broadcasting and Electronic Media, 34*(3), 299-311.

Garramone, G. M., & Smith, S. J. (1984). Reactions to political advertising: Clarifying sponsor effects. *Journalism Quarterly, 61*(4), 771-775.

Getz, K. (1991, August). Selecting corporate political tactics. In J. Wall & L. R. Jauch (Eds.), *Academy of Management best papers* (51st annual meeting, Miami Beach, FL). Briarcliffe Manor, NY: Academy of Management.

Gilkinson, H., Paulson, S. F., & Sikkink, D. E. (1954). Effects of order and authority in an argumentative speech. *Quarterly Journal of Speech, 40*(2), 183-192.

Ginn, R. D. (1989). *Continuity planning: Preventing, surviving and recovering from disaster.* Oxford, UK: Elsevier Advanced Technology.

Gitlin, T. (1980). *The whole world is watching: Mass media in the making of the New Left.* Berkeley: University of California Press.

Goldenberg, E. N. (1975). *Making the papers.* Lexington, MA: D. C. Heath.

Gruner, C. (1967). Effect of humor on speaker ethos and audience information gain. *Journal of Communication, 17*(3), 228-233.

Gruner, C. (1970). The effect of humor in dull and interesting informative speeches. *Central States Speech Journal, 21*(3), 160-166.

Grunig, J. E., & Hunt, T. (1984). *Managing public relations.* New York: Holt, Rinehart & Winston.

Gunning, R. (1968). *The technique of clear writing* (2nd ed.). New York: McGraw-Hill.

Hahn, D. (1970). The effect of television on presidential campaign. *Today's Speech, 18,* 8-10.

Hall, E. T. (1966). *The hidden dimension.* Garden City, NY: Doubleday.

Hass, R. G. (1981). Effects of source characteristics on cognitive responses and persuasion. In R. E. Petty, T. M. Ostrom, & T. C. Brock (Eds.), *Cognitive responses in persuasion* (pp. 141-172). Hillsdale, NJ: Lawrence Erlbaum.

Haukkala, A., Uutela, A., Vartianen, E., Burton, D., & Johnson, C. A. (1994). Social inoculation against cigarette advertisements in a culture allowing cigarette advertising and in another banning it. *Community Health, 17,* 13-18.

Hayakawa, S. I. (1949). *Language in thought and action.* New York: Harcourt Brace.

Heath, R. L., & Associates. (1988). *Strategic issues management.* San Francisco: Jossey-Bass.

Heider, F. (1946). Attitudinal and cognitive organization. *Journal of Psychology, 21*(first half), 107-112.

Herzog, H. (1944). What do we really know about daytime serial listeners? In P. Lazarsfeld & F. N. Stanton (Eds.), *Radio research: 1942-43.* New York: Duell, Sloan, & Pearce.

Hiam, A. (1990). Exposing four myths of strategic planning. *Journal of Business Strategy, 11*(5), 23-29.

Hilgard, E. R. (1956). *Theories of learning.* New York: Appleton-Century-Crofts.

Hofstede, G. (1980). Motivation, leadership, and organization: Do American theories apply abroad? *Organization Dynamics, 9,* 42-63.

Hofstetter, C. R., Schultze, W. A., & Mulvihill, M. M. (1992). Communication media, public health, and public affairs: Exposure in a multimedia community. *Health Communication, 4*(4), 259-271.

Hon, L. C. (1997). What have you done for me lately? Exploring effectiveness in public relations. *Journal of Public Relations Research, 9,* 1-30.

Hon, L. C. (1998). Demonstrating effectiveness in public relations: Goals, objectives, and evaluation. *Journal of Public Relations Research, 10*(2), 103-136.

Horton, D. L., & Mills, C. B. (1984). Human learning and memory. *Annual Review of Psychology, 35,* 361-394.

Hovland, C. I., Harvey, O. J., & Sherif, M. (1957). Assimilation and contrast effects in reaction to communication and attitude change. *Journal of Abnormal and Social Psychology, 55*(2), 244-252.

Hovland, C. J., Janis, I. L., & Kelley, H. H. (1953). *Communication and persuasion.* New Haven, CT: Yale University Press.

Hovland, C., & Mandell, W. (1952). An experimental comparison of conclusion-drawing by the communicator and by the audience. *Journal of Abnormal and Social Psychology, 47,* 581-588.

Hovland, C. I., Mandell, W., Campbell, E. H., Brock, T., Luchins, A. S., Cohen, A. R., McGuire, W. J., Janis, I. L., Feirabend, R. L., & Anderson, N. H. (1957). *The order of presentation in persuasion.* New Haven, CT: Yale University Press.

Hovland, C. I., & Pritzker, H. A. (1957). Extent of opinion change as a function of amount of change advocated. *Journal of Abnormal and Social Psychology, 54*(2), 257-261.

Howard, C., & Mathews, W. (1985). *On deadline: Managing media relations.* Prospect Heights, IL: Waveland.

Hume, S. (1989, November/December). Reporting disasters: What's the media thinking of? *Content,* pp. 19-21.

Hunt, J. M., Smith, M. F., & Kernan, J. B. (1985). The effects of expectancy disconfirmation and argument strength on message processing level: An application to personal selling. In E. C. Hirschman & M. B. Holbrook (Eds.), *Advances in consumer research* (Vol. 12, pp. 450-454). Provo, UT: Association for Consumer Research.

Ingstrup, O. (1990). Unpublished speech by Commissioner of Correctional Services, Government of Canada, Ottawa, Ontario.

Ireland, R. D., Hitt, M. A., & Williams, J. C. (1992). Mission statements: Importance, challenge, and recommendations for development. *Business Horizons, 35,* 36-43.

Iyengar, S., & Kinder, D. R. (1987). *News that matters: Television and American opinion.* Chicago: University of Chicago Press.

Jackson, L. D. (1992). Information complexity and medical communication, the effects of technical language and amount of information in a medical message. *Health Communication, 4*(3), 197-210.

Jackson, S., & Allen, M. (1987, May). *Meta-analysis of the effectiveness of one-sided and two-sided argumentation.* Paper presented at the annual meeting of the International Communication Association, Montreal, Canada.

Jahoda, M., & Warren, N. (1966). Introduction. In M. Jahoda & N. Warren (Eds.), *Attitudes: Selected readings* (pp. 7-12). Baltimore, MD: Penguin.

Jamieson, K. H., & Campbell, K. K. (1988). *The interplay of influence: Mass media and their publics in news, advertising, politics* (2nd ed.). Belmont, CA: Wadsworth.

Janis, I. L., & Feshbach, F. (1954). Effects of fear-arousing communications. *Journal of Abnormal and Social Psychology, 49,* 211-218.

Jersild, A. (1928). Modes of emphasis in public speaking. *Journal of Applied Psychology, 12,* 611-620.

Johnson, J. D., & Meishoke, H. (1992). Cancer-related channel selection. *Health Communication, 4*(3), 183-196.

Johnson, M. A. (1997). Public relations and technology: Practitioner perspectives. *Journal of Public Relations Research, 9*(3), 213-236.

Johnson-Cartee, K. S., & Copeland, G. A. (1991). *Negative political advertising: Coming of age.* Hillsdale, NJ: Lawrence Erlbaum.

Johnston, D. D. (1994). *The art and science of persuasion.* Dubuque, IA: William C. Brown/Benchmark.

Kahle, L. R., Poulos, B., & Sukhdial, A. (1988). Changes in social values in the United States during the past decade. *Journal of Advertising Research, 28,* 35-41.

Kanter, R. M. (1991). Championing change: An interview with Bell Atlantic's CEO Raymond Smith. *Harvard Business Review, 69,* 118-130.

Katz, E., Haas, H., & Gurevitch, M. (1997). 20 years of television in Israel: Are there long-run effects on values, social connectedness, and cultural practices? *Journal of Communication, 47*(2), 3-20.

Kaufman, R. (1992). *Strategic planning plus: An organizational guide.* Newbury Park, CA: Sage.

Keen, P. G. W. (1991). Redesigning the organization through information technology. *Planning Review, 19*(3), 4-15.

Kennedy, J. F. (1963, June 25). Speech given at city hall, West Berlin, Federal Republic of Germany. http://www.geocities.com/newgeneration/Ichbin.htm.

Kinkead, R. W., & Winokur, D. (1992, October). How public relations professionals help CEOs make the right moves. *Public Relations Journal, 48*(10), 18-23.

Koballa, T. R., Jr. (1986). Persuading teachers to reexamine the innovative elementary science programs of yesterday: The effect of anecdotal versus data-summary communications. *Journal of Research in Science Teaching, 23*(5), 437-449.

Kosslyn, S. M. (1981). The medium and the message in mental imagery: A theory. *Psychological Review, 88,* 46-66.

Krugman, H. E. (1965). The impact of television advertising: Learning without involvement. *Public Opinion Quarterly, 29*(3), 349-356.

Krugman, H. E. (1997). Memory without recall, exposure without perception. *Journal of Advertising Research, 37*(4), 7-14.

Langer, E. J. (1978). Rethinking the role of thought in social interaction. In J. H. Harvey, W. J. Ickes, & R. F. Kidd (Eds.), *New directions in attribution research* (Vol. 2, pp. 35-58). Hillsdale, NJ: Lawrence Erlbaum.

Larson, C. U. (1982). Media metaphors: Two perspectives for the rhetorical criticism of TV commercials. *Central States Speech Journal, 33*(4), 533-546.

Lauzen, M. M. (1995). Toward a model of environmental scanning. *Journal of Public Relations Research, 7*(3), 187-204.

Lefkowitz, M., Blake, R. R., & Mouton, J. S. (1955). Status factors in pedestrian violation of traffic signals. *Journal of Abnormal and Social Psychology, 51,* 704-706.

Leiss, W., Kline, S., & Jhally, S. (1986). *Social communication in advertising.* Toronto: Methuen.

Leonard, J. (1978). And a picture tube shall lead them. In R. Atwan, B. Orton, & W. Vesterman (Eds.), *American mass media: Industries and issues* (pp. 374-382). New York: Random House.

Leventhal, H., & Perloe, S. I. (1962). A relationship between self-esteem and persuasibility. *Journal of Abnormal and Social Psychology, 64*(5), 385-388.

Leventhal, H., & Trembly, G. (1968). Negative emotions and persuasion. *Journal of Personality and Social Psychology, 36,* 154-168.

Leventhal, H., Watts, J. C., & Pagano, F. (1967). Effects of fear and instructions on how to cope with danger. *Journal of Personality and Social Psychology, 6*(3), 313-321.

Lewin, K. (1951). *Field theory in social sciences: Selected theoretical papers* (D. Cartwright, Ed.). New York: Harper.

Lewis, J. D. (1990). Using alliances to build market power. *Planning Review, 18*(5), 4-9, 48.

Lind, E. A. (1982). The psychology of courtroom procedure. In N. L. Kerr & R. M. Bray (Eds.), *The psychology of the courtroom* (pp. 13-38). New York: Academic Press.

Lipset, S. M. (1967). *The first new nation.* New York: Anchor.

Lund, F. H. (1925). The psychology of belief: A study of its emotional and volitional determinants. *Journal of Abnormal and Social Psychology, 20*(2), 174-196.

Lusterman, S. (1988). *Managing federal government relations.* New York: Conference Board.

Lutz, K. A., & Lutz, R. J. (1977). Effects of interactive imagery on learning: Applications to advertising. *Journal of Applied Psychology, 62*(4), 493-498.

MacInnis, D. J., & Price, L. L. (1987). The role of imagery in information processing. *Journal of Consumer Research, 13*(4), 473-491.

MacLeod, A. G. (Director). (1993). *Acts of defiance* [Videotape]. Montreal: National Film Board.

Magdenko, L. (with Disman, M., & Raphael, D.) (n.d.). *A theoretical framework for the study of visuals in health promotion.* Toronto: Centre for Health Promotion.

Maslow, A. H. (1954). *Motivation and personality.* New York: Harper.

McAlister, A. (1980). Mass communication and community organization for public health education. *American Psychologist, 35*(4), 375-379.

McClelland, D. C. (1961). *The achieving society.* Princeton, NJ: Van Nostrand.

McClelland, D. C., Atkinson, J. W., Clark, R. A., & Lowell, E. L. (1953). *The achievement motive.* New York: Appleton-Century-Crofts.

McCombs, M. E. (1978). Public response to the daily news. In L. K. Epstein (Ed.), *Women and the news* (pp. 1-14). New York: Hastings House.

McCombs, M. E. (1994). News influence on our pictures of the world. In J. Bryant & D. Zillmann (Eds.), *Media effects: Advances in theory and research* (pp. 1-16). Hillsdale, NJ: Lawrence Erlbaum.

McCombs, M. E., & Shaw, D. L. (1972). The agenda-setting function of mass media. *Public Opinion Quarterly, 36*(2), 176-187.

McCombs, M. E., & Shaw, D. L. (1976). Structuring the "unseen" environment. *Journal of Communication, 26*(2), 18-22.

McCroskey, J. C. (1966). Scales for the measurement of ethos. *Speech Monographs, 33,* 65-72.

McCroskey, J. C., & Mehrley, R. S. (1969). The effects of disorganization and nonfluency on attitude change and source credibility. *Speech Monographs, 36,* 13-21.

McDermott, R. J., Hawkins, M. J., Moore, J. R., & Cittadino, S. K. (1987, March). AIDS awareness and information sources among selected university students. *Journal of American College Health, 35*(5), 222-226.

McGuire, W. J. (1961). The effectiveness of supportive and refutational defenses in immunizing and restoring beliefs against persuasion. *Sociometry, 24*(2), 184-197.

McLoughlin, B. (1990, Summer). Who shapes the agenda? *Manager's Magazine,* pp. 38.

Medvene, L. J., & Bridge, R. G. (1990). Using television to create more favorable attitudes toward community facilities for deinstitutionalized psychiatric patients. *Journal of Applied Social Psychology, 20*(2), 1863-1878.

Meng, M. (1992, March). Early identification aids issues management. *Public Relations Journal, 48*(3), 22-24.

Merritt, S. (1984). Negative political advertising: Some empirical findings. *Journal of Advertising, 13*(3), 27-38.

Meyboom, P. (1989, Summer). Read the signs: Manage the crisis. *Manager's Magazine,* pp. 25-28.

Meyer, A. D., Brooks, G. R., & Goes, J. B. (1990, Summer). Environmental jolts and industry revolutions: Organizational responses to discontinuous change [Special issue]. *Strategic Management Journal,* pp. 93-110.

Meyer, A. J., Nash, J. D., & McAlister, A. L. (1980). Skills training in a cardiovascular health education campaign. *Journal of Consulting and Clinical Psychology, 48*(2), 129-142.

Meyerowitz, B. E., & Chaiken, S. (1987). The effect of message framing on breast self-examination attitudes, intentions, and behaviors. *Journal of Personality and Social Psychology, 52,* 500-510.

Meyrowitz, J. (1985). *No sense of place: The impact of electronic media on social behavior.* New York: Oxford University Press.

Mintzberg, H. (1973). *The nature of managerial work.* New York: Harper & Row.

Mitchell, A. (1983). *The nine American lifestyles: Who we are and where we are going.* New York: Macmillan.

Mitchell, A. A., & Olson, J. C. (1981, August). Are product attribute beliefs the only mediator of advertising effects on brand attitude? *Journal of Marketing Research, 18*(3), 318-332.

Mitroff, I. I., & Pearson, C. M. (1993). *Crisis management: Diagnostic guide for improving your organization's crisis preparedness.* San Francisco: Jossey-Bass.

Moffitt, M. A. (1994). A cultural studies perspective toward understanding corporate image: A case study of State Farm Insurance. *Journal of Public Relations Research, 6,* 41-66.

Mogielnicki, R. P., Neslin, S., Dulac, J., Balestra, D., Gillie, E., & Corson, J. (1986). Tailored media can enhance the success of smoking cessation clinics. *Journal of Behavioral Medicine, 9*(2), 141-161.

Monahan, J. L. (1995). Using positive affect when designing health messages. In E. Maibach & R. L. Parrott (Eds.), *Designing health messages* (pp. 81-98). Thousand Oaks, CA: Sage.

Monroe, A. H. (1945). *Principles and types of speech.* Glenview, IL: Scott, Foresman.

Montgomery, K. C. (1990). Promoting health through entertainment television. In C. Atkin & L. Wallack (Eds.), *Mass communication and public health: Complexities and conflicts* (pp. 114-128). Newbury Park, CA: Sage.

Morgan, G. (1992). Proactive management. In D. Mercer (Ed.), *Managing the external environment: A strategic perspective* (pp. 24-37). Newbury Park, CA: Sage.

Munn, W. C., & Gruner, C. R. (1981). "Sick" jokes, speaker sex, and informative speech. *Southern Speech Communication Journal, 46*(4), 411-418.

Musto, L. (1993, Fall). Unpublished paper on homelessness, produced for the Canadian Mortgage and Housing Corporation, Ottawa, Ontario, Canada.

Naisbitt, J. (1961, March). The great holiday massacre: A study of impact. *Traffic Safety, 58,* 12-15, 36, 48-49.

Nakra, P. (1991). The changing role of public relations in marketing communications. *Public Relations Quarterly, 36,* 42-45.

National Performance Review. (1997). *Serving the American public: Best practices in performance measurement.* Washington, DC: Government Printing Office. (http://www.npr.gov/library/papers/benchmark/nprnotebook.html; in 1998, the name was changed to National Partnership for Reinventing Government)

Newcomb, T. M. (1953). An approach to the study of communicative acts. *Psychological Review, 60*(6), 393-404.

Newhagen, J. E., & Reeves, B. (1991). Emotions and memory responses for negative political advertising: A study of television commercials used in the 1988 presidential election. In F. Biocca (Ed.), *Television and political advertising. Vol. 1: Psychological processes* (pp. 197-220). Hillsdale, NJ: Lawrence Erlbaum.

Nimmo, D., & Combs, J. (1990). *Mediated political realities* (2nd ed.). New York: Longman.

Nisbett, R. E., & Gordon, A. (1967). Self-esteem and susceptibility to social influence. *Journal of Personality and Social Psychology, 5,* 268-279.

Novak, M. (1982). Television shapes the soul. In G. Gumpert & R. Cathcart (Eds.), *INTERMEDIA: Interpersonal communication in a media world* (pp. 334-347). New York: Oxford University Press.

Nugent, J. (1987). Positively negative. *Campaigns and Elections, 7,* 47-49.

Nunnally, J. C., & Bobren, H. M. (1959). Variables governing the willingness to receive communications on mental health. *Journal of Personality, 27,* 275-290.

Ogilvy, D. (1985). *Ogilvy on advertising.* New York: Vintage.

O'Keefe, D. J. (1990). *Persuasion: Theory and research.* Newbury Park, CA: Sage.

O'Keefe, G. J. (1989). Strategies and tactics in political campaigns. In C. T. Salmon (Ed.), *Information campaigns: Balancing social values and social change* (pp. 259-284). Newbury Park, CA: Sage.

Osborne, M. (1967). Archetypal metaphor in rhetoric: The light-dark family. *Quarterly Journal of Speech, 53*(2), 115-126.

Osgood, C. E., & Tannenbaum, P. H. (1955). The principle of congruity in the prediction of attitude change. *Psychological Review, 62,* 42-55.

Paivio, A. (1971). *Imagery and verbal processes.* New York: Holt, Rinehart & Winston.

Pattakos, A. N. (1992). Growth in activist groups: How can business cope? In D. Mercer (Ed.), *Managing the external environment: A strategic perspective* (pp. 107-118). Newbury Park, CA: Sage.

Patton, B. R., & Giffin, K. (1981). *Interpersonal communication in action: Basic text and readings* (3rd ed.). New York: Harper & Row.

Pauchant, T. C., & Mitroff, I. I. (1992). *Transforming the crisis-prone organization: Preventing individual, organizational, and environmental tragedies.* San Francisco: Jossey-Bass.

Pavlik, J. V. (1987). *Public relations: What research tells us.* Newbury Park, CA: Sage.

Perelman, C. (1982). *The realm of rhetoric* (W. Klubach, Trans.). Notre Dame, IN: University of Notre Dame Press.

Perry, S. D., Jenzowsky, S. A., King, C. M., Yi, H., Hester, J. B., & Gartenschlaeger, J. (1997). Using humorous programs as a vehicle for humorous commercials. *Journal of Communication, 47,* 20-39.

Persinos, J. F. (1994, September). Has the Christian right taken over the Republican party? *Campaigns & Elections,* 21-24.

Peters, T. (1990). Part one: Get innovative or get dead. *California Management Review, 33,* 9-26.

Peterson, P., Jeffrey, D. B., Bridgwater, C. A., & Dawson, B. (1984). How pronutrition television programming affects children's dietary habits. *Developmental Psychology, 20,* 55-63.

Petty, R. E., & Cacioppo, J. T. (1981). *Attitudes and persuasion: Classic and contemporary approaches.* Dubuque, IA: William C. Brown.

Petty, R. E., & Cacioppo, J. T. (1986). *Communication and persuasion: Central and peripheral routes to attitude change.* New York: Springer-Verlag.

Pfau, M., & Parrott, R. (1993). *Persuasive communication campaigns.* Boston: Allyn & Bacon.

Picard, R. G. (1991). News coverage of the contagion of terrorism. In A. O. Alali & K. K. Eke (Eds.), *Media and terrorism* (pp. 49-62). Newbury Park, CA: Sage.

Plowman, K. D., ReVelle, C., Meirovich, S., Pien, M., Stemple, R., Sheng, V., & Fay, K. (1995). Walgreens: A case study in health care issues and conflict resolution. *Journal of Public Relations Research, 7*(4), 231-258.

Pollay, R. W. (1989). Campaigns, change and culture: On the polluting potential of persuasion. In C. T. Salmon (Ed.), *Information campaigns: Balancing social values and social change* (pp. 185-198). Newbury Park, CA: Sage.

Postman, N. (1966). The literature of television. In C. S. Steinberg (Ed.), *Mass media and communication* (pp. 257-277). New York: Hastings House.

Priest, R. F., & Sawyer, J. (1967). Proximity and peership: Bases of balance in interpersonal attraction. *American Journal of Sociology, 72*(6), 633-649.

Privy Council Office. (1989). *Crisis management.* Ottawa, Ontario: Government of Canada, Minister of Supply and Services Canada.

Privy Council Office. (n.d.). *Communications information in the M.C. Memorandum to Cabinet (instructions).* Ottawa, Ontario: Government of Canada.

Prosser, M. H. (1970). Introduction. In M. H. Prosser (Ed.), *Sow the wind: Reap the whirlwind* (Vol., 1, pp. v-vii). New York: William Morrow.

Prothro, J. W., & Grigg, C. M. (1960). Fundamental principles of democracy: Bases of agreement and disagreement. *Journal of Politics, 22*(2), 276-294.

Ramsey, S. (1993). Issues management and the use of technologies in public relations. *Public Relations Review, 19*(3), 261-275.

Ranney, A. (1983). *Channels of power: The impact of television on American politics.* New York: Basic Books.

Ray, M. L. (1977). When does consumer information processing research actually have anything to do with consumer information processing. In W. D. Perreault, Jr. (Ed.), *Advances in consumer research* (Vol. 4, pp. 372-375). Provo, UT: Association for Consumer Research.

Reagan, J., & Collins, J. (1987). Sources for health care information in two small communities. *Journalism Quarterly, 64*(2/3), 560-563, 676.

Reardon, K. K. (1991). *Persuasion in practice.* Newbury Park, CA: Sage.

Reddin, C. (1998, June). *Communicating for productivity.* Paper presented at the annual meeting of the Canadian Communication Association, Learned Societies, Ottawa, Ontario.

Redding, J. C., & Catalanello, R. F. (1994). *Strategic readiness: The making of the learning organization.* San Francisco: Jossey-Bass.

Redman, S., Spencer, E. A., & Sanson-Fisher, R. (1990). The role of mass media in changing health-related behaviour: A critical appraisal of two models. *Health Promotion International, 5*, 85-101.

Reese, S. D. (1991). Setting the media's agenda: A power balance perspective. In J. A. Anderson (Ed.), *Communication yearbook 14* (pp. 309-340). Newbury Park, CA: Sage.

Reese, S. D., & Danielian, L. H. (1989). Intermedia influence and the drug issue: Converging on cocaine. In P. J. Shoemaker (Ed.), *Communication campaigns about drugs: Government, media, and the public* (pp. 29-45). Hillsdale, NJ: Lawrence Erlbaum.

Reeves, B., Newhagen, J., Maibach, E., Basil, M., & Kurz, K. (1991). Negative and positive television messages: Effects of message type and context on attention and memory. *American Behavioral Scientist, 34*(6), 679-694.

Reid, A. (1988). Public affairs research. In W. J. Wright & C. J. DuVernet, *The Canadian public affairs handbook: Maximizing markets, protecting bottom lines* (pp. 117-146). Toronto: Carswell.

Reilly, A. H. (1991, August). Communication in crisis situations. In J. L. Wall & L. R. Jauch (Eds.), *Academy of Management best papers* (51st annual meeting, Miami Beach, FL). Briarcliffe Manor, NY: Academy of Management.

Rhee, J. W. (1997). Strategy and issue frames in election campaign coverage: A social cognitive account of framing effects. *Journal of Communication, 47*(3), 26-48.

Robert, M. M. (1990). Managing your competitor's strategy. *Journal of Business Strategy, 11*(2), 24-29.

Roberts, D. F., & Maccoby, N. (1985). Effects of mass communication. In G. Lindzey & E. Aronson (Eds.), *Handbook of social psychology: Vol. 11* (3rd ed., pp. 562-568). New York: Random House.

Roberts, M., & McCombs, M. E. (1994). Agenda setting and political advertising: Origins of the news agenda. *Political Communication, 11*(3), 249-262.

Robinson, G. (1990, November). *Post-Oka Communications Symposium* [Transcript]. Symposium conducted by the Department of National Defence, National Defence Headquarters, Ottawa, Ontario.

Robinson, J. P., & Levy, M. (1996). News media use and the informed public: A 1990s update. *Journal of Communication, 46*(2), 129-135.

Roelofs, H. M. (1992). *The poverty of American politics: A theoretical interpretation.* Philadelphia: Temple University Press.

Rogers, E. M., & Dearing, J. W. (1988). Agenda-setting research: Where has it been, where is it going? In J. Anderson (Ed.), *Communication yearbook 11* (pp. 555-594). Newbury Park, CA: Sage.

Rogers, E. M., & Shoemaker, F. F. (1971). *Communication of innovations.* New York: Free Press.

Rogers, E. M., & Storey, J. D. (1987). Communication campaigns. In C. Berger & S. H. Chaffee (Eds.), *Handbook of communication science* (pp. 817-846). Newbury Park, CA: Sage.

Rokeach, M. (1960). *The open and closed mind.* New York: Basic Books.

Rokeach, M. (1968). *Beliefs, attitudes and values.* San Francisco: Jossey-Bass.

Rokeach, M. (1973). *The nature of human values.* New York: Free Press.

Rokeach, M. (1979). *Understanding human values.* New York: Free Press.

Roper, B. W. (1985, May). *Public attitudes toward television and other media in a time of change.* New York: Television Information Office.

Rose, M. (1991). Activism in the 90s: Changing roles for public relations. *Public Relations Quarterly, 36*(3), 28-32.

Rosnow, R. L., & Robinson, E. J. (1967). Primacy-recency. In R. L. Rosnow & E. J. Robinson (Eds.), *Experiments in persuasion* (pp. 99-104). New York: Academic Press.

Ross, M. W., & Carson, J. A. (1988). Effectiveness of distribution of information on AIDS: A national study of six media in Australia. *New York Journal of Medicine, 88*(5), 239-241.

Rosser, C., Flora, J. A., Chaffee, S. H., & Farquhar, J. W. (1990). Using research to predict learning from a PR campaign. *Public Relations Review, 16*(2), 61-77.

Rossi, P., & Freeman, H. (1989). *Evaluation: A systematic approach.* Newbury Park, CA: Sage.

Rossiter, J. R., & Percy, L. (1983). Visual communication in advertising. In R. J. Harris (Ed.), *Information processing research in advertising* (pp. 83-125). Hillsdale, NJ: Lawrence Erlbaum.

Roth, L. (1990, November). *The "Mohawk Crisis": Reflections on French, English, and Mohawk media coverage.* Paper presented at the Post-Oka Communications Symposium hosted by the Department of National Defence, National Defence Headquarters, Ottawa, Ontario, Canada.

Ruiz, M. S., Marks, G., & Richardson, J. L. (1992). Language acculteration and screening practices of elderly Hispanic women. *Journal of Aging and Health, 4*(2), 268-281.

Ryan, C., Carragee, K. M., & Schwerner, C. (1998). Media, movements, and the quest for social justice. *Applied Communication Research, 26*(2), 165-181.

Salmon, C. T. (1989). Campaigns for social "improvement": An overview of values, rationales, and impacts. In C. T. Salmon (Ed.), *Information campaigns: Balancing social values and social change* (pp. 19-53). Newbury Park, CA: Sage.

Salomon, G. (1987). *Interaction of media, cognition, and learning: An exploration of how symbolic forms cultivate mental skills and affect knowledge acquisition.* San Francisco: Jossey-Bass.

Sandell, K. L., Mattley, C., Evarts, D. R., Lengel, L., & Ziyati, A. (1993, May). *The media and voter decision-making in campaign 1992.* Paper presented at the annual meeting of the International Communication Association, Miami, FL.

Saussure, F. de (1966). *Course in general linguistics* (W. Baskin, Trans.). New York: McGraw-Hill.

Saxer, U. (1993). Public relations and symbolic politics. *Journal of Public Relations Research, 5*(2), 127-151.

Scanlon, T. J. (1990, November). *Post-Oka Communications Symposium* [Transcript]. Symposium conducted by the Department of National Defence, National Defence Headquarters, Ottawa, Ontario, Canada.

Schooler, C., Flora, J. A., & Farquhar, J. W. (1993). Moving toward synergy: Media supplementation in the Stanford five-city project. *Communication Research, 20*(4), 587-610.

Schultz, D. E. (1990). *Strategic advertising campaigns* (3rd ed.). Lincolnswood, IL: National Textbook.

Schwartz, T. (1974). *The responsive chord.* New York: Anchor.

Seitel, F. P. (1984). *The practice of public relations* (2nd ed.). Toronto: C. E. Merrill.

Sereno, K. K., & Hawkins, G. J. (1967). The effects of variations in speakers' nonfluency upon audience ratings of attitude toward the speech topic and speakers' credibility. *Speech Monographs, 34,* 58-64.

Serini, S. A. (1993). Influences on the power of public relations professionals in organizations: A case study. *Journal of Public Relations Research, 5,* 1-26.

Settle, R. B., & Golden, L. L. (1974). Attribution theory and advertiser credibility. *Journal of Marketing Research, 11,* 181-185.

Shaw, D. L., & McCombs, M. E. (1977). *The emergence of American political issues: The agenda-setting function of the press.* St. Paul, MN: West.

Shelley, J. M. (1991). Evaluation of a mass media-led campaign to increase Pap smear screening. *Health Education Research, 6*(3), 267-277.

Simon, R. (1986). *Public relations: Concepts and practices.* Columbus, OH: Grid.

Simons, H. W., Berkowitz, N. N., & Moyer, R. J. (1970). Similarity, credibility, and attitude change: A review and a theory. *Psychological Bulletin, 73,* 1-16.

Sogaard, A. J., & Fonnebo, V. (1992). Self-reported change in health behaviour after a mass media-based health education campaign. *Scandinavian Journal of Psychology, 33*(2), 125-134.

Solomon, D. S. (1982). Mass media campaigns for health promotion. *Prevention in Human Services, 2*(1/2), 115-128.

Sonnenberg, F. K. (1992). Partnering: Entering the age of competition. *Journal of Business Strategy, 13*(3), 49-52.

Soumerai, S. B., Ross-Degan, D., & Kahn, J. S. (1992). Effects of professional and media warnings about the association between aspirin use in children and Reye's syndrome. *Milbank Quarterly, 70,* 155-182.

Sponberg, H. (1946). A study of the relative effectiveness of climax and anti-climax order in an argumentative speech. *Speech Monographs, 13,* 35-44.

Standing, L. (1973). Learning 10,000 pictures. *Quarterly Journal of Experimental Psychology, 25*(2), 207-222.

Stephenson, D. R. (1984). Are you making the most of your crises? *Public Relations Journal, 40*(6), 16-18.

Stephenson, W. P. (1967). *The play theory of mass communication.* Chicago: University of Chicago Press.

Sternthal, B., & Craig, C. S. (1973). Humor in advertising. *Journal of Marketing, 37*(4), 12-18.

Stoffels, J. D. (1982). Environmental scanning for future success. *Managerial Planning, 3*(3), 4-12.

Stuyck, S. C. (1990). Public health and the media: Unequal partners. In C. Atkin & L. Wallack (Eds.), *Mass communication and public health: Complexities and conflicts* (pp. 71-77). Newbury Park, CA: Sage.

Sutton, S. (1982). Fear-arousing communications: A critical examination of theory and research. In J. R. Eiser (Ed.), *Social psychology and behavioral medicine* (pp. 303-337). New York: John Wiley.

Swenson, R. A., Nash, D. L., & Roos, D. C. (1984). Source credibility and perceived expertness of testimony in a simulated child-custody case. *Professional Psychology, 15,* 891-898.

Synnott, G., & McKie, D. (1997). International issues in PR: Researching research and prioritizing priorities. *Journal of Public Relations Research, 9*(4), 259-282.

Tannenbaum, P. H., Macaulay, J. R., & Norris, E. L. (1966). Effects of combining congruity principle strategies for the reduction of persuasion. *Journal of Personality and Social Psychology, 3*(2), 233-238.

Tannenbaum, R., & Schmidt, W. H. (1958). How to choose a leadership pattern. *Harvard Business Review, 36*(2), 95-101.

Taylor, S. E., & Thompson, S. C. (1982). Stalking the elusive "vividness" effect. *Psychological Review, 89*(2), 155-181.

Thomsen, S. R. (1995). Using online databases in corporate issues management. *Public Relations Review, 21*(2), 103-122.

Tompkins, P. K. (1984). The functions of human communication in organization. In C. C. Arnold & J. W. Bowers (Eds.), *Handbook of rhetorical and communication theory* (pp. 659-719). Boston: Allyn & Bacon.

Tregoe, B. B., & Tobia, P. M. (1990). An action-oriented approach to strategy. *Journal of Business Strategy, 11,* 16-21.

Tuggle, C. (1991). Media relations during crisis coverage: The Gainesville student murders. *Public Relations Quarterly, 36*(2), 23-32.

U.S. Department of Health and Human Services. (1997). *Strategic plan.* Washington, DC: Author. (http://aspe.os.dhhs.gov/hhsplan/intro.htm)

Vasquez, G. M. (1996). *Journal of Public Relations Research, 8,* 57-77.

Walker, G. F. (1994). Communicating public relations research. *Journal of Public Relations Research, 6*(3), 141-162.

Wallack, L., Dorfman, L., Jernigan, D., & Themba, M. (1993). *Media advocacy and public health: Power for prevention.* Newbury Park, CA: Sage.

Wallack, L., & Sciandra, R. (1990/1991). Media advocacy and public education in the community intervention trial to reduce heavy smoking (COMMIT). *International Quarterly of Community Health Education, 11*(3), 205-222.

Wallack, L. M. (1983). Mass media campaigns in a hostile environment: Advertising as anti-health education. *Journal of Alcohol and Drug Education, 28*(2), 51-63.

Walster-Hatfield, E., Aronson, E., & Abrahams, D. (1966). On increasing the persuasiveness of a low prestige communicator. *Journal of Experimental Social Psychology, 2,* 325-342.

Wanta, W., & Hu, Y. (1994). The effects of credibility reliance and exposure on media agenda setting. *Journalism Quarterly, 71,* 90-98.

Warnecke, R. B., Langenberg, P., Wong, S. C., Flay, B. R., & Cook, T.D. (1992). The second Chicago televised smoking cessation program: A 24-month follow-up. *American Journal of Public Health, 82*(6), 835-840.

Weaver, D. (1994). Media agenda setting and elections: Voter involvement or alienation? *Political Communication, 11*(4), 347-356.

Webster, F. (1980). *The new photography.* London: Platform.

Weiss, W. (1966). Repetition in advertising. In L. Bogart & R. A. Bauer (Eds.), *Psychology in media strategy: Proceedings of a symposium sponsored by the Media Research Committee of the American Marketing Association.* Chicago: American Marketing Association.

Wewers, M. E., Ahijevych, K., & Page, J. A. (1991). Evaluation of a mass media community smoking cessation campaign. *Addictive Behaviors, 16*(5), 289-294.

White, J., & Dozier, D. M. (1992). Public relations and management decision making. In J. E. Grunig (Ed.), *Excellence in public relations and communication management* (pp. 91-108). Hillsdale, NJ: Lawrence Erlbaum.

Wilde, G. J. S. (1993). Effects of mass media communications on health and safety habits: An overview of issues and evidence. *Addiction, 88*(7), 983-996.

Wilhelmsen, F., & Bret, J. (1972). *Telepolitics.* Plattsburgh, NY: Tundra.

Williams, R. M., Jr. (1970). *American society: A sociological interpretation* (3rd ed.). New York: Knopf.

Williams, S. L., & Moffitt, M. A. (1997). Corporate image as an impression formation process: Prioritizing personal, organizational, and environmental audience factors. *Journal of Public Relations Research, 9*(4), 237-258.

Williams, W., & Semlak, W. (1978). Campaign '76: Agenda setting during the New Hampshire primary. *Journal of Broadcasting, 22*(4), 531-540.

Wimmer, R. D., & Dominick, J. R. (1997). *Mass media research: An introduction* (5th ed.). Belmont, CA: Wadsworth.

Windahl, S., & Signitzer, B. H. (with Olson, J. T.). (1992). *Using communication theory.* Newbury Park, CA: Sage.

Winski, J. M. (1992, January 20). Who we are, how we live, what we think. *Advertising Age,* pp. 16-20.

Wober, J. M. (1988). Informing the British public about AIDS. *Health Education Research, 2*(3), 19-24.

Yankelovich, D. (1981). *New rules: Searching for self-fulfillment in a world turned upside down.* New York: Random House.

Yankelovich, D. (1991). *Coming to social judgment: Making democracy work in a complex world.* Syracuse, NY: Syracuse University Press.

Yeric, J. L., & Todd, J. R. (1983). *Public opinion: The visible politics* (1st ed.). Itasca, IL: F. E. Peacock.

Yeric, J. L., & Todd, J. R. (1989). *Public opinion: The visible politics* (2nd ed.). Itasca, IL: F. E. Peacock.

Zajonc, R. B. (1980). Feeling and thinking: Preferences need no inferences. *American Psychologist, 35*(2), 151-175.

Zielske, H. A., & Henry, W. (1980). Remembering and forgetting television ads. *Journal of Advertising, 20,* 7-13.

Author Index

Subject Index

on lifestyle changes, 177
Stanford Heart Prevention Program as
good example of, 159, 181
use of multiple sources, 179
See also Media; Media, agenda setting;
Proxemics of television; Television
Message content, 162-168
boomerang effect, 165, 170
creativity and humor, 167
emotional appeals, 165-166
explicit vs. implicit conclusions, 163-164
fear appeals, 166
news content, 173
one-sided vs. two-sided argumentation,
162
positive vs. negative content, 164-165
reference group appeals, 167-168
supporting materials, 162
visual and vivid content, 164
See also Message design; Message
strategies; Messages; Messages,
organization of
Message design, 146-174
affective dimension, 151
function of trigger signals, 146-147.
See also Trigger signals
novel stimuli, 149
"pictorial superiority effect," 155
"pseudoevents," 153-154
primacy effect, 156
role of metaphor, 147-149.
See also Metaphor
selective attention, 149
selective exposure, 149
selective perception, 149
selective retention, 155
textual factors, 155
timing, strategic decisions on, 171-172
use of emotion, 156, 161
use of familiar stimuli, 152
use of humor, 151, 156
use of repetition, 151, 172
use of visual cues, 146, 151, 161
See also Message content; Message
strategies; Messages; Messages,
organization of
Messages:
audience response to, 149-154
design of, 146-174. *See also* Message
design

effect of source credibility on reception
of, 131-133. *See also* Source
credibility
for crisis communication planning, 92,
103
for strategic planning, 39-40
for support planning, 77-78
framing of, 154, 184
impact of belief systems on reception of,
115-118. *See also* Belief systems
limitations of media for conveyance of,
178-179. *See also* Media
necessity for coordination of, 194
organization, 168-169
rank ordering of, 40
role of audience values in accepting, 119
role of personality in receiving, 128
scope of, 39-40
strategies for, 170-174
tactical considerations related to, 82
target audiences 40, 104.
See also Target audiences
textual factors, 155
themes of, 39-40
timing of, 83
uses of trigger stimuli, 122, 161
using appeals to logic, emotion and
credibility, 80-81
See also Message content; Message
design; Message strategies;
Messages, organization of
Messages, organization of, 168-169
climactic vs. anticlimactic ordering, 169
effect on persuasive impact, 168
primacy vs. recency effects, 168-169
psychological ordering of information,
168
See also Message content; Message
design; Message strategies;
Messages; Persuasion
Metaphor, 123, 147
ambiguity of, 126, 147-149
archetypal metaphors, 125
coding and decoding, 147-148
functions of, 147-149
paradigmatic or associative (vertical)
relations, 124
role of the iconic, 147-148
syntagmatic (horizontal) relationships,
124

role of in receiving messages, 128.
 See also Messages
Persuasion Theory:
 conscious vs. unconscious appeals, 161
 "critical mass," 172
 effect of discrepancy, 171
 effect of message organization, 168
 Elaboration Likelihood Model, 161
 importance of duration, 172
 incremental vs. preventative innovations,
  171
 timing of messages, 171-172
 using emotion, 161
 See also Message content; Message
  design; Message strategies;
  Messages; Messages,
  organization of

Proxemics of Television, 139-143
 applications to political communication,
  140-144
 audience perceptions of communicators,
  143, 176
 perceived distances separating audiences
  from communicators, 139-141
 See also Media; Media, agenda setting;
  Media, effectiveness of;
  Television

Resources, sharing of. *See* Cooperative
  strategies
Rank ordering. *See* Communication
  priorities
Required support systems for crisis
  management, 98-99
 alternative communication channels, 98
 alternative sites for operation, 98-99
 budgetary concerns, 99.
  See also Financial resources
 necessary documents, 98
 personnel requirements, 99

Signal behavior:
 function in advertising, 123-127
 role of metaphor, 123-127.
  See also Metaphor
 role of metonymy, 124

vs. symbolic behavior, 123
 See also Trigger signals
Situation audits, 8
 evaluation of environment, 8
 evaluation of past performance, 8
 evaluation of resource needs, 8
 identification of stakeholders, 8
Social action campaigns. *See* Support plans
  for communication, campaigns
Social marketing campaigns. *See* Support
  plans for communication, campaigns
Source credibility, 131
 and reception of messages, 131
 effect on communication strategies, 138
 effect of media on, 131-133, 137, 138.
  See also Media
 effect of proxemics on, 138-143.
  See also Proxemics of television
 effect of similarity on, 138
 factors of, 133-138. *See also* Source
  credibility factors
 importance for communication, 131,
  132
 role in advertising, 131
 "sleeper effect" (*disassociation
  hypothesis), 138*
 three modes of persuasion, 132-133
Source credibility factors:
 composure,136-137
 consistency, 134-135
 dynamism, 136
 ethos, 134
 expertise, 133, 135
 extroversion, 136
 family orientation, 135
 likeability, 136
 similarity to audience, 138
 sociability, 136
 trustworthiness, 133-134, 135
Stakeholders:
 consultative strategies of, 215-218.
  See also Consultative strategies
 cooperative strategies of, 214-215.
  See also Cooperative strategies
 credibility of, 207
 defined, 194-195
 factors influencing private agendas of,
  217
 levels of involvement, 217-218

About the Author

Sherry Devereaux Ferguson is Professor and Chair of the Communication Department at the University of Ottawa, Canada. She received a PhD from Indiana University and a master's degree from the University of Houston. She received the NCA PRIDE (Public Relations Innovation, Development, and Educational) award for her book on strategic planning for issues management—*Mastering the Public Opinion Challenge* (Irwin, 1994). Previous books include *Organizational Communication* (Transaction Publishers, 1988) and *Intercom: Readings in Organizational Communication* (Hayden, 1980). Recently, she has written articles that appeared in the *Communication Yearbook* (1998), *U.S. Image Around the World* (1998), and the *Canadian Communication Journal* (1998). She has acted as consultant to many federal government departments, including the Department of Foreign Affairs, the Department of Justice, the Privy Council Office, Health Canada, Secretary of State, Communications Canada, the Canadian Space Agency, the National Research Council, the Department of Fisheries and Oceans, the Bureau of Management Consultants, Indian and Northern Affairs, and Transport Canada. Other consulting assignments include work for Petro Canada, the Canadian Council of Catholic Bishops, Canadian Satellite Communications, Inc., the Addiction Research Foundation, and the Center for Health Promotion at the University of Toronto. She was an invited faculty member at the annual Management Institute,

Canadian Council for Public Affairs Advancement, 1997, and priority speaker at sessions sponsored by the International Quality Control and Productivity Center of Chicago, 1998. She was also speaker at International Communications Management conferences in Toronto and Calgary (1999). She has trained managers and executives in issues management and strategic planning techniques for more than a decade. Recently, she acted as a member of a high-level advisory panel charged with defining curriculum needs for federal government communication officers, and she was a member of the 1998 National Communication Association (United States) task force on public relations curricula.